PRAISE FOR *WHEN THE LION ROARS*

"Carl Gallups is an author who has the well-recognized gift of making complex topics understandable and enjoyable to study. In *When the Lion Roars*, he has done it once again! You will soon discover what so many seem to be missing these days - with every turn of the page you will become increasingly convinced that we are living in the most profoundly prophetic days since Jesus Christ first walked the earth in the flesh. Captivating! Essential!"

—PAT BOONE, SINGER, SONGWRITER AND AUTHOR

"Carl Gallup's prophetic detective work will stoke the fire of urgency and expectancy in even the coldest heart. Carl's passion for biblical prophecy and the return of Jesus is contagious. He is indeed coming soon! Are you ready?"

—JOEL RICHARDSON, *NEW YORK TIMES* BEST SELLING AUTHOR OF
THE ISLAMIC ANTICHRIST

"Do we need another prophecy book? 'No!' What we need is a review about what has happened biblically in the last few decades and how that corresponds with present and coming events. Author, Carl Gallups, accomplishes this in his latest book *When the Lion Roars.*"

—DR. HERMAN BAILEY, HOST OF "IT'S TIME WITH HERMAN & SHARRON"

"*When the Lion Roars* is a must read whether you are a serious student of biblical prophecy or if you have been intimidated by the complexity of studying it. Carl puts modern events into the lens of biblical prophecy in a way that will have you thinking."

—MIKE LEMAY, HOST OF *STAND UP FOR THE TRUTH*

"*When the Lion Roars* offers uniquely prophetic insight into biblical end-time events through a Hebraic-central understanding and at the same time keeps you on the edge of your seat! Amazing wisdom and understanding to help prepare the bride of Messiah Yeshua fo̶

—MESSIANIC RABBI ZEV PORAT, FOUNDE

WHEN THE LION ROARS

UNDERSTANDING THE IMPLICATIONS
OF ANCIENT PROPHECIES FOR OUR TIME

CARL GALLUPS

WHEN THE LION ROARS

All scripture references are NIV unless otherwise noted. THE HOLY BIBLE, NEW INTERNATIONAL VERSION®, NIV® Copyright © 1973, 1978, 1984, 2011 by Biblica, Inc.® Used by permission. All rights reserved worldwide.

Other translations used: American Standard Version (ASV) Public Domain. Holman Christian Standard Bible (HCSB) Copyright © 1999, 2000, 2002, 2003, 2009 by Holman Bible Publishers, Nashville Tennessee. All rights reserved. International Standard Version (ISV) Copyright © 1995-2014 by ISV Foundation. ALL RIGHTS RESERVED INTERNATIONALLY. Used by permission of Davidson Press, LLC. King James Version (KJV) (public domain). New American Standard Bible (NASB) Copyright © 1960, 1962, 1963, 1968, 1971, 1972, 1973, 1975, 1977, 1995 by The Lockman Foundation. New English Translation (NET) NET Bible® copyright ©1996–2006 by Biblical Studies Press, L.L.C. http://netbible.com All rights reserved. The Webster Bible (WBT) (public domain). Young's Literal Translation (YLT) (public domain)

Published by WND Books, Washington, D.C. WND Books is a registered trademark of WorldNetDaily.com, Inc. ("WND")

Cover by Vi Yen Nguyen

WND Books are available at special discounts for bulk purchases. WND Books also publishes books in electronic formats. For more information call (541) 474-1776, e-mail orders@wndbooks.com or visit www.wndbooks.com.

Paperback ISBN: 978-1-944229-37-5
eBook ISBN: 978-1-944229-38-2

Library of Congress Control Number: 2016023260

Printed in the United States of America
16 17 18 19 20 21 LBM 9 8 7 6 5 4 3 2 1

For Pam, Brandon, Hannah, and Parker. You are my dearest earthly treasures from the Lord.

CONTENTS

PART I: UNDERSTANDING THE PROPHETIC NATURE OF OUR TIMES

PART II: THE PROBLEMS OF BIBLICAL PROPHECY

PART III: THE PROFOUND PROPHETIC MARKERS OF OUR TIMES

ACKNOWLEDGMENTS

DR. JACK GOLDFARB SR. (1929–2016), a fellow servant in the kingdom work, a pastor on staff with me, a dear brother in the Lord, and one of the dearest friends I have ever had. I will see you in glory, my brother. Thank you, Bonnie, for sharing your husband's life with me.

The People of Hickory Hammock Baptist Church in Milton, Florida, you have stood by my side since 1987, as together we have been advancing the kingdom of Jesus Christ. Thank you for your prayers, encouragement, kindness, and consistency. You are God's ministry blessing to my life.

Brandon Gallups and Mike Shoesmith, thank you so much for your invaluable research assistance and biblical insight. The contributions you made to this work were invaluable. I have enjoyed our personal discussions, as well as our routine radio broadcast analysis of many of the topics within this work.

Joseph and Elizabeth Farah, you have been gracious and patient with me for years. You are the ones God used to catapult my gospel ministry platform into the world. I will forever be in your debt for your investment in my life and ministry. Your dedication to professionalism and excellence has been an inspiration and lesson to my own life. Your unwavering commitment to the kingdom work is a light to many. God bless you both!

Geoffrey Stone, Renée Chavez, Michael Thompson, Mark Karis, George Escobar, and the entire crew at WND, WND Films, and WND Books, over the years you have tirelessly applied yourselves to the daunting task of making my material as excellent as possible, and available to the world. Beyond the professional relationship we have enjoyed, I also count you as friends.

FOREWORD

WHAT YOU ARE ABOUT TO READ WILL CHANGE YOUR LIFE. How do you write a fresh work on prophecy and keep it pertinent to the rapidly changing times in which we now live? Just as Carl Gallups has done. *When The Lion Roars* is relevant and as gripping as the title suggests, and is impossible to put down once you open its pages. The theme of each chapter pops right out of today's headlines; then Pastor Gallups masterfully juxtaposes the current events with the predictive Word of God. From the push for globalism by world leaders and the implosion of the Middle East, to the global anxiousness of our day and the staggering technological advancements that even experts say are threatening to spiral out of control, Pastor Gallups weaves it all together with the thread of biblical prophecy that foretold the alignment of nations that would rise up against a miraculously returned Israel in the last days. He takes you on a journey through topics that you will be continually merging into your daily conversations from this day forward. Yes—this book is *that* relevant.

The reading of *When The Lion Roars* does not require that you hold to a specific end-times view concerning the rapture.

But it will bring to life the stark realization that we are, indeed, living in the most profound days of biblical fulfillment since the first coming of Yeshua Ha-Mashiach.

One thing that always impresses me about Carl Gallups—a seasoned and bestselling author, senior pastor, radio host, and former law enforcement officer—is the amount of sheer investigative work, documentation, and biblical word-study he exhibits. It is enough to keep you glued to the daily news and the prophetic Word of God from this day forth. Yet, it is all laid out, simply and beautifully—and is actually enjoyable to read!

You will soon discover just how significant this work really is as it causes you to reconsider how you relate to the world—including how you worship. I am convinced that the meaning of the few years of earthly existence we are given by Yahweh will take on a new freshness and significance for readers of this book.

The last four chapters—which cover so well the encouragement of the saints to not sit idly by but engage the culture and coming storm—derive, no doubt, from a true pastor's heart, and you can tell the author has been a pastor for a long time. He knows what life and ministry are all about. He possesses a prophetic and practical message today's church so desperately needs to receive.

If you have ever been a bit intimidated by the Bible's prophetic utterances of end time declarations, let your heart be troubled no longer. You finally have your hands on what you have been waiting for.

Now, prepare yourself for the ride of your life—as well as the life to come!

—JOSEPH FARAH, FOUNDER OF WND.COM AND WND BOOKS

INTRODUCTION

MIRED IN A MESS

IT IS AMAZING HOW many times material within certain chapters of this book had to be adjusted while in the middle of writing. Some of the chapters were eventually rewritten entirely. Why? Because as the book was being penned, the world continued to dramatically change, rapidly—especially in the Middle East, the land of biblical prophecy. What a commentary on the prophetic nature of our day!

For example, the bulk of this work began in late 2015. During that time Russian and Chinese troops were arriving in Syria. Russia then entered military agreements with Iran, the ancient land of Persia, and all of that clearly the trappings of biblical prophecy. In the meantime, Turkey was immersed in a re-Islamization process, while ISIS, at the same time, was striving to bring about its apocalyptic visions of an end-of-days, Islamic jihad. However, by March 2016, just as the publisher's manuscript deadline was approaching, conditions in the land of the Bible took another dramatic turn. Saudi Arabia announced it was putting together a coalition of twenty-five to thirty nations and would be training 350,000 troops for possible insertion into the Syrian conflict. The United States announced it was backing Saudi Arabia. Vladimir Putin proclaimed that if these things happened, it would be the beginning of "World War III." Nothing prophetic so far—right? Wow!

Then, by the middle of March 2016, Fox News announced Putin was in the process of pulling his troops out of Syria. This was their assessment of that situation:

> Even as [Putin] backs out of Syria, [he] looks stronger in the region. Meanwhile, the U.S. continues to appear as a lost babe in the woods of a Middle East meltdown.
>
> And, it's important to note, Putin's not talking about a total withdrawal. Russia will retain a military footprint in Syria, just as it has in Croatia. And that residual force can be useful for destabilizing as well as stabilizing purposes.
>
> While the drawdown has begun, the fact of the matter is that Putin will have Assad's back for a long, long time. And that will leave the rest of the Arab world mired in a mess.[1]

I hope not, but it could be that by the time you are reading this book, Putin's World War III has already begun. My fervent prayer is that perhaps it will have been diverted.

Regardless, the Word of God is clear, there is coming a last-days World War III event. That war will be centered in the Middle East. And it will more than likely involve Syria, perhaps Russia, and China as well. A sizable number of Bible scholars believe we may be currently watching that dreaded global war building to a head—right in the midst of our historical generation.

Believe it or not, there is so much more to this book than even all that. We are living in unprecedented prophetic times.

Biblically foretold events are rolling in like a flood. And as you will discover in the pages that follow, we are the first generation to see these events. Furthermore, everything we will examine commenced with the foretold resurrection of the nation of Israel. Imagine that.

Do not fear. There is no need to be concerned with subscribing to a certain eschatological scheme as you begin turning these pages. That is not the purpose of this work. However, what we will do is examine what the Bible clearly reveals about the signs scheduled to accompany the last-days generation. We will then mirror those prophecies against what is actually happening in the world of our day.

From there, you will decide. You will have reliable and documented information at hand so you can make a biblical, historical, and geopolitically accurate decision as to the "season" in which we might be living.

There is no "date setting" in this book. Neither is there an attempt to sensationalize anything beyond the plain truth of what is before us.

This work not only offers prophetic observations, but it also proffers a biblical plan of action for day-to-day living. I pray you will find the advice useful. I trust this will be a volume that you will urge others to read.

Thank you for picking it up. Thank you for turning to the next page. May the Lord bless you as together we take this investigative journey. I truly believe you will be amazed by much of what you will soon be reading and exploring.

Now, I have to get this manuscript to my publisher—before the world changes again! Hang on for the ride!

PART I

UNDERSTANDING THE PROPHETIC NATURE OF OUR TIMES

Since it was customary for the king to consult experts in matters of law and justice, he spoke with the wise men who understood the times.

—ESTHER 1:13

When a trumpet sounds in a city,
Do not the people tremble?
When disaster comes to a city,
Has not the LORD caused it?
Surely the Sovereign LORD does nothing
Without revealing his plan
To his servants the prophets.
The lion has roared—
Who will not fear?
The Sovereign LORD has spoken—
Who can but prophesy?

—AMOS 3:6–8

1

IS THE SKY FALLING?

This is the Voice of Doom speaking! Special bulletin! Flash! The sky is falling! A piece of it just hit you on the head! Now be calm. Don't get panicky . . . Run for your life!
—FOXY LOXY, FROM THE 1943 WALT DISNEY FILM *CHICKEN LITTLE*

THE YELLOWSTONE VOLCANO IS about to blow! Millions expected to die! Twenty states to be obliterated! Global history altered forever!

The year 2016 rounded the corner with the UK's *Express* proclaiming those chilling announcements through its January 7 headlines and article contents.[1]

I normally do not take "Chicken Little" headlines very seriously. But I finally clicked on that article and gave it a look. The report claimed the world had entered a "volcano season" (never heard of that one before!). It also claimed the chances of the Yellowstone volcano blowing within the next seventy to eighty years were about 10 percent.

Aha! *Almost a century away!* And only a *10 percent* chance!

Those last few specific points of clarification rendered the article not nearly as sensational as the headlines had first appeared. However, the piece offered up further distressing prognostications.

Citing a specific scientific research paper, the article continued its woeful news by claiming that a super-volcano eruption could "devastate the planet" and "kill millions." The report also asserted that the "earth's atmosphere would be poisoned with ash and other toxins 'beyond the imagination of anything man's activity and global warming could do over 1,000 years. . . . There are already fears that Yellowstone could blow any time within the next 70 years on a scale that would wipe out the western USA and affect the course of global history.'"[2]

And most distressing is that "due to their far-reaching effects on climate, food security, transportation, and supply chains, these events have the potential to trigger global disaster and catastrophe."[3]

One day later, Fox News anchor Shepard Smith addressed the European Science Foundation's analysis in a live television broadcast. His guest was theoretical physics professor Michio Kaku, a popular television and radio science pundit.

During the show, Smith opined, "But, 10 percent . . . I mean, that's not tiny."

Professor Kaku warned, "We're talking about a sleeping Godzilla underneath Yellowstone . . . if it erupts in a maximum eruption . . . it could literally tear the guts out of the United States of America! Instead of having fifty states of the Union, we would only have thirty states of the Union."

Kaku continued, "But . . . don't panic; we don't expect it to happen in our lifetime . . . however, eventually the law of averages catches up to you."[4]

Yes. . . yes, it always does, doesn't it? Sheesh!

Further bolstering those prophetic concerns, the *Express* article added, "Instances of volcanic eruptions are at their highest for 300 years," and "large earthquakes and tsunamis" have dramatically increased "in the last 2,000 years." Also asserted was the claim that "in the last few decades earthquakes have been the main cause of fatalities and damage around the globe."[5]

Gee, "in the last 2,000 years"? As in, since the time of Christ? Earthquakes? Volcanoes? Tsunamis? Death? Destruction? Global catastrophe? A dramatic increase in intensity? Did Jesus not predict these kinds of things would accompany the last days?

I am a connoisseur of reader comments, especially regarding articles of this nature. Often, the independent observations of readers help to interject a little more perspective and humor upon such portentous claims. Following are a few of the comments left at the *Express* article:[6]

USERNAME: THINKMCFLY
Did you really just write a story saying that maybe a volcano will erupt in over 80 to 100 years? Seriously?

USERNAME: JACKPOD
Say your prayers and make peace with your Maker. The end is upon us.

USERNAME: SUSANCOOK
OMG!! It's bad enough the sky is falling; now the ground wants to get in the act. We're "doomed," I tell you! "Doomed!!"

USERNAME: FOUNDERS1791
"Likely to go off within the next 80 years." Apparently science
and their scientists have become perpetual Steven King fear
mongers with little regard for probability and an obsession with
statistics they consistently interpret wrongly.

USERNAME: TORINO
Yellowstone hasn't erupted for 70,000 years. Before that it was
1.5 million years. Now they predict it'll erupt within 80 years?
Sounds political to me.

So, was the article a reliable report of the very best scientific research available at the time? Or, was it just a sensational,
pseudo-scientific piece designed to garner readership? Who
knows? Time will tell. It seems that something monumentally
tragic, somewhere, is always "about to happen."

Not to be outdone in forecasting potentially devastating
disasters, CNN reported in February 2016, "The worst natural
disaster in the history of North America could . . . hit at any
time."[7] The article addressed the latest research on the Cascadia
subduction zone, a deep-sea earthquake-maker stretching
seven hundred miles along the Pacific Northwest, from British
Columbia's Vancouver Island to Washington to Oregon to
Northern California.

CNN reported, "It's thirty times more energetic than the
San Andreas [fault] . . . If the Cascadia were to experience a
large-magnitude earthquake, the temblor and resulting tsunami
[alone] could kill more than 11,000 people and injure more than
26,000, according to one FEMA model."

Okay . . . wait just a minute. Let me catch my breath.

AS THE WORLD TURNS

But the miserable news did not stop there. Various news reports of the brand-new year also cranked out the following warning narratives:

- ISIS expected to ramp up its global bloody rampage
- Possibility of nuclear war in the Middle East
- Russia and China uniting their military presence in the Middle East
- Russia's Putin warns of World War III
- A coming global economic collapse
- CDC reports sexually transmitted disease epidemics

And the list goes on.

Did it just get darker in the room?

I often find myself saying aloud, "Good grief! What if we are living in the last days? Would anyone even realize it until, perhaps, it was far too late?" Maybe like the days of Noah?

Seriously.

2

EVERYBODY'S TALKING ABOUT IT!

Everybody talks about the weather, but nobody does anything about it.
—ATTRIBUTED TO MARK TWAIN

ACCORDING TO PEW RESEARCH, nearly half of U.S. Christians believe Jesus Christ will return to earth in or before the year 2050.[1] By implication that would mean nearly half of all American Christians believe we are probably living in the end-times. At least that was their thinking in 2010, when this survey was done.

But remember: that particular poll was conducted before the rise of the Islamic State, and before the arrival of Russia and China in the Middle East to begin making military pacts with each other and with Iran. It was also taken before the Iranian nuclear talks of 2014 and 2015, before Christianity was practically eradicated from the Middle East, and before Christians were being routinely crucified, beheaded, and burned alive by ISIS.

The respondents were polled before the massive refugee crisis erupted in the Middle East, dramatically affecting Europe and the United States and raising grave concerns over terrorism and both national and international security. They were also polled before North Korea launched the ballistic missile tests of 2013–2016, before they put satellites in orbit, and before they began leveling threats of nuclear strikes upon their enemies. One has to wonder what those polling numbers might look like among American Christians in the current climate.

WHAT THE VIPS ARE SAYING

Billy Graham turned ninety-five years old in 2013. That same year, he was named by the Gallup polling institution as one of America's Top 10 Most Admired Men. Since 1955, Dr. Graham's name has appeared on that list fifty-six times, more than any other person.[2]

Dr. Graham's worldwide preaching ministry has put him before audiences totaling nearly 215 million people in more than 185 countries. To date, this accomplishment is unmatched by any other gospel preacher. And it is safe to say that millions more have been reached by his preaching through television, video, and films.[3]

In 2013, while writing yet another book, and pondering the prophetic signs as he saw them, Dr. Graham said, "The Bible says there will be signs pointing towards the return of the Lord. I believe *all these signs are evident today*. Regardless of what society says, we cannot go on in the sea of immorality without judgment coming."[4]

Samaritan's Purse president and CEO Franklin Graham declared in a March 2015 Facebook post:

> The Bible tells us that in the end-times there will be "distress of nations with perplexity." This is certainly the case today. The

meltdown of the Middle East. The rise of anti-Semitism in Europe and here in . . . America. China and Russia building their military at cosmic speed. The financial crises worldwide. The political crisis in Washington. Israel is desperate to have peace, but the Bible says "they will seek peace but there shall be none." There is only one ultimate, eternal solution—Jesus Christ and Him alone.[5]

In May 2015, Anne Graham Lotz, appearing on a Fox News radio broadcast with host Alan Colmes, insisted, "We are coming close to the end of human history as we know it." She went on to predict God's soon-coming judgment upon America. Why?

> Everywhere they're telling Him to get out . . . They don't want His name in the Pledge of Allegiance; they don't want Him in the schools; they don't want to say the name of His Son, Jesus, in public settings; they don't even allow chaplains now in the military to pray in the name of Jesus. . . .
>
> God is a gentleman. He doesn't go where He's not wanted. He gradually begins to walk away, and that's what He told Israel in Deuteronomy 28. He said, I'm going to bless you if you turn to me, but if you turn against me, I'll just back away. Then He allows us to be subjected to the things He's been protecting us from.[6]

As of 2010, Christianity was by far the world's largest faith group, with an estimated 2.2 billion claiming to be followers of Jesus Christ, nearly a third of all 7 billion people on the planet.[7]

According to Vatican figures, there are more than 1.2 billion Catholic Christians in the world, making up about half of all those professing to be Christians. And the pope wields enormous influence over every one of them.

In November 2015, Pope Francis delivered a sermon to ten thousand pilgrims in St. Peter's Square. His message was given just days after the now infamous ISIS terrorist attacks in Paris, France. The topic of the pope's message was decidedly apocalyptic. He spoke of the need to always be ready to meet the Lord—even in a martyr's death.

In one portion of his message, Pope Francis emphasized, "In those days the sun will be darkened, and the moon will not give its light, and the stars will be falling from the sky, and the powers in the heavens will be shaken . . . We are called to live the present, but always ready to meet God whenever he may call." The implication of his message was clear to many around the globe: the end is near.[8]

Former Minnesota representative Michele Bachmann has also expressed her views of the prophetic times in which we might be living. Bachmann, a conservative evangelical Christian, stepped down from her congressional responsibilities in 2014, after eight years of service.

In an August 2015 interview on Jan Markell's evangelical radio program *Understanding the Times*, Bachmann proclaimed that President Obama's March 2015 controversial deal with Iran would help bring about the last days and the ultimate return of Jesus Christ. "All the nations of the world signed an agreement that slams the door against Israel and opened it up to enriching and empowering the leading state sponsor of terrorism in the world, whose ultimate goal is the annihilation of the Jewish State," she said.[9]

Markell responded by saying, "That is Zechariah 12:3, folks." She was referring to a scriptural passage that prophesies that "all the nations of the earth" will team up against Jerusalem in the very last days, only to be destroyed in the process.

> ON THAT DAY, WHEN ALL THE NATIONS OF THE EARTH ARE GATHERED AGAINST HER, I WILL MAKE JERUSALEM AN IMMOVABLE ROCK FOR ALL THE NATIONS. ALL WHO TRY TO MOVE IT WILL INJURE THEMSELVES. —ZECHARIAH 12:3

Bachmann, who served on the Permanent Select Committee on Intelligence and the Financial Services Committee while in office, emphasized:

> We know how this is going to turnout [*sic*]. As the prophets fore-told, the prophets longed to live in this day. I'm actually extremely excited. I think we're about to see, if we believers act in concert, I absolutely believe we can see the strong right arm of a holy God prove to the world his power and his strength.
>
> From a biblical perspective, the Lord has allowed us to see how he is using politics, using leaders, using politicians, using foreign policy to bring about where we are today.

THE WHOLE WORLD IS ON EDGE

As 2015 came to a close, the *Financial Times* posted an article titled "Battered, bruised and jumpy—the whole world is on edge." The essence of the article is best expressed in the very first sentence: "In 2015, a sense of unease and foreboding seemed to settle on all the world's major power centers. From Beijing to Washington, Berlin to Brasília, Moscow to Tokyo—governments, media and citizens were jumpy and embattled. This kind of globalized anxiety is unusual."[10]

A few days after the release of that year-end article, the calendar turned the page to 2016. The New Year's headlines in the *Financial Times* reported, "China plunge spreads to global markets." The subheadings read, "Blue-chip CSI 300 index falls 7 percent as share-sale ban set to expire," and, "Global Market Overview Wall Street rattled by China stock slide," as well as, "Markets Insight: China overshadows global outlook for 2016."[11]

By the end of the first day of stock market trading in 2016, CNBC posted these headlines: "Dow closes down triple digits, posts worst opening day in 8 years."[12] That headline brought back memories of the 2008 market crash and the resulting recession/depression.

On January 16, 2016, the UK *Times* reported: "Markets suffer their worst start to the year since Great Depression."[13] Wow. Who would not be depressed over that news?

By early March, that same newspaper reported the world's financial markets had entered a state of alarming instability. The headlines declared, "Global fears as markets lose faith in central banks." The article emphasized that the Bank for International Settlements, known as the central bank for the world's central banks, had affirmed in its last quarterly report, "The uneasy calm in financial markets last year has given way to turbulence."[14]

Of course, financial markets ebb and flow, rise and fall, and even self-correct. Certainly, America's stock market has seen plenty of dark and desperately bleak times in the past.

The difference now, though, is that the world has

dramatically changed, and much of the change has occurred only in the past decade or so. Today our world is intricately and geopolitically connected as never before. Many of the world's financial concerns are associated to the instability in the Middle East, Iran, ISIS, and now China and Russia's involvement in the Middle East. Not to mention an ever-escalating and unprecedented American debt liability—resulting in increasingly dire predictions from financial experts.

DREAMS OF A 2016 APOCALYPSE

It did not help to ease the world's anxieties when the UK's *Express* reported on the first day of January 2016 that the true goal of the radical Islamic terror group ISIS is to "slaughter thousands" and to purposely bring about "the Final Battle" in 2016. Considering the carnage ISIS had already inflicted, the world's anxiety level heightened yet again.

ISIS carried out more than fifty attacks in eighteen countries, killing several thousand people, since it first declared its caliphate in 2014. And 2016 started with the ominous prediction by ISIS expert Theodore Karasik that there would be a huge increase in both the number and the scale of major Islamic terror attacks. Dr. Karasik is a Gulf-based analyst of regional geopolitical affairs; he has extensively studied ISIS's behavior.[15] Even the decidedly left-leaning *Huffington Post* stated, "One must . . . be aware of the power of apocalyptic dreams [of ISIS] in spurring on the violence of men who are completely convinced they are bringing in the final apocalyptic vision of the 'end-times.'"[16]

Back in 2008, a *Forbes* article written by Amir Taheri, author of ten books on Iran, the Middle East and Islam, shocked the prophecy-watching community by disclosing an alarming Shiite prophecy. The original report was supposedly published on an Iranian pro-government website, focusing on a seventeenth-century Shiite prophecy text.

Taheri claimed that imam Ali Ibn Abi-Talib, a cousin and son-in-law of Muhammad, wrote the end-time apocalyptic prediction. Abi-Talib said, "A tall black man will assume the reins of government in the West." The prophecy also asserted that the new ruler of the West would command "the strongest army on earth," and would carry "a clear sign" from the third imam, Hussein Ibn Ali (625–680). The tradition concludes: "Shiites should have no doubt that he is with us."

Forbes further asserted, "In a curious coincidence Obama's first and second names—Barack Hussein—mean "the blessing of Hussein" in Arabic and Persian. His family name, Obama, written in the Persian alphabet, reads O Ba Ma, which means, "He is with us."[17]

Of course, most Bible students give little credence to the "prophecies" of Islam. However, one must remember that almost one-quarter of Earth's population is Islamic. And nearly 15 percent of that Islamic population is Shiite.[18]

As 2015 came to a close, ISIS's apocalyptic goal came up again in, of all places, the GOP presidential undercard debate. In that meeting, Republican presidential candidate and then senator Rick Santorum spoke of ISIS's end-times vision:

> There's all sorts of theological reasons why we may not want to go into Syria to take ISIS. ISIS is a caliphate. They've established a caliphate, the first Sunni caliphate since 1924, when Ataturk disbanded the Ottoman Empire. They've established a caliphate and under Islamic law, "good Muslims" who see them as a legitimate

caliphate are required to follow them. That's why we have people in this country, who see them as a legitimate caliphate, who is a leader of this Sunni Muslim world, they are required under their law to follow them.[19]

Santorum asked, "How do you defeat their caliphate? Well, it's very clear in Islamic law how you do so. You take their land. You have to take land back from the caliphate and in the Islamic world that delegitimizes the caliphate. It makes the caliphate unsuccessful, therefore not blessed by Allah, therefore you should not follow it."

Santorum continued, "I have great hesitancy, based on ISIS' desire to draw us into Syria, and to a particular town in Syria [Dabiq, where Sunni Muslims believe a final battle is to take place], for their own apocalyptic version, to go in with ground troops at this point."

IT'S GETTING CLOSE

From the Graham family to the pope, from the House of Representatives to the Senate, in a national Pew Research Center survey, in pulpits coast to coast, and in United States presidential debates—people around the world are talking about the profoundly prophetic nature of our day. Even ISIS, which is the current focus of military strategies of the world superpowers, is discoursing in apocalyptic/prophetic tones. In fact, they are actually purposing to bring on the final battle that will usher in their mahdi—the ultimate Islamic "messiah."[20]

There are many other examples of prominent and internationally recognized figures, groups, and institutions that believe they see the "signs of the end" as well. A number of them are even speaking of the assuredness of a soon-coming World War III.

Regardless of whether or not they are correct, the point is that what they believe they discern is most certainly being reflected around the planet. There can be no legitimate argument otherwise. The question is, how can we know with any measure of certainty how close we might be to the return of Jesus Christ?

Read on, and decide for yourself.

3

WHEN THE LION ROARS

The lion has roared—who will not fear?   —AMOS 3:8

IF A LION ROARS in the jungle and the natives ignore it, did the lion *really* make a sound?

Well, of course it did! The reality of the lion's presence can be ignored by the villagers if they so choose, but only to their ultimate peril. The lion announced its presence for a reason. The natives would be foolish to simply pretend they didn't hear it.

So it is when the "Lion of prophecy" roars His truth straight from the pages of the everlasting Word of God and into the world of twenty-first-century humanity. Those who have "ears to hear" will understand what God has done. The others will often miss the message entirely.

PERSIA ARISING

During several months in 2014 and into the first months of 2015, the Obama administration held close-to-the-vest talks with Iran, the ancient land of Persia. The discourse was veiled in a shroud of intrigue and involved Iran's aspirations to continue with its program of obtaining nuclear weapons—this after several of Iran's leaders had more than once proclaimed that Israel should be "wiped off the map."[1]

In 2013, Mohammed Razza Hidari, a former representative of the Iranian Foreign Ministry, claimed that if Iran manufactures a nuclear bomb, "it would definitely use it against Israel or against any other enemy state." Hidari also warned that if Iran was ever allowed to stall for more time in its research and development, "it will have the knowledge to make a nuclear bomb in less than a year."[2]

Tensions increased around the world as the secret talks between the Obama administration and Tehran continued. Anxiety especially mounted in the Middle East—the land of Bible prophecy.

PURIM ON THE POTOMAC

It was against this backdrop that Israel's prime minister, Benjamin Netanyahu, traveled to the United States in the spring of 2015. He had been invited by then Speaker of the House John Boehner to address a rare joint session of Congress. Tensions mounted as various pundits insisted that Boehner's invitation, without first being approved by the president, was unconstitutional.

But this was not Netanyahu's first visit to Congress. In 1996 the prime minister delivered his very first speech to the U.S. Congress. In that address he prophetically warned that a nuclear Iran might one day prove to be Israel's greatest threat.

Nineteen years later, well into the twenty-first century, the leader of modern Israel once again ascended to the podium and stood before America's congressional leadership, in spite of opposition to his presence. He began his plea on March 3, 2015, the eve of the Jewish holiday of Purim.

To highlight his congressional message, Netanyahu drew on a passage from the biblical book of Esther, pointing to its prophetic implications as it related to Israel's current plight:

> We're an ancient people. In our nearly 4,000 years of history, many have tried repeatedly to destroy the Jewish people. Tomorrow night, on the Jewish holiday of Purim, we'll read the Book of Esther. We'll read of a powerful Persian viceroy named Haman, who plotted to destroy the Jewish people some 2,500 years ago. But a courageous Jewish woman, Queen Esther, exposed the plot and gave for the Jewish people the right to defend themselves against their enemies.
>
> The plot was foiled. Our people were saved.
>
> Today the Jewish people face another attempt by yet another Persian potentate to destroy us. Iran's Supreme Leader Ayatollah Khamenei spews the oldest hatred, the oldest hatred of anti-Semitism with the newest technology. . . .
>
> But Iran's regime is not merely a Jewish problem, any more than the Nazi regime was merely a Jewish problem. The 6 million Jews murdered by the Nazis were but a fraction of the 60 million people killed in World War II. So, too, Iran's regime poses a grave threat, not only to Israel, but also the peace of the entire world.[3]

As Netanyahu continued his address, he urged the United States not to enter into the potentially disastrous negotiations with the very people who had repeatedly announced their intentions to attack his nation. He once again warned of the dangers of a nuclear-armed Iran and the terrifying scenario that might follow." [U.S. and Iranian negotiations] will all but guarantee that Iran will get those nuclear weapons, lots of them," the Israeli leader said. "We'll face a much more dangerous Iran, a Middle East littered with nuclear bombs and a countdown to a potential nuclear nightmare."[4]

Predictably, opposing speeches were delivered within hours. Shortly following Netanyahu's speech, Obama responded from the Oval Office, sharply reproving the prime minister and the congressional membership siding with him.

A PROPHETIC TIMETABLE?

The Obama government then assured congress that a multinational deal with Iran would indeed take place by March 31, 2015, regardless of Netanyahu's concerns, or the objections of certain factions of Congress.

On April 2, President Obama declared, in a Rose Garden ceremony, that a provisional deal had in fact been reached with Iran, just one day earlier—on April 1. This, indeed, was a remarkably portentous date, because April 1, 2015, just happened to have corresponded with the Jewish calendar date of Nisan 13, the very day on which a Persian court official, Haman, duped king Ahasuerus into signing a devastating accord (see Esther 3). The pact was an agreement to obliterate all the Jews in the Persian Empire. That antagonistic biblical kingdom was the ancient equivalent of modern-day Iran.

THUNDERCLAPS FROM HEAVEN

Was Barack Obama's date change merely coincidental, or was it purposely brought forward as an attempt to chastise, or even mock, Israel's Netanyahu for relating his congressional speech to the Esther account of Haman? Regardless of its foundation, the choosing of that specific date to sign the accord with Iran appeared ominous. At the very least, many saw it as a pompous move on the part of the Obama administration. At the most, it also could have served as a warning sign from God . . . the proverbial lion of prophecy roaring in the jungle.

Joel Richardson, the *New York Times* best-selling author of *The Islamic Antichrist*, declared:

> The God of Heaven and Earth frequently orchestrates world events in such a way as to demonstrate His perspective . . . Those who are quick to brush aside the correspondence of profound global events, particularly as they affect the state of Israel, with important biblical dates often miss what may very well be purposeful thunderclaps from heaven.
>
> It is the cynic that dismisses the possibility of a divine hint as mere coincidence. I think we need to be looking at this very seriously and asking ourselves what it is indicating.[5]

Could Israel's prime minister have been used as a "thunderclap from heaven"? On the day before Netanyahu gave his Purim speech to Congress, the *Jerusalem Post* said of him, "Netanyahu views that his destiny is to protect the Jewish state, and—by extension—the future of the Jews. In his mind, this is why he was fated to come to power. Nothing less."[6]

Is it possible that a "ruler," or "king," or prime minister of Israel could be destined of God to deliver a prophetic message to the world? Absolutely! Most Bible students will know of the prophecies of Moses and King David, as well as other significant leaders of ancient Israel. We also know that God used Pharaoh of Egypt and Nebuchadnezzar of Babylon to proclaim heavenly truth. God can use whomever He wishes.

This is not to proclaim Prime Minister Netanyahu to be a bona fide prophet of God, but it is to say that we must not discount God's ability to use anyone He chooses to reveal the unfolding future. After all, the Lord declared Israel was to be His eternal witness to the world. He promised He would use Israel, in one way or another, to reveal His will to the nations (see Isaiah 43:9–11). Could this not have been one of those heavenly warnings to a last-day's generation?

And what better witness to the modern world, as well as the current global chaos, than the prophetically reborn nation of Israel, represented by its prime minister, standing in the halls of the congress of the greatest superpower the planet has ever known?

WILL A TIGER TURN INTO A KITTEN?

In October 2015, a little more than six months after his Purim speech to Congress, Netanyahu spoke at the United Nations. In that speech, he blasted the multinational nuclear deal with Iran. He insisted the deal would eventually provide the Islamic Republic of Iran with sufficient funds to finance terrorist networks and ultimately to threaten much of the rest of the world. The leader of Israel was still sounding his prophetic trumpet:

> Unleashed and un-muzzled, Iran will go on the prowl, devouring more and more prey. . . . [7]
>
> You think hundreds of billions of dollars in sanctions relief and fat contracts will turn this rapacious tiger into a kitten?
>
> If you do, you should think again. . . .

The greatest danger facing our world is the coupling of militant Islam with nuclear weapons.

And I'm gravely concerned the nuclear deal with Iran will prove to be the marriage certificate for that unholy union.

Netanyahu reminded the audience that seventy years after the murder of six million Jews, Iran's leaders "promise to destroy my country. Murder my people. And the response from this body, the response from nearly every one of the governments represented here has been absolutely nothing! Utter silence! Deafening silence."

"IN OUR TIME THE BIBLICAL PROPHECIES ARE BEING REALIZED."

—BENJAMIN NETANYAHU[8]

Netanyahu then paused for forty-four seconds. During that uncomfortable eternity he stared angrily into the faces of the stunned attendees without uttering a sound. International television cameras swept the room to reveal a nervous General Assembly hall noticeably deficient of many of its delegates.

He continued, "The Jewish people have learned the heavy price of silence. And as the Prime Minister of the Jewish state, as someone who knows that history, I refuse to be silent. . . .

"The days when the Jewish people remained passive in the face of genocidal enemies—those days are over."

In late September 2015, a military superpower with a massive nuclear arsenal delivered military troops to the Middle East, practically overnight. Russia had planted itself in Syria.

After it was there, Russia entered coordinated agreements with Iran, the world's number one state sponsor of terror, and the avowed enemy of Israel. The coordination was Russia's effort to gain Iran's assistance in the propping up of Syria's dictator, Bashar al-Assad.[9]

Furthermore, while Russia insisted Bashar al-Assad must be protected and remain in power in Syria (and while seeking Iran's assistance in the matter), the United States, under the Obama administration, insisted he had to be removed from office and that the Syrian civil war "would not end with Assad in power." Rumors of a looming World War III reverberated throughout the world.[10]

By March 9, 2016, the Associated Press was reporting that Iran had test-launched two ballistic missiles inscribed in Hebrew with the phrase "Israel must be wiped out."[11]

All of this occurred on Israel's back door steps.

Benjamin Netanyahu's warnings appeared to be taking on life.

4

OH, AND BY THE WAY . . .

The Sovereign LORD has spoken—who can but prophesy? —AMOS 3:8

ON THE EVE OF the December 16, 2015, Republican presidential debate, Paul Lalonde, producer and writer of the end-times film *Left Behind*, commented, "So I'm watching the debate tonight and listening to the candidates talking at some length about the politics in the Middle East . . . They even specifically mention the alliance of Iran and Russia . . . And yet not one of the entire panel of self-professed Christians said, 'Oh, and by the way, that's the very alliance that the Bible says will attack Israel in this generation.'"[1]

God has not left His people without warning or understanding. He has given us prophetic markers throughout the generations so that we might be able to at least generally discern where our generation falls along humanity's timeline. We have been given advance intel. Whether or not we pay attention is entirely our choice—but we have not been left in the dark. We can never say, "I didn't know!"

Now, brothers and sisters, about times and dates we do not need to write to you, for you know very well that the day of the Lord will come like a thief in the night. While people are saying, "Peace and safety," destruction will come on them suddenly, as labor pains on a pregnant woman, and they will not escape.

But you, brothers and sisters, are not in darkness so that this day should surprise you like a thief. You are all children of the light and children of the day. We do not belong to the night or to the darkness. (1 Thess. 5:1–5)

Nevertheless, it often seems that a huge part of the current stream of humanity plods along its merry way, oblivious to the profoundly prophetic nature of our day beckoning us to pay attention.

However, for those who have an eye to see and an ear to hear, life is consistently interposed with amazing, *Oh, and by the way, the Bible said that would happen,* events. And practically every one of those prophetic markers affords the believer a fresh opportunity to interject the glorious message of the gospel of Jesus Christ into the world in which we live and move.

THE UNIQUENESS OF OUR TIME

In 1948, in just one day, the nation of Israel impossibly burst back into existence as Isaiah predicted:

Who has ever heard of such things? Who has ever seen things like this? Can a country be born in a day or a nation be brought forth in a moment? Yet no sooner is Zion in labor than she gives birth to her children. (Isa. 66:8)

The following day the new nation was attacked by a coalition of Arab nations. In the ensuing nineteen months, the nascent nation of Israel conquered every military power that dared to lash out against it—oh, and by the way . . .

In 1967 the returned nation of Israel recaptured the city of Jerusalem—oh, and by the way . . .

To this day, Israel, with the prize of Jerusalem firmly in its grip, is living in the backyard of enemies who breathe out threats of imminent destruction. Constantly, they speak of their yearning to drive Israel into the sea.

Additionally, a bursting forth of a decidedly demonic Middle Eastern apocalyptic scenario, centered upon the Euphrates River. has important world leaders and powerbrokers predicting a soon-coming World War III. Some are even proclaiming the dreaded global war has already begun. And, oh, by the way . . .[2]

In the fall of 2014, defense secretary Chuck Hagel delivered what many considered to be disturbing commentary concerning the globally chaotic times. Hagel spoke of a "new world order," and the forming of certain "coalitions of common interests." As you can imagine, prophecy experts perked their ears. When questioned about the ongoing global chaos, Hagel said:

> I think we are living through one of these historic, defining times.
> I think we are seeing a new world order.
>
> What we're seeing in the Middle East with ISIL is going to require a steady, long-term effort. It's going to require coalitions of common interests, which we are forming.[3]

But this was not the only occasion upon which Secretary Hagel made such prophetic sounding and geopolitically alarming comments. On May 6, 2014, Hagel declared:

> This is a time of great global transformation. We are seeing essen-
> tially a new world order evolving and being built. I don't think
> we've seen such a time since right after World War II. And, again,
> the United States is an essential architect of this—of this process.[4]

Secretary Hagel's remarks were unnerving to prophecy
watchers, especially when put in the context of previous comments he made during an appearance on Al Jazeera television.
Al Jazeera is a Middle Eastern news outlet owned by the government of Qatar and boasting an international audience.

In that interview, America's defense secretary characterized
the United States as a *bully* in world affairs. Hagel also expressed
his desire for the United States to enter into negotiations with
Iran, the world's premier state sponsor of terrorism, with *no
preconditions*. At the same time he bestowed empathy upon
Iran, Hagel expressed less-than-favorable affinity for Israel,
America's greatest ally in the Middle East and Iran's target of
desired destruction.[5]

PROPHETIC IMPLICATIONS?

Think of the talking points being bantered about by important
world players: Coalitions of common interests are forming.
Living in globally chaotic times. The rise of a new world order.
The world is on the precipice of World War III. We should
negotiate with Iran without preconditions. A historic defining
time is on the rise. The greatest superpower on the planet is
orchestrating much of the global transformation. America's top
leaders view Israel with increasingly less favorability.

As astounding as the foregoing considerations might be, many see what they believe to be additional biblically connected prophetic matters associated with our day. Consider the following topics of recent prophetic discussion and international headlines:

- The alarming re-Islamization of Turkey[6]
- Pope Francis repeatedly calls for a "new world order"[7]
- Pope Francis officially acknowledges the "State of Palestine"[8]
- An astounding condition of apostasy sweeps the modern church[9]
- The global spread of the LGBT agenda, led by the United States of America[10]
- The deception of the "man-made global warming" farce and its socialist, government-controlling agenda[11]
- The continual call for Israel to give up more land[12]
- The disturbing rise and spread of global anti-Semitism[13]
- The rapid advancement of biblically prophesied last-days technologies.[14]
- The unprecedented, prophetic presence of China and Russia in the Middle East and their teaming up of military capabilities[15]
- The unparalleled raising of the "Palestinian flag" over the United Nations as an acknowledgment of the nonexistent "State of Palestine"[16]
- The massive influx of Muslim "refugees" in Europe and the United States—seen as a potential "Trojan Horse" infiltration tactic of ISIS[17]
- The rapid acceleration of the post-Christian era in the world's largest Christian nation, the United States[18]
- The distressing acceleration of sexually transmitted infections (STIs) worldwide, with more than 1 million new cases each day[19]

- A full one-third of the entire population of the United States currently infected with an STI[20]
- A global HIV/AIDS epidemic[21]
- An unprecedented international fascination with the occult, demons, Satanism, and exorcisms—popularized and proliferated through worldwide communication and information technologies[22]
- The intentional efforts of ISIS to bring about an apocalyptic end-times war in order to usher in the Islamic "messiah"[23]
- The profusely documented and unprecedented worldwide persecution of Christians[24]
- The widely reported potential for the total extermination of Christianity in the Middle East[25]
- The UN and World Bank agenda of a 2030 global marking system—to identify every person on the planet[26]
- The persistent Islamic outcry for Israel and Jerusalem to be captured and the Jews to be expelled from the land.[27]

Remember: only one book in the history of humanity dared to undertake the unthinkable task of documenting scores of prophetic utterances concerning the end of days. And that book recorded these predictions more than two thousand years before they would actually come to pass. That book is the Bible, the holy Word of God.

There is only one generation in the past two thousand years that has seen many of those specific prophecies in the process of rapid convergence.

That generation is ours.

PART II

THE PROBLEMS OF BIBLICAL PROPHECY

"But you, Daniel, roll up and seal the words of the scroll until the time of the end. Many will go here and there to increase knowledge. . . . [but] none of the wicked will understand."

—DANIEL 12:4, 10

5

READY OR NOT, HERE HE COMES!

Christians have been expecting the imminent end of the world for millennia . . . But it keeps not ending.
—ORSON SCOTT CARD, *ENDER'S SHADOW*

IN 2013, A POPULAR Internet news site printed an article about Dr. Billy Graham's latest end-times warnings. In the comment section of the Graham article, a poster identified as SteelerGrrl wrote a rebuttal directed to Dr. Graham's attention:

> The signs have been converging for decades. Remember that book Hal Lindsey wrote in 1970, Billy? The Late Great Planet Earth? I do, because I read it when I was ten. Then there was the 1988 scare, and Harold Camping's 1994? Then Y2K, and 9/11, Left Behind and 2012. Trust me, it's been done to death.
>
> Yet people still buy the books and believe it.[1]

When I read SteelerGrrl's post, I was struck by what proved to be a profound reminder for me: some Christians, perhaps many, do not appear to have a proper sense of prophetic time.

The hard truth of the matter is that there will come a generation that will actually see the return of the Lord Jesus Christ, whether the unbelieving world likes it or not. All the mocking and scoffing they might muster will not stop the biblical prophecies from being fulfilled.

And we have been assured in the Word of God that scoffers will come in each generation, right up to the end:

> Woe to those . . . who say, "Let God hurry, let him hasten his work so we may see it. The plan of the Holy One of Israel—let it approach, let it come into view, so we may know it." (Isa. 5:18–19)

> Above all, you must understand that in the last days scoffers will come, scoffing and following their own evil desires. They will say, "Where is this 'coming' he promised? Ever since our ancestors died, everything goes on as it has since the beginning of creation." (2 Peter 3:3–4)

We are confident Jesus will do just as He said. And since we have clear prophecies that speak of certain events that will take place relatively close to His second appearance on earth, would we not be wise to examine those prophecies in light of what is already happening in the world around us? A reasonable person would say yes.

THE TWO-STRAND CORD OF PROPHECY REVELATION

There are two important factors to consider when examining any specific generation concerning the prophetic potentiality of those days. They are (1) the *rapid convergence factor*, and (2) the *gradual revelation principle*. Let's take a look at each.

THE RAPID CONVERGENCE FACTOR

One of the oldest of the major prophetic signposts we have examined thus far occurred in 1948 with the unparalleled rebirth of the nation of Israel. The remaining unprecedented markers have all happened since then, many of them taking place in only the last couple of decades. It would seem, to many students of biblical prophecy, that Daniel's prediction of the end coming "like a flood" might also be a mark of our day: "The end will come like a flood," he wrote. "War will continue until the end, and desolations have been decreed" (Dan. 9:26).

If only *one* prophetic occurrence were present in our specific age of human history, we would still have to take a serious look at the phenomenon. But what if three or four clearly prophetic signs converged within just a few years, or even a few decades, of each other? Most would consider a phenomenon of that magnitude to be extremely relevant to prophecy interpretation.

So, what do we say when, in our own generation, close to two dozen profusely documented phenomena are in the works—all of which have distinctive ties to biblical end-time prophecy? The odds against such an occurrence are overwhelming. When a particular generation observes a rapid convergence of clear and reliably documented prophetic signs, it is time to take notice. God is up to something!

THE GRADUAL REVELATION PRINCIPLE

The gradual revelation principle speaks to the epic period of time that is often involved in prophecies advancing to the stage of rapid convergence. It is this element of gradual revelation that causes many to overlook the significance of events happening within their lifetime.

Consider this important truth by examining it against the prophetic complexity of Jesus' arrival in the world the first time. Centuries before the prophesied incarnation, God's people pored over the Scriptures and compared them to the events of their generation. Some generations may have observed only a few of what they believed to be important signs as they looked for Messiah's coming. In subsequent generations, perhaps even more signals of His arrival were observed.

But as certain messianic prophecies finally began to come together, the wise ones took note. In fact, even magi from the East were logging important convergences. Their years of study and observation, and their trek of several months, finally led them to the house in Bethlehem where the young child lived with his mother and earthly father. This probably put the Magi in Bethlehem at about a year to a year and half after the actual birth of Jesus had taken place (see Matthew 2).

However, a year or so before the visit of the Magi, even shepherds were told of His birth, and they were told how this event related to the fulfillment of prophecy. Yet, it would be a full thirty years later before a single one of those shepherds (if they were still living at the time) would have had the opportunity (if they were even in the area of Judea at the time) to see Him begin His ministry! *Thirty years!* And even then, it would be three more years before they would see (or hear of) the fulfillment of the prophecies of His sacrificial death and resurrection.

Meanwhile, in the midst of those thirty-three years, it was just *life*—plain old, everyday, going-to-the–salt-mines, keeping-watch-over-their-flocks-by-night *life*. Just like our lives!

How often we forget this. Most of the time there is simply a lot of everyday, routine, ho-hum living that has to be eked out between factors of sometimes not-so-obvious prophetic fulfillment. It is often the very chore of living out the daily routine (sprinkled with naysayers and mockers along the way) that causes many to overlook prophetic happenings. This is one of the reasons why it was possible for the people in the days of Noah to go on "eating, and drinking, marrying and giving in marriage," even though there was a huge ship in the prophet's backyard for 120 years (Matt. 24:38)! Day by day, no "rain of judgment" fell. And life had to be lived. So obviously Noah was some kind of nut, right?

While Jesus was living out the prophecies of His ministry, right in front of the world of His day, most of the Jewish religious elite (the ones who should have known of the foretelling) missed the event entirely! And so did the majority of the crowd under the teaching of those elders.

Why did they miss it? They missed the fulfillment largely because the Man standing before them did not fit the boxed-in view they had created of the Messiah they were expecting! He did not fit their charts, graphs, maps, and eschatological schemes. He did not fit what the "learned ones" had been teaching the crowds about what would actually accompany the coming of Messiah. Entire schools of eschatology had developed, and each of these schools was in the regular business of vehemently protecting its turf!

On top of all that, the Romans were in control of Judea. There were taxes to be paid and taskmasters to be placated and families to be raised and . . . *sigh*. So the religious elite declared themselves to be indisputably correct. And they declared Jesus to be a heretic.

They even accused Jesus of being demon possessed, and

worthy of death. Is there any wonder Jesus wept over Jerusalem? He was finally on the earth, in keeping with all the prophecies, standing among them. Yet, they utterly missed Him. (See Luke 19:41–44; John 1:11).

So, in the name of God, outside the city of God, within a stone's throw of the temple of God, they nailed the Son of God to a Roman cross—all the while thinking they were doing God a favor. Wow!

From the first clear prophecies of Messiah's coming, to the final fulfillment, there were at least a thousand years of history to be lived out. From the moment of His actual birth until the day they put Jesus on the cross was another thirty-three years. The unfolding of the prophecies that finally led to the apex moment was slow—very slow. However, the prophecies gradually piled up until they began to rapidly converge, and then . . . *bam!* There it was! *Fulfillment.*

Even then, the obviousness of the matter was only for those who had "eyes to see" and "ears to hear" because, in the midst of everyday life, those who were not spiritually attuned were not equipped to *see* it. (See Ezekiel 12:2.)

Both of these principles might best be summed up in the words of Michael Snyder, founder of the *Economic Collapse* blog:

> Many Christians have been sitting back and waiting for one giant "event" to happen, but the truth is that small steps toward a one world government, a one world economy and a one world religion are happening almost constantly now . . . The apostle John warned that these things would happen nearly 2,000 years ago, and now they are playing out right in front of our eyes. When will people finally start to wake up?[2]

WHAT DOES "END-TIME" MEAN?

The following terms are frequently used interchangeably: *end times, end of days, time of the end, last days, the great day, the day of the LORD, that day, the coming of the Lord, the coming of the Son of Man,* and so forth. Most of those terms come from the text of the Bible itself.

It is important to remember, however, that none of these terms mean the end of all things. In fact, properly understood, they all lead to a blissful understanding for the believer. Each of these terms speaks to the promised time when Jesus Christ will return and set up His eternal kingdom. Of course, His appearing will be preceded by the day of God's wrath, when His holy punishment is poured out on the unbelieving world. Then the wickedness of humankind and the reign of Satan will end, and Christ Himself will reign eternally. Indeed, this is a blessed promise for the born-again child of God.

It is the profoundness of this truth that caused the apostle Paul, when speaking about the coming of the Lord, to declare, "Therefore encourage one another with these words" (1 Thess. 4:18).

PROPHECY IS CENTRAL TO THE BIBLICAL MESSAGE

According to *The Encyclopedia of Biblical Prophecy* by J. Barton Payne, there are 1,239 prophecies in the Old Testament and 578 prophecies in the New Testament, for a total of 1,817. These prognostications are contained in 8,352 of the Bible's verses.

Since there are 31,124 verses in the Bible, the 8,352 verses that contain prophecy constitute 26.8 percent of the Bible's entire contents. In other words, more than one-quarter of the Bible is centered upon prophetic utterances.[3]

Of those multitudinous prophecies, more than half of them have already been fulfilled. This fact should be an assurance to the reasonably minded person that the other half will also be accurately fulfilled, and that the remaining prophecies would obviously point to the time of the end.[4]

Since the probability for any *one* of the prophecies to actually have been fulfilled in the first place averages less than one in ten (by conservative calculations), and since most of the prophecies are independent of one another, the odds for all these prophecies having been fulfilled by chance without error are less than one in 10^{2000}—a statistical impossibility.[5] Regardless, fulfilled biblical prophecy stands before history as God's witness of the truthfulness of His Word.

In a *Time*-CNN poll, more than one-third of Americans said that since the terrorist attacks of September 11, 2001, they have been thinking more about how current events might be leading to the end of the world. While only 36 percent of all Americans believe that the Bible is God's Word and should be taken literally, 59 percent say they believe that events predicted in the book of Revelation will come to pass.[6]

That same poll also revealed that almost one out of four Americans believes that 9/11 was predicted in the Bible, and nearly one in five believes that they will live long enough to see the end of the world. Even more significant, over one-third of those Americans who support Israel, report that they do so because they believe the Bible teaches that the Jews must possess their own country in the Holy Land before Jesus can return.

> JUST AS IT WAS IN THE DAYS OF NOAH, SO ALSO WILL IT BE IN
> THE DAYS OF THE SON OF MAN. PEOPLE WERE EATING, DRINKING,
> MARRYING AND BEING GIVEN IN MARRIAGE UP TO THE DAY NOAH
> ENTERED THE ARK. THEN THE FLOOD CAME AND DESTROYED
> THEM ALL. —LUKE 17:26–27

Many would sympathize with SteelerGrrl's heartfelt concerns about prophecy sensationalism. But to effectually proclaim that the world "keeps not ending," as proclaimed at the opening of this chapter,[7] and to therefore pay no attention to what's happening around us now—that is simply not a valid way to approach the subject of end-time prophecy. Too many biblical prophecies have been perfectly rendered for us to ignore those prophecies that are yet to be fulfilled.

However, day by day we must get on with our lives. There are flocks in the fields that must be watched by night. At the same time we must endeavor to never lose sight of the urgency of the last days—those days that actually began two thousand years ago, when Jesus walked out of the tomb alive.

We are in the final hour.

6

WERE THEY MISTAKEN?

I, or any mortal at any time, may be utterly mistaken as to the situation he is really in.

— C. S. LEWIS, *A GRIEF OBSERVED*

JUST BEFORE THE TURN of the twenty-first century, the president of a fairly large denomination penned the following, very misguided words:

> Wars have always been with us. Natural disasters have plagued humanity for millennia. Societies have been breaking down, and violence has been erupting, for centuries . . . Someday, the end will indeed come. But rumors about the end have been greatly exaggerated. The world has had many disasters since the last days began nearly two thousand years ago, and I am sure there will be many more. God can end the world whenever he wants to, and I will be happy for the great day to come, but I do not see any biblical proof that it will be very soon.[1]

Sadly, his words express the sentiments of a number of people, even within today's Christian community.

The naysayers sometimes tell us that if we would just take a look at what Jesus truly declared about the end-times, we would discover that even He was utterly confused about the matter. The same is true, they claim, with the original disciples and the congregants of the early church. In fact, practically *every* generation since the time of Christ has seen itself as potentially dwelling in the "last days." How do we answer those contentions?

A number of scholarly works have been written to address the misinformation regarding this topic, verse by verse. Largely, these works seek to interpret what Jesus said, what the New Testament writers claimed, and what the early church must have thought about this subject, *in the proper context*. I will not reproduce that detailed material in this chapter. Rather, I will hit on the high points to provide a correct biblical and historical understanding of the "last days." A proper understanding is essential before we continue with the premise of this book.

JESUS SETTLES THE MATTER OF TIMING

The issue of what Jesus knew about His own return is truly settled in Luke 17, regardless of the arguments to the contrary. In this passage Jesus is speaking to His disciples, specifically about His eventual return and His ultimate kingdom rule. Observe His assurances:

> "The time is coming when *you will long to see* one of the days of the Son of Man, *but you will not see it*. People will tell you, 'There he is!' or 'Here he is!' Do not go running off after them. For the

Son of Man in his day will be like the lightning, which flashes and lights up the sky from one end to the other. *But first he must suffer* many things and be rejected *by this generation.*" (Luke 17:22–25, emphasis added)

Jesus could not have been any clearer: the Twelve would *not* see His return. But, when He did return, He told them, there would be no mistaking the event. In the meantime, though, He was on a specific mission, with His first coming, to fulfill His foretold suffering and sacrifice.

His *second coming*, however, would happen in a different "day," sometime *after* the generation of their day.

There simply is no contextual or linguistic reason to believe Jesus was ever mistaken about the immediacy of His return.

WERE THE DISCIPLES MISTAKEN?

But did not the New Testament believers and writers think they were living in the time of the end as well? The honest answer to that question is both yes and no.

Certainly, the early believers longed to see the return of Jesus in their day. Why would they not? They had just witnessed His resurrection and His ascension, as well as the birth of the church through the giving of the Holy Spirit. This is probably the reason that for the nascent period of the early church the Scripture records that they met "every day" and "broke bread" (Acts 2:46).

The early Christians assembled themselves each day precisely because they thought Jesus might return at any moment, and certainly during their lifetime. Eventually, more definitive preaching on the matter, especially by Paul and John, convinced the church otherwise. In time, we see a more balanced approach to the early church's worship and evangelism practices emerging through the pages of the New Testament, as well as in the writings of some of the early church fathers.

I am convinced this emerging maturity occurred because of a very important reason: both John and Paul testified to an experience of being "caught up to heaven," during which each was shown the end of days.

Paul's "catching up" was a full thirty years before John's experience. Since this is so, then they both (according to what they wrote and preached) also must have known that the endtimes and the return of Jesus would not occur for at least several thousand more years!

This is no small matter. Think of the burden these men must have borne. They were each given the signs of prophetic fulfillment that must precede the second coming of the Lord, yet they also had to encourage the church of their day as well as the future church—for the next two thousand years! Seldom does one hear a prophecy teacher mention this important fact. Yet, here again is another example of the extremely important gradual revelation principle we have already discussed.

In light of this truth, consider the following passages of scripture, perhaps with a fresh contextual perspective. First, we read the words of the apostle Paul:

> I must go on boasting. Although there is nothing to be gained, I will go on to visions and revelations from the Lord. I know a man [from verse 1 we know that Paul was speaking of himself!] in Christ who fourteen years ago *was caught up to the third heaven*. Whether it was in the body or out of the body I do not know—God knows.

And I know that this man—whether in the body or apart from the body I do not know, but God knows—*was caught up to paradise and heard inexpressible things*, things that no one is permitted to tell. (2 Cor. 12:1–4; emphasis added)

Here Paul was speaking of the years at the very beginning of his ministry. He said he was "caught up to paradise." This is similar to the words John the Revelator would use of his own "come up here!" experience some thirty years later (see Revelation 4:1–2).

We know that Paul subsequently became an important prophet and end-times preacher to the early church. He often expanded upon specific last-days events, such as: the last trumpet, the catching away of the saints, the return of Christ, the resurrection body with which the saints would return, the days of the Antichrist and his unprecedented ability to deceive the world, the last-days apostasy, and so forth. It cannot be denied—Paul claimed he was caught up to the throne room of God and saw *our days* . . . and beyond.

The apostle John was in the same boat with Paul in this regard. Sometime in the AD 90s, John was also caught up to paradise. Observe John's words:

After this I looked, and there before me was a door standing open in heaven. And the voice I had first heard speaking to me like a trumpet said, "Come up here, and I will show you what must take place after this." At once *I was in the Spirit, and there before me was a throne in heaven* with someone sitting on it. (Rev. 4:1–2, emphasis added)

Surely, based on all that John saw during the course of his vision, he could see that the end was not coming anytime soon. How could he not have known? He may not have been given a specific date, but certainly he would have known the second coming of Jesus would not occur until many years into the future.

Since Paul also knew this truth, I believe this is why he could so confidently tell the Thessalonian church:

> Concerning the coming of our Lord Jesus Christ and our being gathered to him, we ask you, brothers and sisters, not to become easily unsettled or alarmed by the teaching allegedly from us— whether by a prophecy or by word of mouth or by letter—asserting that the day of the Lord has already come. Don't let anyone deceive you in any way, for that day will not come until the rebellion occurs and the man of lawlessness is revealed, the man doomed to destruction. He will oppose and will exalt himself over everything that is called God or is worshiped, so that he sets himself up in God's temple, proclaiming himself to be God. (2 Thess. 2:1–4)

Obviously, false teachers were proclaiming, at least to the church at Thessalonica, that the day of the Lord had, somehow, already come. Paul straightened out the matter by directly tying *that day* to the appearance of the Antichrist.

Whether the Antichrist will show up before or after the rapture is not important here. What is important is that Paul knew when the Second Coming would occur—sometime in the *future*—because he had been shown the event at the throne of God! He assured the early church that monumental things had to first take place before Jesus Christ returned and set up His kingdom—namely, the Antichrist must appear. And notice that Paul did not announce to the first-century church that this had *already* happened, or that it was anywhere near happening, only that it *would* happen in the future.

The apostle Peter, one of the chief leaders of the early church, also warned the saints about the danger of growing impatient while expecting the Lord's return. In addition to the menace of impatience, they were told that there would be scoffers—especially as the world continued on what appeared to be its *normal* course before the Day of the Lord was ultimately fulfilled. (2 Peter 3:3–9)

In that passage, Peter referred to a day being "like a thousand years," and a thousand years being "like a day" to the Lord (v. 7). This was probably his way of hinting to the early church that the Day of the Lord may yet be a while off. Peter was telling his readers that instead of worrying about the exact timing of the event, they should be grateful for the Lord's long-suffering. That is a lesson we would do well to heed today.

THE FINAL ANALYSIS

Even though a portion of the early church probably thought they would see the return of the Lord in their lifetime, they would eventually come to recognize that certain prophetic fulfillments had to first occur. They also understood that the last days began with the resurrection of Jesus, regardless of how long it might be before His ultimate return, so they were in the beginning of *the last hour* of Earth's opportunity to get right with God through Christ.

In time, they must have learned that the resurrection of Israel would have to take place in the last days, and that Jerusalem would need to be in the possession of the resurrected Israel before the Lord returned. The Scriptures are very clear about these requirements. Surely the early church, primarily made up of Jews, would have been familiar with those major prophecies.

Furthermore, by the time of John's writings, the Romans had already destroyed the temple in Jerusalem and had expelled the Jews from the city. After the middle of the second century, there were few Jews at all living in the land of Judea. Obviously, there was not much "human" hope for the early church regarding Israel being restored and Jerusalem being recaptured in their lifetimes. Yet, they prayed, and they waited; they still hoped, and they still watched—just as we should.

WHERE IS THAT UNIQUE GENERATION?

Ultimately the early church came to understand that it would indeed be a unique generation that witnessed all the events required to fulfill the last-days' ultimate prophecies.

Amazingly, they *have* happened—in our day—every one of them! And, they have occurred *only* in our day, along with so many more potentially prophetic manifestations.

We are the only historical generation to see Israel's return to their land and to take possession of Jerusalem once again. We are the only generation to see the prophetic, Ezekiel 38 alignment of the nations taking place—those nations that were pre-ordained to come against a *last-days* resurrected Israel. And we are the *only* generation to witness the achievement of this very specific last-days prediction—by Jesus Himself: "And this gospel of the kingdom *will be preached in the whole world* as a testimony to all nations, and then the end will come (Matt. 24:14, emphasis added).

No other generation has witnessed the fulfillment of this definitive end-times declaration, except ours. Only we possess the technology necessary to affect the prophecy's fulfillment.

And *now* it's happening.

PART III

THE PROFOUND PROPHETIC MARKERS
OF OUR TIMES

People can see the future only when it coincides with their own wishes, and the most grossly obvious facts can be ignored when they are unwelcome.

—GEORGE ORWELL

7

MEET GEORGE JETSON

Scientific truth is marvelous, but moral truth is divine; and whoever breathes it's air and walks by its light has found the lost paradise.
—HORACE MANN, *A FEW THOUGHTS FOR A YOUNG MAN*

THE JETSONS PREMIERED IN 1962 on ABC. It was the network's first show to be broadcast in color. But this futuristic way of viewing life through an animated television family apparently did not strike a resonant chord in the American '60s. Perhaps the concept proved to be a bit too much to wrap our minds around back in those ancient days. I mean, come on! Flying cars and video telephones? Impossible! *The Jetsons* lasted a mere twenty-four episodes before being canceled.

The production company Hanna-Barbera (of the *Flintstones* and *Scooby-Doo* fame) gave the *Jetsons* still another shot by reviving it in 1985. But the new episodes ran only two years before being canceled again.

FROM SCIENCE FICTION TO SCIENCE FACT

Despite its overall lack of appeal among American television viewers, the *Jetsons* proved to be astonishingly prescient about where the future of technology was aimed. From the show's initial airing until the present, almost two dozen Jetson science fiction technologies are in use today.

If you are familiar with the show, you will get a kick out of the following list. Here are the most obvious Jetson impossibilities that are now reality:

- flying cars
- 3-D printed food products
- jet packs
- robotic helpers and housekeeping machines
- holograms
- drones
- belt conveyors (moving sidewalks)
- smartwatches with video chat
- flat-screen TVs
- large-screen video telephone chat
- instant food preparation devices
- the PillCam (a capsule with a camera inside that can be swallowed by a patient, allowing the doctor to observe inside the body on a computer screen)
- nanotechnology
- talking alarm clocks
- dog treadmills
- a tablet device that displays the daily news reports

Surprisingly, there even appears to be a reference to man-made pollution and, perhaps, climate change in the *Jetsons*'s animated presentation. In the world of the Jetson family, everybody in the upper class lives "in the sky," in elevated buildings. We later discover that they dwell in these lofty perches because pollution has run amok down below!

The most apparent reference is when Mr. Spacely, George Jetson's boss, says his company was founded in 1937, where it continued to flourish until massive surface pollution necessitated a shift to the elevated condos seen in the series. George Jetson also mentions that grass is "ancient history," and that if you want to go to the surface of the planet, you have to pass through the "smog layer."[1]

Why did I take you into this TV-land blast from the past? I did it to illustrate the amazing rapidity with which our world of technology is advancing. Just a little over a hundred years ago, humans were still walking everywhere they went, or using carriage and wagon devices pulled by animals, or riding animals. In those short hundred years we went from horse and buggy to space travel—and everything in between.

We now travel through the air, into the depths of the oceans, over the surface of the water, and into outer space—and all at incredible speeds. The six thousand years prior to the very recent technology explosion were rather boring when it came to communication, information, and transportation technologies. Not any longer.

But what does technology have to do with Bible prophecy? you ask? Absolutely *everything*!

IT HAS BECOME APPALLINGLY OBVIOUS THAT OUR TECHNOLOGY HAS EXCEEDED OUR HUMANITY. —ATTRIBUTED TO ALBERT EINSTEIN

It is a fact that none of the last-day's prophecies in the Bible would be able to come to fruition unless some truly space-age technology had been born, and then globally employed. Heck, when the Bible first mentioned these technologies, the entire globe had yet to be discovered! Yet, the Bible routinely speaks of the global population seeing or hearing or experiencing something, or receiving a "mark"—and at the same time!

I have a feeling that if ol' George Jetson could visit our generation, he might be astounded at what he would experience. Even George's world could not have anticipated what we now take for granted—namely, that our knowledge base is *doubling* every twelve years.

How in the world could that fact, as amazing as it might sound, have any connection with end-time prophecy? Are you curious to know the answer?

Keep reading and find out.

8

MANY WILL GO TO AND FRO

If an alien came to visit, I'd be embarrassed to tell them that we fight wars to pull fossil fuels out of the ground to run our transportation. They'd be like, "Whaaaaat?"

—NEIL DEGRASSE TYSON

THE OLD TESTAMENT BOOK of Daniel has something incredible to say about the technological advancements that were to be expected by the last-days generation. Observe one of the closing verses of this Old Testament apocalyptic book as the New International Version and the King James Version translate it:

> "But you, Daniel, roll up and seal the words of the scroll until the time of the end. Many will go here and there to increase knowledge." (Dan. 12:4)

> But thou, O Daniel, shut up the words, and seal the book, even to the time of the end: many shall run to and fro, and knowledge shall be increased. (Dan. 12:4 KJV)

Notice the twenty-five-hundred-year-old words "seal the words of the scroll until the time of the end." The implication appears to be that even though Daniel was given the future predictions contained in his book, a large portion of its contents would be unintelligible. But not forever, only until the time of the end.

In other words, something monumental would happen in the very last days that would cause prophecy to be unveiled and the truth of it distributed globally. Many biblical scholars now believe that God may have been speaking of the advent of computer technology and, more specifically, Internet communication and language translation technologies.

But, the prescient passage also declares, "Many will go here and there to increase knowledge." The Hebrew word *shuwt*, translated as "will go here and there" means "to push forward," or by specific implication "to travel."[1]

Obviously, there is something very important being declared about the rapid increase of travel capabilities in the time of the end. Remember: travel was arduous and limited in Daniel's day. Along with the prediction about vastly improved modes of travel is the corresponding promise—knowledge will increase.

The word *increase* comes from a Hebrew word that is versatile in translation. *Rabah* means to bring in or increase in abundance. It can also mean to heap up or to multiply exceedingly.[2]

Following is another explanation of the unbelievably prophetic times in which we live. Information expansion is occurring so rapidly we can barely wrap our minds around it:

Today at the Techonomy conference in Lake Tahoe, CA, the first panel featured Google CEO Eric Schmidt. As moderator David Kirkpatrick was introducing him, he rattled off a massive stat.

Every two days now we create as much information as we did from the dawn of civilization up until 2003, according to Schmidt. That's something like five exabytes of data, he says.

Let me repeat that: we create as much information in two days now as we did from the dawn of man through 2003.[3]

Stated another way, Daniel is told that the very last days would be marked by a dramatic (exponential) and unprecedented increase in information, communication, and transportation technologies. Only the last one hundred years of global history have seen that prophecy literally come to pass. However, only the last several decades have witnessed an explosion of those prophetic technological advancements. Consider the following words from a popular modern technology publication, written in 2013:

Buckminster Fuller created the "Knowledge Doubling Curve"; he noticed that until 1900 human knowledge doubled approximately every century. By the end of World War II knowledge was doubling every 25 years. Today things are not as simple, as different types of knowledge have different rates of growth. For example, nanotechnology knowledge is doubling every two years and clinical knowledge every 18 months. But on average human knowledge is doubling every 13 months. According to IBM, the build out of the "internet of things" will lead to the doubling of knowledge every 12 hours.[4]

INTERNET OF THINGS

What, you might ask, is this "internet of things,"? *Forbes* author Jacob Morgan explains:

Simply put this is the concept of basically connecting any device with an on and off switch to the Internet (and/or to each other). This includes everything from cell phones, coffee makers, washing machines, headphones, lamps, wearable devices and almost anything else you can think of. . . .

By 2020 there will be over 26 billion connected devices. . . . (Some even estimate this number to be much higher, over 100 billion). The IoT is a giant network of connected "things" (which also includes people). The relationship will be between people-people, people-things, and things-things.

How does this impact you? The new rule for the future is going to be, "anything that can be connected will be connected."[5]

In February 2016, the United States director of national intelligence, James Clapper, in testimony before a Senate panel, claimed, "In the future, intelligence services might use the [Internet of things] for identification, surveillance, monitoring, location tracking, and targeting for recruitment, or to gain access to networks or user credentials."[6]

In 2015, Samsung stirred up a firestorm of controversy after announcing a television that would listen to everything said in the room in which it is located. In the fine print accompanying the television, it literally warned people not to talk about sensitive information in front of the TV set.[7]

But not to worry, Samsung assured its customers the information collected would be safe, and would not be sold to third parties, nor would it be used in any way that violates privacy. Yeah, right.

However, Bruce Schneier, security expert and the chief technology officer of CO3 Systems warned, "Whether it's your TV listening to your voices or your cellphone knowing where you are, or your thermostat knowing who's in the room, this kind of thing is the future . . . [but] they can be hacked. We know again and again that there are vulnerabilities in the system and we've seen many times where criminals and government take advantage of this [technology]."[8]

Gee. Ya think?

Please bear with me a moment as I don my tinfoil hat; I have a question or two. So, if a "smart" TV can listen to everything being said in your living room and then send that information to a third party—why couldn't that same TV "watch" everything you are doing as well? Common sense tells us, "Of course it could!" And could the hidden microphones and cameras also be live and working, even if the TV is not turned on? Of course they could. Considering the NSA's and CIA's record of harvesting information on private citizens and the building of databases on them—how scary is that possibility? Just a thought.

Think of it. Practically everything on earth (people and things) will eventually be connected and communicating to each other. In a world run by benevolent, right-minded people, this kind of technology could be an amazing innovation, especially in cases of legitimate national security concerns. But in our culture of ever-diminishing moral certitude, even the thought of such a technological planet sends shock waves and trepidation through many of us. I mean, after all, what could possibly go wrong with this scenario of future life? George Orwell, anyone?

Analyzing the new technology from a prophecy standpoint, one has to ask: If everything in the world is one day connected—how hard would it be for a malevolent, antichrist system to control every action, thought, and movement of those forced to endure its power? According to the technology experts (without even knowing what they are admitting), we are just a few years away from realizing that kind of terrible supremacy.

Are you still not convinced? Consider the following technology headlines, taken from various respected information sources. These announcements burst upon the scene at the close of 2015 and at the opening of 2016:

- "Scientists Ponder How to Create Artificial Intelligence That Won't Destroy Us: Researchers take responsibility for the futuristic monster they may build"[9]
- "Robots to outnumber humans by 2040"[10]
- "VR [virtual reality] porn is here and it's scary how realistic it is" [11]
- "Rise of the Robots Will Eliminate More Than 5 Million Jobs" [12]
- "Company Claims It Will Soon Resurrect the Dead: Looks to preserve human brain before you die"[13]
- "Could this be humanity's LAST century? Expert says 're-engineering our children' will lead to the creation of a new species"[14]
- "The Terminator could become real: Intelligent AI robots capable of destroying mankind"[15]
- "Meet Knightscope's Crime-Fighting Robots: Robot Cops Are Real"[16]
- "Will YOU live forever? Presidential candidate claims technology to transform us into immortal cyborgs is within reach"[17]
- "Could we soon 'speak' telepathically? Mind-reading computer deciphers words from brainwaves before they are spoken"[18]
- "10 sex robots you can actually make love to TODAY"[19]
- "New Technique Allows Scientists to Read Minds at Nearly the Speed of Thought"[20]

Did you notice those headlines contain an awful lot of talk about robots, even "killer" robots? This is no longer science fiction; it is the new science fact. The tech experts tell us we had better get used to it.

In February 2016, the *Daily Mail* reported, "Killer robots that can execute without human intervention will become a reality within years unless there is a global agreement to ban them, warns a leading scientist. Wendell Wallach, an ethicist at Yale University, will today call on the US government to outlaw such machines on the basis they violate international humanitarian law."[21]

Bart Selman, professor of computer science at Cornell University, said of the new technology of intelligent robots, "We will be in sort of symbiosis with those machines and we will start to trust them and work with them . . . This is the concern because we don't know the rate of growth of machine intelligence, how clever those machines will become."[22]

How clever the machines will become? Really? That's our newest technology concern? Good grief! Whatever happened to the good old days of hiding under your desk at school, practicing for a mere nuclear attack? But, how does one hide from the Terminator?

And we have barely scratched the surface of the real-life technological wizardry that is right around the corner. Please do not get me wrong; I really do love my technology! I am not one of those old fuddy-duddies balking at everything new that comes along. I would be hard-pressed to get along without my microwave oven, cell phone, Internet connection, and Bluetooth devices! But sex robots, frozen-resurrected-brains, uncontrollable killer robots, and television sets that listen to everything discussed in our homes while sending information back to the mother ship? Come on! How much weirder can it get?

You have no idea. Prepare yourself.

9

AM I STILL HUMAN?

"Fancy thinking the Beast was something you could hunt and kill!" said the head. [. . .] "You knew, didn't you? I'm part of you? Close, close, close! I'm the reason why it's no go? Why things are what they are?
—WILLIAM GOLDING, *LORD OF THE FLIES*

DEALING WITH SOLDIER ROBOTS, cop robots, and killer robots is one thing. Adjusting to a part-human/part-machine (or something worse) is another situation altogether.

As if the technology headlines of near reality could not become any more frightening, consider the potential nightmare scenario of transhumanism. Simply put, transhumanism is the theory that the human race can evolve beyond its current physical and mental limitations, aided and accomplished purely by means of science and technology. The term *transhumanism* means "beyond human." Please do not dismiss this idea as mere science fiction. It is not. The technology is real and is already being employed, and its ethical considerations are being actively debated. Following is a good definition of the concept:

What does it mean to be human? Biology has a simple answer: If your DNA is consistent with Homo sapiens, you are human—but we all know that humanity is a lot more complex and nuanced than that. . . . If you were to build a human from scratch, from the bottom up, at some point you cross the threshold into humanity . . . Likewise, if you slowly remove parts from a human, you cross the threshold into inhumanity. Again, though, we run into the same problem: How do we codify, classify, and ratify what actually makes us human?

Does adding empathy make us human? Does removing the desire to procreate make us inhuman? If I physically alter my brain to behave in a different, non-standard way, am I still human? If I have all my limbs removed and my head spliced onto a robot, am I still human? . . .

In the next decade, given the continued acceleration of computer technology and biomedicine, we will be forced to confront these questions and attempt to find some answers.[1]

And what do the transhumanism supporters say to the scientific opposition and the concerned religious groups? Following is an explanation of the transhumanist's modifying statements as posted in the *Huffington Post* in May 2015:

Many major scientific breakthroughs and advances in the last few centuries have been challenged by luddites and anti-science naysayers, who usually warned that ethics were being negated or outright broken. But human ethics, at least when it concerns science, is bound to the idea of helping the human being to live better. . . . It also could make the next generation of human beings stronger and healthier, giving parents more choice in what they might want out of a child, including eye color, height, gender, athletic skill, and intelligence.

Critics—many of them fundamentally religious—worry that genetic engineering will create a race of nonhuman beings who resemble monsters. Their fears are overblown and tied more to Hollywood horror movies than actual science.[2]

Please note that the overblown fearmongers are none other than those fundamental religious people. Also observe the writer's focus on the fears of those who are concerned—calling those fears overblown. Really? Not according to developmental biologists specializing in chimera research. *Chimera* is the term used to describe genetically modified organisms composed of cells from two or more individual organisms, whether of the same or different species. In other words, it is a composite organism.

A research organization called the Company of Biologists publishes the journal *Development*, which focuses on "Advances in Developmental Biology and Stem Cells." In an article titled "Ethical Considerations in Chimera Research" professor of medical ethics Göran Hermerén claims:

> Different kinds of human-animal chimeras might raise different ethical issues—according, for example, to which tissues the human cells contribute to or how long the chimeric animal survives. Chimeras that include human neural tissue are of particular concern, because the cognitive capacities of the chimeras might be affected, and because of the prevailing special status of humans in our culture.[3]

Even the renowned Brookings Institute, one of Washington's oldest think tanks, has weighed in on the ethical considerations of chimera research and development. A 2011 article titled "Endowed by Their Creator? The Future of Constitutional Personhood," summarizes this startling and far-sighted issue:

In the coming century, it is overwhelmingly likely that constitutional law will have to classify artificially created entities that have some but not all of the attributes we associate with human beings. They may look like human beings, but have a genome that is very different. Conversely, they may look very different, while genomic analysis reveals almost perfect genetic similarity. They may be physically dissimilar to all biological life forms—computer-based intelligences, for example—yet able to engage in sustained unstructured communication in a way that mimics human interaction so precisely as to make differentiation impossible without physical examination.[4]

The decidedly liberal *New York Times* similarly reported:

An advisory committee of the Food and Drug Administration is set to begin two days of meetings tomorrow to consider radical biological procedures that, if successful, would produce *genetically modified human beings. This is a dangerous step.* These techniques would *change every cell in the bodies of children born as a result of their use,* and these alterations would be passed down to future generations.[5]

By April 2015, Chinese scientists proclaimed they had genetically modified human embryos for the very first time. In an article on the website ScienceDaily, Professor Robin Lovell Badge spoke out about the lurid new technology:

There has been much excitement among scientists about the power of these new gene editing methods, and particularly about the CRISPR/Cas9 system, which is relatively simple to use and generally very efficient. The possibility of using such methods to genetically modify human embryos, and therefore humans, [transhumanism] has been on the cards since these methods were first described, and recently these prospects have been brought to the attention of the public through several commentaries made by senior scientists and commentators, some of whom have called for a moratorium to halt any attempts.[6]

CRISPR/CAS9

Very simply put, the CRISPR/Cas9 system is a recently discovered but preexisting ancient biological mechanism that allows scientists to edit genomes with unprecedented accuracy and flexibility.

Cas9 is an enzyme that snips DNA. CRISPR (Clustered Regularly Interspaced Short Palindromic Repeats) is a collection of DNA sequences that tells Cas9 exactly where to snip. All biologists have to do is feed Cas9 the right sequence, called a guide RNA, and then cut and paste small portions of DNA sequence into the genome wherever desired. With the CRISPR/Cas9 discovery, it is theoretically possible to adjust the genomes of any living thing, including humans. Precise genome engineering has the potential to alter the entire world, including every one of earth's ecosystems.[7]

WHERE IT'S ALL HEADED

Is "digital immortality" headed our way within the next few decades? The Science & Tech section of the *Daily Mail* ran an article in February 2016 claiming just such a possibility:

> If you're under the age of 40, there is a good chance you will achieve "electronic immortality" during your lifetime.
>
> This is the idea that all of your thoughts and experiences will be uploaded and stored online for future generations.
>
> That's according to a futurologist who not only believes technology will let humans merge with computers, that this will create an entirely new species called Homo optimus.
>
> And, he claims this could occur as soon as 2050. . . .
>
> He believes that within the next 35 years, humans will "live" online, and our pets could even "talk" to us, like real-life Furbies.
>
> He also claims transhumanism, the idea we can make people technologically better, will be the norm by 2050.[8]

Tom Horn is a longtime television and radio personality as well as an author and publisher. He also serves as the CEO of SkyWatchTV.[9]

Horn and his team have amassed enormous amounts of research on the topic of transhumanism. In October 2015, Horn released *Inhuman*, a three-hour documentary thoroughly dissecting the subject.[10]

In a review of the film on Amazon, the reviewer claims, "Cybernetics, bioengineering, nanotechnology, machine intelligence, and synthetic biology are each poised to create mind-boggling game-changes to everything we have known until now about Homo sapiens. . . Transhumanism intends the use of these powerful new fields of science and technology as tools that will radically redesign our minds, our memories, our physiology, our offspring, and even perhaps—as Professor Joel Garreau,

Lincoln Professor of Law, claims—our immortal souls. . . .

"[This is] an unprecedented time in earth's history already being called the 'Hybrid Age,'" the review concludes.[11]

BRAIN-MACHINE INTERFACE

The genetic considerations of transhumanism are just the beginning. There is also the subject of human/computer brain interfacing. The Defense Advanced Research Projects Agency (DARPA) is an agency of the U.S. Department of Defense, responsible for the development of emerging technologies, especially for use in military applications. A number of DARPA technologies eventually trickle down into everyday civilian and commercial use, as the technologies become refined for such purposes. Examples of DARPA technologies in common use today are: GPS, digital speech translation, and the Internet.

In January 2016, in the Tech & Science section of *Newsweek*, an article titled "U.S. Military Plans Cyborg Soldiers with New DARPA Project" reported:

> The U.S. military is working on an implantable chip that could turn soldiers into cyborgs by connecting their brains directly to computers. The brain-machine interface is being developed by the Defense Advanced Research Projects Agency (DARPA), which claims the neural connection will "open the channel between the human brain and modern electronics."
>
> It is not the first time DARPA researchers have attempted to build a brain-machine interface. . . .
>
> Initial applications of DARPA's device are likely to be within a military context, though such technologies often filter down to find commercial and civilian applications.[12]

There you have it—hidden in plain sight. The U.S. government, in conjunction with the military, is exploring the technological possibilities of transforming our fighting forces into "cyborgs." We are living in the days when "conspiracy theories" are consistently exposed as "conspiracy reality."

WE ARE THE FUTURE. LIKE IT OR NOT. AND IT NEEDS TO BE MOLDED, GUIDED, AND HANDLED CORRECTLY BY THE STRENGTH AND WISDOM OF TRANSHUMAN SCIENTISTS. —ZOLTAN ISTVAN[13]

Now that you understand the implications of the quickly expanding and scientifically possible reaches of transhumanism research, and the related technological developments of gene modification and brain machine interfacing, observe a few more recent technology headlines:

"World's First Genetically Modified Human Embryo Raises Ethical Concerns"[14]

"Horrifying Human Animal DNA Experiments Shows Transhumanism and Hybrids"[15]

"Scientists create animals that are part-human: Stem cell experiments leading to genetic mixing of species"[16]

"Brain Computer Interface and Artificial Brain: Interfacing Microelectronics and the Human Visual System"[17]

"Genome Surgery: Precise and easy ways to rewrite human genes"[18]

"The new frontier of genome engineering with CRISPR-Cas9"[19]

"Elites Pouring Billions into Gene Therapy Research: But who will actually benefit from advances in anti-aging treatment?"[20]

"Scientists take a step closer to ETERNAL LIFE as they PRESERVE and REVIVE brain."[21]

Do any of these headlines sound bizarrely "end of days" to you? The unnerving truth is that each of these technologies is now reality, or near reality, and they are no longer merely the stuff of science fiction and television cartoons.

As emphasized previously, I am not opposed to the marvels of technology, and especially the legitimate and ethical advancements used to alleviate human suffering. As a matter of fact, advanced communication, transportation, and information technologies are the mainstay of worldwide gospel ministry endeavors. And there certainly are many more altruistic uses arising from such technological advancements.

However, we can be absolutely certain that desperately wicked people will also have their hands on this technology as well. And they will continue to amass the fruit of the tree of the knowledge of good and evil. Whatever their selfish and lustful minds are capable of devising, they will be able to accomplish.

Sound familiar?

THE PROPHETIC BOTTOM LINE
We currently possess the technology capable of bringing to life

every single prophetic end-of-days technology found in the Bible. We are the first generation in Earth's history to see the words of Daniel's prophecy, and John's Revelation, take a literal form. Most of that techno-advancement has occurred within only the last two decades or less. Furthermore, since many of us have grown up with this technology, a large portion of the planet has no idea of the biblical implications of any of it.

Do you now understand how a worldwide marking system could be implemented—today? Can you envision how a one-world currency, or one-world government system could take shape overnight, once the right chips fell into place? Can you imagine how all the world could see something, or be forced to do something—at the same time? Do you now appreciate the dreadful possibilities of an otherwise potentially wonderful technology falling into the hands of unthinkably evil people and governments?

OUR FUTURE IS A RACE BETWEEN THE GROWING POWER OF TECHNOLOGY AND THE WISDOM WITH WHICH WE USE IT.
—STEPHEN HAWKING[22]

As it turns out, George Jetson's fanciful world of futuristic gadgets might prove to be rather boring in our near future. Come to think of it, the Jetsons didn't even have cell phones! How outrageous!

As for our world, we might find ourselves agreeing with Dorothy's assessment in *The Wizard of Oz* when the tornado dumped her and her little dog into Munchkinland, "Toto, I've a feeling we're not in Kansas anymore."

For numerous students of Bible prophecy, it appears we might be far beyond Dorothy's predicament. Instead, we may have found ourselves in the land of Daniel's end of days.

Need the lion roar any louder?

But, hang on.

He does.

10

BACK TO THE FUTURE

MARTY MCFLY: Hey, Doc, we better back up. We don't have enough road to get up to 88 [mph].
DR. EMMETT BROWN: Roads? Where we're going, we don't need roads!
—*BACK TO THE FUTURE* (1985)

THERE IS AN ANCIENT Persian legend about the inventor of the game of chess. When the emperor of a vast kingdom was presented with the gift of his first chessboard, he was so pleased that he, in return, offered a gift to its inventor. He promised to grant the creator of this new and fascinating game one wish— any wish.

The recipient of the king's graciousness thought for a moment and then replied, "All I want is rice."

"Really? Just *rice*? How *much* rice?" the king asked.

The inventor placed a single grain of rice on the first square of the chessboard. He looked up at the king and smiled. Before the king could speak, the inventor further requested that the gift of rice simply *double* for each of the sixty-four squares represented on the board. He leaned back in his chair and asked the ruler, "Is this arrangement agreeable to you?"

The king quickly agreed, believing he had received the best end of the deal. After all, how much could a handful of rice grains on each of the chessboard squares set him back?

So, what did the emperor finally owe? By the time he arrived at the final square, the king owed two to the sixty-fourth power, or 18,446,744,073,709,551,616 grains of rice.[1]

That amount of rice would have weighed in at 461,168,602,000 metric tons, which would be a mountain of rice larger than Mount Everest. That tonnage is around 1,000 times the global production of rice in 2010 (464,000,000 metric tons).[2]

As it turned out, the king was forced to forfeit the entire kingdom's wealth to keep his hasty promise.

The story is often used as a teaching tool to illustrate the mind-boggling power of exponential growth rate. A mere doubling effect can quickly produce an astronomical number. And as we discovered in the last chapter, it is the power of the unmitigated explosion of technology, and the new knowledge that comes with it, that is rapidly changing our world. It is changing the way we live into something completely unrecognizable by the generations that came just before us.

"EXPONENTIALS CAN'T GO ON FOREVER, BECAUSE THEY WILL GOBBLE UP EVERYTHING."—CARL SAGAN[3]

THE FUTURE IS NOW. . .

Technology gurus insist the very near future will be far more astonishing than most of us can imagine. We have entered into the part of the technology growth curve that will soon catapult into inconceivably aggressive expansion. The force of that expansion will launch the world into an age of what many, just a few years ago, would have called pure science fiction. We are said to be in the "knee" of this curve at this very moment. Numerous prophecy watchers believe this is precisely the age of humankind to which the prophet Daniel referred in Daniel 12:4.

On their own merits, much of the upcoming technological advancements could prove to be wonderful stuff. But when one considers that we are the only generation in history to be on the brink of unparalleled technological advancements, perhaps thrusting us into the days of the Antichrist's reign, it gives the serious Bible student cause for reflection.

MOORE'S LAW

The basis for our current predictions of the technology boom comes from a concept known as *Moore's law*, so named because of an observation made by Intel cofounder Gordon Moore in 1965.

Moore observed that the number of transistors per square inch on integrated circuits had doubled every year since their initial invention. Moore's law predicted that this same doubling trend would continue into the foreseeable future. And even though there have been a number of naysayers, Moore's prediction has remained astoundingly accurate for the last fifty years.[4]

Nevertheless, for those who claim that Moore's law will eventually reach its limit of capabilities within current technology achievements—never fear. It is now being declared that around the year 2020, quantum computing will take over from the computer chip, and will be infinitely more advanced than anything we have yet to see. Quantum computing could raise the rate of growth even higher than already expected! [5]

But for now, Moore's prediction is the observable fact of ongoing technology progression. These advancements have enabled the production of everything from pocket-sized smartphones to utterly immersive first-person video games, and the ongoing computerization of the world's financial and intercontinental weapons systems.

In 2013, an article published by Mainstay Technologies, which expounded the possible ramifications of Moore's law equation, made a shocking admission: "Exponential growth. It's scary, and it's exhilarating."[6]

So you see, even the technology gurus, who live and die by the industry's exhilarating innovations, admit that the rate at which today's technology is advancing the future could also be considered downright scary. Yes, indeed.

Apparently it is not merely a bunch of biblical prophecy professors who see the prospect for real danger lying just ahead in our brave new world.

A PERFECT FUTURE

Would you like an example of some of the potentially frightening components we may see in our world in fewer than thirty years? Consider the following technology predictions:

> When graphing exponential growth, we eventually reach a point where growth seems "vertical." This stage of growth is often referred to as the Technological Singularity. It is a time that seems

incomprehensible, and will be possible through our creating sentient Artificial Intelligence, which will have *intelligence level far superior to our own.*

Once this is possible, and if it advances in our favour—*all of mankind's most intractable problems will be conquered*—We are talking about immortality; curing cancer and all current diseases; correcting global warming; efficiently harnessing the power of the sun for free energy; mind uploading—which will allow us to live in virtual realities, travel deep space, and transfer our minds into alternate bodies/robots (all solving the overpopulation problem).

A perfect future is painted above, and technologically, that future is possible by 2045 . . .

Nothing is certain. But if exponential growth continues, everything will be possible.[7]

Ponder for a moment the dreams of the technology leaders of the next generation as just expressed. Please take careful note of the world they intend to build: A perfect future. Everything will be possible, all mankind's problems will be solved, humans will achieve immortality, and we will be able to upload our minds into alternate bodies and even into robots while living in virtual realities. Does it seem possible that a biblical antichrist world might lie just around the corner? Naw—couldn't be!

Consider the following description of our planned future as given by a business and industry technology consulting firm:

Eighteen to twenty years out, technological advancements will be hundreds of thousands to a million times more advanced. That makes our first fourteen years of exponential growth seem flat lined (no progress), when in fact, it will be 4,000 times more advanced than today.

This is the time period that "The Singularity" is supposed to occur. This means that bio, nano, robotic and computer technology will become so rapid, so advanced, and so profound that today's limited understanding does not allow us to describe, within reason, what life will be like.

In the early 2040's, the rapid pace of improved changes will be hundreds of millions of times faster than today as each year passes. Evolution will bring about artificial general intelligence (AGI). AGI will come in the form of intelligent machines that have the ability to create and improve its own software and hardware, and evolve according to its own interests (if interests still exist).

Without the fear of death, poverty, boredom, disease, pain, or even maintenance, preoccupation with self-interests may diminish or even dissolve. "Living" may become a spontaneous series of events.[8]

In 2012, Vivek Wadhwa, writing for *Forbes*, penned a technology article about the accelerated advances in synthetic biology. He wrote:

Genome data will readily be available for millions, perhaps billions, of people . . .

We can now "write" DNA. Advances in "synthetic biology" are allowing researchers, and even high-school students, to create *new organisms* and *synthetic life forms*. Entrepreneurs have developed software tools to "design" and "compile" DNA. There are startups that offer DNA synthesis and assembly as a service. DNA "printing" is priced by the number of base pairs to be assembled (the chemical "bits" that make up a gene).

Today's cost is about 30 cents per base pair, and prices are falling exponentially. Within a few years, it could cost a hundredth of this amount. Eventually, like laser printers, DNA printers will be inexpensive home devices.[9]

There you have it. Hang around just a few short decades and technology leaders will save us all, using their most wonderful techno gadgets! World peace, no more hunger, and the added benefit of guaranteed security for everyone! No more poverty, disease, pain—as a matter of fact—no more *death*! A virtual paradise on earth! God-like promises from God-wannabes! Don't worry; be happy! And all of it brought to you by the magnificent world of rapid-fire technological innovation engineered by its transcendent leaders. Won't that just be fabulous? What could possibly go wrong?

Of course, it is highly probable that some of the predictions may be delayed in their actual fulfillment by a few decades. It is also possible that some of the currently dreamed-about technology will ultimately prove to be unpopular and, therefore, not in enough demand to be produced. However, many of the techno dreams spoken of in this chapter are already in place, and are currently being employed. And the fact that the others are actually doable, whether they are employed or not, is what stokes the apprehension of many.

The preceding examples of technology prognostications bring several important passages of scripture to mind:

> For you yourselves know very well that the day of the Lord will come like a thief in the night. While people are saying, "Peace and safety," destruction will come on them suddenly, as labor pains on a pregnant woman, and they will not escape. (1 Thess. 5:2–3)

And then the lawless one will be revealed, whom the Lord Jesus will overthrow with the breath of his mouth and destroy by the splendor of his coming. The coming of the lawless one will be in accordance with how Satan works. He will use all sorts of displays of power through signs and wonders that serve the lie, and all the ways that wickedness deceives those who are perishing. They perish because they refused to love the truth and so be saved. For this reason God sends them a powerful delusion so that they will believe the lie and so that all will be condemned who have not believed the truth but have delighted in wickedness. (2 Thess. 2:8–12)

During those days people will seek death but will not find it; they will long to die, but death will elude them. (Rev. 9:6)

Then I saw a second beast, coming out of the earth. It had two horns like a lamb, but it spoke like a dragon. It exercised all the authority of the first beast on its behalf, and *made the earth and its inhabitants worship* the first beast, *whose fatal wound had been healed*. And it performed great signs, even causing fire to come down from heaven to the earth in full view of the people. Because of the signs it was given power to perform on behalf of the first beast, it *deceived the inhabitants of the earth*. It ordered them to set up an image in honor of the beast who was wounded by the sword and yet lived. The second beast was given power to give breath to the image of the first beast, so that the image could speak and cause all who refused to worship the image to be killed. It also *forced all people*, great and small, rich and poor, free and slave, *to receive a mark* on their right hands or on their foreheads, so that they *could not buy or sell* unless they had the mark, which is the name of the beast or the number of its name.

This calls for wisdom. Let the person who has insight calculate the
number of the beast, for it is the number of a man. That number
is 666. (Rev. 13:11–18, emphasis added)

So, we see that more than two thousand years ago the
Word of God predicted the end-times generation would see
technologies (signs and wonders?) that would promise world
peace, individual safety, immortality, and financial security. We
would see images that lived, instantaneous healing from mortal
wounds, and many wondrous signs of power coming down from
the heavens. Surely John was thrust at least into the twenty-first
century and beyond.

The Bible further warns us that eventually a global marking
system would serve as the final assurance that all of humankind
could be equitably served by the benevolent provider—at least
that is what the godless world will think he/it is. However, the
Word of God tells us this one would actually be the abomination
of desolation of Daniel's vision (see Daniel 9). He would also
be known as the "son of perdition" of Paul's "catching up" (see
2 Thessalonians 2:1–4 KJV) and John's apocalyptic beast rising
up out of the sea (see Revelation 13:1–10)—the demonically
embodied entity that forces everyone to "receive a mark" (v. 16)

We are the first generation in history to hear people glow-
ingly speak of these things, in the techno-flowery language of
the unredeemed, but also we are the first generation to possess
every piece of technology to make them happen—including
the mystery of 666.

11

THE SOLUTION TO EVERYTHING

It is so stupid of modern civilization to have given up believing in the devil when he is the only explanation of it.
—RONALD KNOX (1888–1957) BRITISH CLERGYMAN

IN 1931, UNIVERSAL PICTURES produced a controversial but wildly popular movie called *Frankenstein*. The movie introduces Dr. Heinrich "Henry" Frankenstein, a zealous young scientist, and his devoted assistant, Fritz, as they are in the process of piecing together a manufactured human body. The pair of mad scientists had been secretly collecting the body parts from various sources over a period of time. Dr. Frankenstein's intense aspiration was to create human life through various electrical devices with which he had been experimenting and finally had perfected.

The movie commences with actor Edward Van Sloan appearing from behind a stage curtain to convey a friendly word of warning to the anxiously awaiting (and relatively innocent) 1930s audience:

> We are about to unfold the story of Frankenstein, a man of science who sought to create a man after his own image without reckoning upon God. It is one of the strangest tales ever told. It deals with the two great mysteries of creation—life and death. I think it will thrill you. It may shock you. It might even—horrify you. So if any of you feel that you do not care to subject your nerves to such a strain, now's your chance to—uh, well, we warned you.

State censorship boards in Massachusetts, Pennsylvania, and New York summarily cut several objectionable scenes from the movie. Those same states also protested a line they considered to be particularly blasphemous. Dr. Frankenstein, enthused to learn that his creature is alive, cries, "It's alive! It's alive! In the name of God! Now I know what it feels like to be God!" The deleted line was eventually restored to the movie in the late 1990s—when the times became a little more "tolerant"[1]

I know what it feels like to be God . . . According to the inferences of scripture, and especially Revelation 13, this experience is the ultimate desire of Satan himself. And a monumental part of the god-desire-nature of the beast of that chapter is the global marking system imposed upon all humankind. This will be a coordinated event employed to literally control the world and every human in it.

Since John's words were first penned in the book of Revelation, biblical scholars have pondered this passage's fulfillment possibilities: "It [the Antichrist, or beast] also *forced all people*, great and small, rich and poor, free and slave, *to receive a mark* on their *right hands or on their foreheads*, so that they *could not buy or sell* unless they had the mark, which is the name of the beast or the number of its name. This calls for wisdom. Let the person who has insight calculate the number of the beast, for it is the *number of a man. That number is 666*" (Rev. 13:16–18).

The first-century church undoubtedly considered that this marking system might have been the emperor worship identification card or tattoo that was required during the reign of the delusional caesars. Those despots demanded that all people worship them at dedicated shrines. Of course, many Christians refused to do so, and they paid with their lives.

As technology began to climb up the exponential curve in the last century, some people became apoplectic over the rise of social security numbers and fingerprint technology. More recently we have worried about national databases, national ID cards, video and electronic surveillance systems, credit cards, bar codes, and microchip implants. Now we are focusing on biometric scanning and identification devices.

Consider some of the latest headlines and quotes speaking to the power of biometric technologies:

- RFID [radio frequency identification] chips [in humans]; a key to more or less freedom?[2]
- "DFBA [the U.S. Department of Defense Forensics and Biometrics Agency] represents the synthesis of Department of Defense (DoD) capabilities in forensics and biometrics."[3]
- Biometrics: Who's Watching You?[4]
- "The World Bank is calling on governments to work together to implement standardized, cost-effective identity management solutions. . . . The UN's . . . [goal is] getting legal ID into the hands of everyone in the world by . . . 2030 [using biometric technologies]."[5]
- "'The future is in the palm of your hand' [literally!] . . . thanks to the proliferation of biometric technology."[6]

- Biometric technology that goes beyond fingerprints
- Ready for ID by body odor? Or the butt-scan?
- Neither are we. But in the brave new world of the biometric revolution, biomarkers like scent and derrière shape could open doors—literally. Or start your car. Or let you vote.
- This is not the distant future. Around the world, governments are rolling out massive biometric identification programs. [7]
- Ray Kurzweil: In the 2030s, Nanobots in Our Brains Will Make Us "Godlike". . . .
- . . . So as we evolve, we become closer to God. Evolution is a spiritual process. There is beauty and love and creativity and intelligence in the world—it all comes from the neocortex. So we're going to expand the brain's neocortex and become more "godlike."[8]
- "India Launches Universal ID System with Biometrics"[9]

THE UN AGENDA 2030

It is no longer difficult to imagine that the global identification system of Revelation 13 might easily be implemented within our lifetime. No fanciful paranoia need be involved in considering the prospects of it—just plain fact. It is being openly spoken of in today's media headlines. The people discussing such things are not tinfoil hat–wearing conspiracy theorists, wild-eyed prophecy handwringers, or clinical therapy patients; they are today's revered scientists, researchers, technology experts, government officials, and the mainstream media.

In November 2015, a popular Internet news website ran an article titled "The UN Plans to Implement Universal Biometric Identification for All of Humanity by 2030."[10]

The article referenced United Nations documents touting the UN's highly publicized 2030 agenda, as well as promoting a leading biometrics company called FindBiometrics. Note that company's definition of the science of biometrics:

> At the most basic, biometrics can be best explained by breaking down the word: bio, as in biological; and metric, as in measurement. That is to say, biometrics are biological measurements. Thanks to the unique nature of many of these measurements, biometrics are *particularly suited for identification*. Fingerprints, facial measurements, the patterns that your veins make and even the way you walk—all of these characteristics and more are unique to you and you only.
>
> At FindBiometrics, we focus on the technologies that measure biometrics and apply them to identity verification. Sometimes that means proving to a computer that you are you and are allowed to access your email, other times it means law enforcement officers uncovering wanted crooks. In every case biometrics allow for a high level of efficiency and assurance when it comes to *every transaction dealing with identity and credentialing*.[11]

So let's think about this for a moment. We have a one-world organization called the United Nations clinging to an impassioned vision of developing a one-world-government system. And that organization is coupling with leading biometrics companies and world banking systems to employ the very latest technology to identify every single human on the planet. Without shame, FindBiometrics claims the tracking technology will be used to trace *every transaction dealing with identity and credentialing*. Notice the word *every*. Do not let the swank of the claim pass you by.

You should read the ominous boast as: "We will soon know where you are at all times. We will know what you are doing, what you are purchasing, whom you are with, and how you are feeling as you do whatever it is that you are doing. By 2030, we will be able to grant or deny access to your bank, computer, phone, and anything else we want to. Eventually, we will be able to biometrically connect every person to almost everything on the planet! Think of how wonderful this new world order will make your life!"

"WHILE PEOPLE ARE SAYING, 'PEACE AND SAFETY . . .'"

You can bet the implementation of such biblically prophetic technology will be made upon the altar of *peace and safety* for all *mankind*. All manner of altruistic promises will be brought forth, including guaranteed protection from terrorist attacks, and the eradication of poverty from the planet. The new *State* will brag that pervasive criminal activity will all but be eliminated. Many would venture to guess that the whole world would actually welcome the paradigm shift. Perhaps the citizens of the brave new world would even *worship* the one who brings this promised Utopia to fruition.

In case you might be tempted to think I am being a bit overdramatic, listen to Secretary-General Ban Ki-moon's 2015 speech endorsing the United Nations' draconian global vision:

> Today is the start of a new era. We have travelled a long way together to reach this turning point. . . .
>
> Today, we are ready to hand over this agenda to world leaders for endorsement at the Summit later this month. Agenda 2030 aims high. . . . It aims to foster human *well-being, prosperity, peace and justice* on a healthy planet. It pursues respect for the human rights of all people and gender equality. It speaks to *all people in*

all countries and *calls for action from everyone everywhere*. It aims to inspire and create genuine partnerships among all countries and actors.

This agenda marks a paradigm shift. It completes the unfinished business of the MDGs [Millennium Development Goals]. . . . It breaks new ground in the way it links peace and security to sustainable development . . . It presents solutions to deal with root causes of the complex problems in our world today, from migration and conflict to exclusion, *violence* against women *and humanitarian crises*, and it prioritizes the vulnerable and marginalized, vowing *to leave no one behind*. . . .

At this month's Summit, we expect Heads of State and Government to not only endorse the new Agenda, but to affirm their strong political commitment to its timely implementation. I am delighted that more than 150 world leaders, as well as His Holiness Pope Francis will join us to start this new era for sustainable development. We must all now act with utmost ambition—and mobilize maximum political will. . . .

. . . With today's resolution, the United Nations has brought the international community to the cusp of decisions that can help realize the founders' dream of a *world of peace and dignity* for all.

I thank you for having taken the world so far *on our collective journey towards a better world for all the world's peoples*. Let us all now work with determination to reach that destination.[12]

Couple the secretary-general's remarks with the following claims of the FindBiometrics Company:

[We have] demonstrated that reliable, biometric ID cards can affordably be used on a large scale. It offers hope for the UN's

Sustainable Development Goal of getting legal ID into the hands
of everyone in the world by the year 2030 with its Identification
for Development (ID4D) initiative.[13]

Whether or not this particular UN agenda will be implemented is yet to be seen. However, according to the Bible, an
agenda very similar to it will eventually be put into place—complete with the technology to force every single human being on
the planet to comply.

The resolve for such an agenda already exists. It even has a
name: Agenda 2030. The technology for the plan is already in
place. Regardless of the myriad of false concerns of past generations regarding a worldwide marking system, we are finally at
the threshold of its reality, and we are the first generation in
history to be so situated. And when it does happen, who might
contend with such a "beast"? Who could oppose such power?
Who would be able to resist its demands?

Sound familiar? Sound probable? Sound biblically prophetic?
It certainly should—for it was written.

AND THEY ALSO WORSHIPED THE BEAST AND ASKED, "WHO IS LIKE

THE BEAST? WHO CAN WAGE WAR AGAINST IT?" —REVELATION 13:4

12

MYSTERY OF THE AGES

Wherever God erects a house of prayer, the Devil always builds a chapel there;
And 'twill be found, upon examination, the latter has the largest congregation.

—DANIEL DEFOE

REVELATION 13 HAS PROVEN to be one of the deepest and most contemplated biblical mysteries. Even John said it would take a mind of "wisdom—or insight"—to finally discern the fulfillment of the prophecy:

> And [the beast] was given authority over every tribe, people, language and nation. All inhabitants of the earth will worship the beast—all whose names have not been written in the Lamb's book of life. . . . [The second beast, the false prophet] . . . also forced all people, great and small, rich and poor, free and slave, to receive a mark on their right hands or on their foreheads, so that they could not buy or sell unless they had the mark, which is the name of the

beast or the number of its name. This calls for wisdom. Let the person who has insight calculate the number of the beast, for it is the number of a man. That number is 666. (Rev. 13:7–8, 16–18)

Obviously, only one generation in history would ultimately live it, and if most scholars are correct, the technology will be used for seven years or less. But will the world's population understand what is actually happening to them when "the mark" finally becomes a reality?

WHAT DOES IT MEAN?

Over the last two thousand years, there has been much speculation as to how the actual marking system and the 666-identification process will ultimately manifest itself. I will not rehash all those potentials in this chapter.

But I do want you to at least consider something you may not have thought of before. Until now, we really have not had the technology against which to compare the possibility. We will commence with a revealing word-by-word study of the passage in question.

FORCED TO RECEIVE A MARK

The prophecy declares that the beast will force every human being on the planet to receive a mark. The mark will be used as identification to determine who can "buy or sell." In other words, without the mark, the sustaining of daily life will eventually become impossible.

The word *force* certainly does not have to mean every human on the planet will be held down or constrained (a nearly impossible task) in order to be identified by the new world system. It could also mean that the mode of the planned individual identification system will be automatically applied, without individual choice in the matter. You can be compelled to do something without being violently or physically accosted—or even touched. You could even be "scanned" and permanently identified without your knowledge, or permission! That specific technology is already being employed in major cities across the globe.

The New Testament word used for *mark* is Strong's #5480 (*charagma*). That Greek word means a scratch, an etching, an imprint, a badge, or a stamp. The specific type of technology that will be employed in the *marking* is not mentioned in the scripture. So, there are any number of modern possibilities for how this mark might be made.

Some translations of Revelation 13:16 say that people will "receive" the mark (NIV, KJV). Others say the mark will be "given" (NASB, HCSB). But the International Standard Version (ISV), renowned for its consistency in providing the most literal translation possible, translates the verse as, "The second beast forces all people . . . to be marked." It makes no mention of being *given*, or having *received* the mark. The ISV simply acknowledges that people will *be* "marked" or identified somehow; it does not state by what means.

Why are there so many obvious variations present within these reliable and scholarly translations?

The Greek word translated *receive* in this verse is Strong's #1325 (*didomi*). This word can also mean the "mark" in question would simply be brought forth, offered up, granted, allowed, produced, merely furnished, given over, or even "shown" to someone. The Blue Letter Bible entry for #1325 even outlines the proper use of the word:

I. to give

II. give something to someone

   A. of one's own accord to give one something, to his advantage.[1]

The receiving of the mark is also mentioned in Revelation 14:9: "A third angel followed them and said in a loud voice: 'If anyone worships the beast and its image and receives its mark on their forehead or on their hand . . .'" The Greek word for "receive" in that verse is Strong's #2983 (*lambano*), which means to "lay hold of," though it can also be correctly used in the sense of "to associate *with* one's self as companion."[2]

Note, then, that in both chapters of Revelation, the verbs often translated *receive* or *take* can also denote an "offering up" or "furnishing" of the mark, rather than the physical forcing of an actual stamp or insignia upon the person.

A REVELATORY MOMENT

Aha! Now we are seeing very different potential understandings of the prophetic scenario. Perhaps it is time to rethink this matter of the beast's *mark* and the vehicle by which it might be employed.

We know that in the two thousand years since this passage was written, the technologies enabling us to identify people have certainly changed in spades. Accordingly, we now know the "mark" does not have to be forcibly *applied* to or stamped upon a person—but rather, it can be "offered up," but in a way that leaves the person very little choice in the matter.

As you will discover, we currently possess the technology for that exact type of human identification plan. The UN is talking about the plan, and preparing for it, even now. It seems as though the Holy Spirit may have chosen the perfect words to use, in order to transcend all generations. Imagine that.

Revelation 14:9 goes on to declare that the mysterious identification scheme will involve the right hand or the forehead. Some translations say it will be "in" (KJV, WBT) the hand or forehead; others say it will be placed "on" or "upon" (NIV, ASV) the hand or forehead. Again, we must ask—Why the variation in translations?

The Greek word for "in" or "on" is *epi* (*Strong's* #1909). It is a complex prefix (with multiple modes of interpretation depending upon context in application) occurring in loanwords from Greek, where it means "upon," "on," "over," "near," "at," "before," and "after" (*epicedium*; *epidermis*; *epigene*; *epitome*); and used in the formation of new compound words (*epicardium*; *epinephrine*).[3]

Again, like the words "mark" and "receive," this biblical word could have a myriad of modern-day fulfillment potentialities and still be completely within its correct Greek interpretation.

The word can easily mean that the mark would be *scanned*; perhaps some piece of technology would *pass over* or *come near* the hand or forehead? Already, fingerprints and iris scans identify passengers at many of the world's airports and other heavily frequented public places where individual identification and security are important. Are lightbulbs coming on over your head? Keep reading.

THE NUMBER OF A MAN

Now we arrive at the truly fascinating part of the equation. This is the element John declared to be a mystery, a riddle requiring wisdom and insight to decipher. In Revelation 13:17–19, we are told that the number of the beast is 666. We are also told that this number is both the number of the beast's name and the number of "a man"; "man's number" (NET); or "a human multitude" (ISV; the footnote to this verse adds, "Or is a multitude of a man; or is the number of a human being"). Apparently the beast and humankind share something very similar—expressed in some type of numerical code.

For centuries, Bible students have fretted over the questions, How could the fact that everyone receives a 666 stamped on their forehead or hand be missed? How could it serve any useful purpose for *everyone* to have the very same number? And, would not the literal application of such a number to one's forehead or hand be so obvious as to cause, perhaps, a worldwide rebellion, rather than bringing an atmosphere of world peace? But, keep reading. It could be that the answers to these riddles are right before us.

The Greek word for *man* is *Strong's #444, anthropos*. This is the word from which our word *anthropology* derives—the study of humankind. As a matter of fact, the Greek *anthropos* allows the translation to be either a singular human being or humanity in general, depending on the context in which the word is used. This is probably why the International Standard Version renders the word as "a human multitude," meaning *all of humanity shares this number.*

Now, that is interesting! The "multitude" including both global humanity *and* the beast have this one thing in common: they share an identical *number code.* The code of "humanity" is somehow tied to the number 666. And this *code* may very well be the secret to unlocking the mystery of the last-days marking system.

Read on to discover what this number code might be.

13

THE TIE THAT BINDS

Time is the best appraiser of scientific work, and I am aware that an industrial discovery rarely produces all its fruit in the hands of its first inventor.

—LOUIS PASTEUR

THE ELEMENT CARBON OCCURS naturally as carbon 12, an isotope that makes up almost 99 percent of the carbon in the universe. Carbon 12 is the most abundant element in the universe. It is present in all forms of carbon-based life.

In the human body carbon is the second most abundant element by mass (about 18.5 percent) after oxygen. Carbon 12 is also one of the five elements that make up human DNA. Thus carbon 12 is indeed *the most crucial element for the existence of humanity*.[1]

But here is the real shocker about carbon 12: its mass number is 12, and it contains 6 protons, 6 neutrons, and 6 electrons. Yes, you see it correctly. The chemical "number" of carbon 12 (the stuff of life itself!) is *666*. Therefore, it can correctly be stated, with scientific accuracy, that 666 is the main identifying chemical number of humankind. Or, stated another way, "666 is the *number of man*."

Carbon was not even officially classified as an element until near the end of the eighteenth century. In 1787, four French chemists wrote a book outlining a method for naming chemical substances. The name they used, carbone, is based on the earlier Latin term for charcoal—*charbon*.[2]

Out of over 6,000 years of human history, we have only known about Carbon-12 for the last 230 years! And only in the last several decades have biblical scholars begun to seriously examine the *666* correlations to the very element that to identify us as human beings, through our DNA—carbon 12. Do the words "Seal it up, Daniel, until the time of the end" have a new ring for you now (Dan. 12:4, paraphrased)?

THE OMNIPRESENT POTENTIAL

While writing this chapter, my son, Brandon, called me from Guatemala, where he was on a mission excursion. He and his son, Parker, were building homes for Third World communities. During the call he told me they had been deep in the jungles of Guatemala, and in one place the villagers told him that they rarely ever saw a white person. He instantly became the newest celebrity in the village.

Brandon went to a small banking facility in the village to see if he could get his U.S. currency exchanged into the local currency. The bankers refused to do so, saying they did not want U.S. currency in their bank!

"But Dad," Brandon said, "it was interesting. You know what they did have in that little jungle bank? They had a biometric fingerprint scanner on the counter and insisted that every villager use it—or they couldn't use the bank's services!

"On top of that," he continued, "a large number of the villagers had cell phones, coded for use by scanning their fingerprint over the surface of the screen!"

So, here is a village so far back in the Guatemalan jungle that it rarely sees white people, yet biometric scanning devices are in place and already "marking" the individual villagers, as well as giving them access to the Internet and to the world!

Knowing what we now understand about the Greek words in Revelation 13, as well as the wanton growth of today's ever-present technologies and the universally planned use of them to "identify" every person on the planet by the year 2030, allow me to present a thought-provoking scenario . . .

THE 666 SCENARIO?

What if the end-time marking system involves something as simple as the number we already carry around inside us? What if the number by which all humankind will be identified in the days of Antichrist is simply the individual coding of the human DNA and/or other biometrically measurable information unique to each human on the planet? Remember: we have only learned how to "access" this "code" within the last several decades.

And suppose the apostle John were given this chemical/mathematical information more than two thousand years ago as a huge clue, one that would be revealed to the exact generation that would need to understand it. Could this have been why John declared that the unraveling of this end-time mystery "calls for wisdom" (Rev. 13:18)?

Think of it. Each person already has a completely unique identifying system/number within his or her own body. There is no need to round everyone up in the world and *implant* anything, or to invent a workable numbering system by which everyone in the world would have to be identified. The number is already there. Since you are a carbon-based life form, you already have a distinctive mathematical identifier implanted in your body—you came into this world with the number. You were *marked* from the moment you were conceived. It is your exclusive DNA "stamp."

It is a scientific fact that identical twins have identical DNA. But they do not have duplicate fingerprints, retina scans, facial vein patterns, facial measurement ratios, or gaits. Each of these exclusive identifiers, as well as a number of others, can be measured biometrically and easily scanned to single out an individual for identification. And it can all be accomplished without ever touching the individual being marked. Also, the "number" can be "offered up" by the individual so that it officially becomes that individual's "mark."

Is it possible that John saw some type of futuristic biometric scanning device being *passed over* the retina (forehead area) or the hand (digital fingerprint scanner, DNA swath, biometric palm recognition device) in the world of the Antichrist? It is definitely a linguistic possibility, and the method for implementation of such a plan is already achievable with current know-how.

If this scenario is anywhere near the truth of the final fulfillment of Revelation 13:16, it is easy to see how it could be brought to fruition very soon—say, by 2030 or so. Nothing overtly invasive need be done to any individual, much less every human in the world. The only requirement would be to place the technological devices throughout the world, especially in frequented places, like financial institutions, grocery stores, medical offices, workplaces, water supplies, and so forth. It would not take long before practically every person on the planet, including jungle villagers, would pass through one of these devices, each having his or her bio number recorded in a universal database. People could also be issued a card bearing the same harvested information in the form of a biochip.

If anyone refused to participate in the scheme, the solution would be simple. He or she would not be allowed to buy or sell—ever again. In fact, to "hide" from the technology, a person would have to disappear, *forever*, into the mountains or deep jungles and live like a primitive. Pretty hefty penalty for refusing to participate; would you not agree?

Another important observation—the language of Revelation 13 does not insist that the marking system of the end-time beast (implemented by the second beast—the false prophet) is some form of a certificate of "worship." The scripture clearly indicates that the peoples of the earth are *already* worshipping the beast before the marking system is implemented.

Apparently, it is this worshipful exaltation of the beast that enhances his spirit of presumptuousness, ultimately resulting in a global identification system. The scripture is clear; the "mark" is employed to determine who buys and sells. The marking system's primary use is to dominate the world—apparently through technological means. And the mark will determine if you get to eat—*or not*.

THE BOTTOM LINE

Of course, the preceding interpretation is not the only possible scenario. However, we have come a long way in the last two thousand years since John first saw the vision of the Antichrist days. As a matter of fact, we have taken a monumental leap, and only in the last couple of decades.

On the other hand, if one prefers the theory that the "mark" will actually be "received" or "taken" (in the most literal interpretation), and would be visible on the hand or forehead—never fear—that technology can be employed immediately as well.

Software company Chaotic Moon recently developed a "tech tattoo" that is easily embedded into a person's arm and can store and monitor your medical and financial information. The tattoo can also monitor your vital signs, heart rate, and everything else it needs in order to notify you that you are getting sick. Further, this "mark" is being touted as having the ability to track missing children and to check up on soldiers in combat.[3]

In a predictive 2007 technology piece, *NBC Nightly News* reported that by 2017, use of microchip implants embedded under the skin may well be commonplace.[4]

By 2015, the envisioned biochip technology was already in use and being used voluntarily, with "home kits" made available for self-insertion of the chip.[5]

However, the major power influencers of the world couldn't care less what our favorite interpretation of Revelation 13 might be. They are chomping at the bits to set in motion the global human identification agenda. It is now only a matter of *when*. The date they have set is 2030. We shall see. It may not happen by then. But, according to the Word of God—something like this *will* eventually happen . . . count on it.

Of course, as I pointed out near the beginning of this book, there is the matter of the *rapture of the church* to consider.

Some believe the church will be raptured before the

Antichrist is even revealed; thus there is no need to be concerned about a "mark." Others believe the Antichrist will be revealed to the church and the rapture will not occur until after his rule begins, so they will have to make decisions about the mark. My purpose is not to urge you to choose a side, but to illustrate how close the world has come to realizing the fulfillment of John's Revelation prophecy—especially the coming global marking system. The truth is, we are either very close to the rapture of the church—or, believers are in for some extremely tough decisions . . . and perhaps incredibly soon. Either way, we are a uniquely prophetic generation. No generation before us even came close to possessing the technology that could make the Revelation prophecy of a global identification system an immediate reality. We now possess that technology, and global power brokers are planning for its implementation within the next few years. These plain facts can no longer be disputed.

However, we have yet to examine the greatest prophetic sign of all—the one that biblically and historically proves we are living in *the time of the end*.

That revelation comes next.

14

THE REVENANT NATION

I remember how it was in 1948 when Israel was being established and all my Jewish friends were ecstatic, I was not. I said: what are we doing? We are establishing ourselves in a ghetto, in a small corner of a vast Muslim sea. The Muslims will never forget nor forgive, and Israel, as long as it exists, will be embattled.

—ISAAC ASIMOV

"THE JEWS THOUGHT WE forgot Palestine and that they had distracted us from it," he said. "Not at all, Jews. We did not forget Palestine for a moment. With the help of Allah, we will not forget it . . . The pioneers of the jihadist fighters will surround you on a day that you think is distant and we know is close. We are getting closer every day."

With those words on Christmas Day 2015, the year 2016 commenced for Israel. ISIS leader Abu Bakr al-Baghdadi made the public statement in a rare recording, his first open declaration in almost seven months.

"Be confident that [Allah] will grant victory to those who

worship him," Baghdadi said, "and hear the good news that [ISIS] is doing well. The more intense the war against it, the purer it becomes and the tougher it gets."

"Jews," he warned, "soon you shall hear from us in Palestine which will become your grave."[1]

When Baghdadi leveled those threats, prophecy students around the world remembered Jesus' haunting words spoken two thousand years earlier, "When you see Jerusalem being *surrounded by armies*, you will know that its desolation is near" (Luke 21:20; emphasis added). Baghdadi's statements also correlated with the ominous words of Yahweh in Zechariah 12:2–3: "I am going to make Jerusalem a cup that sends all the surrounding peoples reeling. Judah will be besieged as well as Jerusalem. On that day [the time of the end], when all the nations of the earth are gathered against her . . ."

The year 2016 certainly began on a prophetic note, distinctively for Israel.

UNIQUELY SITUATED IN HISTORY

Israel is the only independent nation-state to ever exist in the land of "Palestine," having defined borders, a recorded lineage of kings, a unique and internationally recognized monetary system, an established government, a distinctive military organization, a capital, foreign emissaries, and international trade agreements and treaties. And while it is true that there were many tribal people in the region before the Israelites, and some were even ethnic colonies of Egypt, there is not a single historical source indicating that a classically defined independent nation-state existed in that particular expanse of real estate before Israel. It is also a fact that since Nebuchadnezzar overran Judah and destroyed Israel's temple in Jerusalem (587–607 BC), no offi-cially recognized nation-state has ever existed in that region. Nor has there ever been a recognized "Palestinian nation" or "Arab nation" in that location.

Israel's *return* to the land in 1948 is nothing short of one of the most monumental miracles ever witnessed by the world. Never before had any nation's inhabitants, which were scattered around the globe for two millennia, returned to their original homeland and reestablished their language and national heritage, to once again become a politically, militarily, and economi-cally independent nation—never. The statistical improbability of such a geopolitical occurrence is staggering, and remains unequaled in world history.

A growing number of Bible scholars believe Israel's modern "resurrection" is the most definitive prophetic marker to stand as a witness to this end-time generation. They would claim, "With the rebirth of Israel, the last-days 'countdown clock' began. The witness of the olive tree has begun" (see Romans 11; Revelation 11:4).

THE CANAANITE CONTROVERSY

But what about the relatively recent claim, "Today's Palestinian Arabs are descendants of the ancient Canaanites and therefore were some of the very first people to inhabit the area"?

Hussein ibn Ali al-Hashimi (1854-1931), sharif of Mecca and the guardian of the Islamic Holy Places in Arabia, admitted that the Palestinian Arab's ancestors had been in the region no longer than a thousand years. Other renowned Palestinian Arabs have also acknowledged that their association with the area came long after the ancient Jews. For example, in statements before the Anglo-American Committee in 1946, Arab representatives claiming a legitimate connection to Palestine of more than a thousand years dated that connection no further back than the seventh-century conquest of Muhammad's followers.[2]

The Bible indicates that the ancient Canaanites lived alongside the Jordan River (see Numbers 33:51–52; Joshua 22:10–11). Archaeological confirmation of the name Canaan in ancient Near Eastern sources is found almost entirely during the period wherein the region was a colony of the New Kingdom of Egypt (16th–11th century BC). The usage of the term *Canaanite* nearly disappeared following the late Bronze Age collapse (ca. 1206–1150 BC).[3]

ISRAELITES RELATED TO THE CANAANITES?

Canaan is first revealed in Scripture as one of Noah's grandsons (Gen. 9:18). Later, we discover that God promised the land of Canaan to Abraham, and eventually delivered it to Abraham's direct descendants (the Israelites) through his wife, Sarah (Gen. 12:5–7; 17:8, 20–21).

Respected Bible scholars assert that archaeological and textual evidence confirms that the early Israelites were themselves Canaanites, or at the very least, directly related to them.[4]

Even though the Bible appears to contrast the Canaanites' ethnicity as being different from the ancient Israelites', modern scholars Jonathan Tubb and Mark Smith have proposed that the kingdoms of Israel and Judah are actually a subset of the Canaanite culture. This assertion is based on their archaeological and linguistic interpretations:

> Despite the long regnant model that the Canaanites and Israelites

were people of fundamentally different culture, archaeological data now casts doubt on this view. The material culture of the region exhibits numerous common points between Israelites and Canaanites in the Iron I period (ca. 1200–1000 BC). The record would suggest that the Israelite culture largely overlapped with and derived from Canaanite culture.[5]

In short, Israelite culture was largely Canaanite in nature. Given the information available, one cannot maintain a radical cultural separation between Canaanites and Israelites for the Iron I period.[6]

Another scholarly examination states:

The Hebrew tribes were originally Syrians, *i.e.* Aramæans *Highlanders* and probably, . . . they were in reality kindred tribes with, and spoke the same language as the Canaanites or *Lowlanders*, whence the Hebrew language called in [Isaiah 19:18] "the (lip) language of Canaan."[7]

The Hebrew Bible describes the Israelite conquest of Canaan in the books of Joshua, Judges, 1 and 2 Samuel, and 1 and 2 Kings. Scholarly studies of the earliest historical writings and archeological discoveries have largely concluded that modern Israel legitimately lays a nationalistic claim upon the land. It is a claim that goes back more than three thousand years. The nation of Israel appears to be the only people who can reliably make such a claim, in spite of the politically correct historical revisionism of today.

NOT BY YOUR RIGHTEOUSNESS

Regardless of who was in the area first, the Lord made it clear to the Israelites that the *only* reason they were possessing the land was because He had ordained it, and because the nations they would drive out had become exceedingly wicked. They were not "entitled" to the land—only the intention of God made their nation possible:

> After the LORD your God has driven them out before you, do not say to yourself, "The LORD has brought me here to take possession of this land because of my righteousness." No, it is on account of the wickedness of these nations that the LORD is going to drive them out before you. It is not because of your righteousness or your integrity that you are going in to take possession of their land. (Deut. 9:4–5)

Not only did God establish Israel in the land, but He also declared He would reestablish them there—in the last days. To this day, Israel still exists in that particular spot as the only nation that has ever existed there! Just as Yahweh said it would be.

A FAKE ISRAEL?

There are those who insist that the nation of Israel, as we know it today, is nothing more than a "fake" Israel—a mere fabrication of man's political maneuvering. That might be an interesting proposition, except that there is not a solitary passage of scripture, in either the Old or New Testaments, that prophesies a fake Israel returning to the land in the last days.

If a fake Israel were going to arise at *any* point in history, would that not be indescribably important for God's people to know? Would it not have been prolifically expounded in the Scriptures? Of course it would! I cannot imagine God knowing of such an event, one that would cause such anxiety in the world, without having given us a single word about it.

> "WHO ASSISTS THE FAKE ZIONIST REGIME, WHO SUPPORTS THEM, WHO CLEARS THE ROAD FOR THEM, WHO STANDS BEHIND THEM?"
>
> —AYATOLLAH ALI KHAMENEI[8]

Conversely, the Bible is replete with prophecies about the actual return of Israel in the last days. And the Bible is clear that when Israel did in fact return, it would be *a sign* to the other nations that Yahweh alone is God, and His Word is true.

Israel is one of the greatest miracles Yahweh has ever directly displayed to His creation. The existence of today's Israel is the promise of dozens of prophecies, each over two thousand years old, proclaiming they would one day return. From the Babylonian, Persian, Greek, and Roman captivities right up to the days of the Holocaust there was no nation of Israel. Now there is, against all odds, a monument to the truthfulness of God's promise. And we are forced to acknowledge the miracle practically every day. Is there any wonder, then, that haters of Israel are so vehement in their desire to see its demise?

As long as Israel is in the land, standing as an independent nation, speaking the Hebrew language, and living the Hebrew culture, it declares the glory of Yahweh, the truthfulness of His Word, and the veracity of the gospel of Jesus Christ.

Those who *hate* Israel's existence are among the likes of Hitler, Mussolini, Stalin, radical Islam, Islamic terrorist organizations, Iran's Ayatollah Khamenei, Iran's Mahmoud Ahmadinejad, enemies of evangelical Christianity, anti-Zionists, Bible detractors, and supremacist hate groups. I refuse to align myself with such groups. Instead, I align myself with Yahweh, who indisputably was the very first *Zionist*! (See 2 Kings 19:21, Psalm 2:6; 53:6, Matthew 21:5; Revelation 14:1.)

IF THE ARABS PUT DOWN THEIR WEAPONS TODAY, THERE WOULD BE NO MORE VIOLENCE. IF THE JEWS PUT DOWN THEIR WEAPONS TODAY, THERE WOULD BE NO MORE ISRAEL. —BENJAMIN NETANYAHU

From the Balfour Declaration of 1917 to the UN decision of 1947, how is it that, in the case of Israel alone, the hand of God must be discounted in the affairs of humankind? Does the Bible not declare it is God Himself who ultimately establishes all the peoples and nations of the earth? (See Genesis 12:2; 17:3–5; Jeremiah 18:6–10, Isaiah 14:26.)

How Yahweh chooses to "establish" a nation is no concern of ours. The resurrected Israel is a miracle of God—His hand is all over it—plain and simple. There is only one place in all eternity wherein Israel's entire history was prophesied, including its ultimate return, and that is the Bible. Further, there is only one nation in history to be resurrected according to those prophecies—the nation of Israel. And Yahweh told us exactly *why* He would use Israel, throughout history, in this remarkable fashion:

> You were shown these things so that you might know that the LORD
> is God; besides him there is no other. (Deut. 4:35)

And there's the rub.

TOUGH DAYS TO COME

Many Bible scholars believe the budding nation of Israel still
has a dreadful time of travail ahead of it. Observe the prophecy
of Jeremiah:

> "'The days are coming,' declares the LORD, 'when I will bring
> my people Israel and Judah back from captivity and restore them
> to the land I gave their ancestors to possess,' says the Lord." . . .
> How awful that day will be! No other will be like it. It will be
> a time of trouble for Jacob. (Jer. 30:3, 7)

The days wherein the resurrected Israel will be viciously
attacked and almost destroyed (see also Ezekiel 38), often
known as *the time of Jacob's trouble*, may rapidly be ascending
upon the world scene, even in our day. It also appears as
though Israel will be left all alone in those days. Jeremiah 30:14
tells the nation, "All your allies have forgotten you; they care
nothing for you."

Zechariah 12:3 indicates this as well: "On that day, . . . all
the nations of the earth [will be] gathered against her."

However, in the end of it all, Israel will prevail. Yahweh has
promised to personally deliver His people from ultimate destruction (Eze. 38–39, Jer. 30:7, 11, 17) while chastising those
nations that turned their back on His beloved (Jer. 30:16). God
declared He would do these things to show Israel and all the
nations of the world that He is the Lord, and His word is true.

"I will make known my holy name among my people Israel. I will no longer let my holy name be profaned, and the nations will know that I the LORD am the Holy One in Israel. It is coming! It will surely take place, declares the Sovereign LORD. This is the day I have spoken of." (Eze. 39:7–8)

On May 14, 1948, the lion roared. The prophetic blast still echoes around the world. We are the only generation to hear it so clearly.

We ignore the signal at our own peril.

15

FORETOLD FROM THE BEGINNING

[I believe in the] rebuilding of Judea as an independent nation.

—JOHN QUINCY ADAMS

BEFORE THEY TOOK THE first step across the Jordan River and into the promised land, the children of Israel were warned that one day they would cease to be a nation because of their eventual rebellion against God. However, they were also assured that because of God's great love for them, they would ultimately be restored as a nation once again—in the last days.

Observe the words of Deuteronomy 30:1–4:

"When all these blessings and curses I have set before you come on you and you take them to heart *wherever the LORD your God disperses you among the nations,* and when you and your children return to the LORD your God and obey him with all your heart and with all your soul according to everything I command you today, then the LORD your God will restore your fortunes and have compassion on you *and gather you again from all the nations where he scattered*

122

you. Even if you have been banished to the most distant land under the heavens, from there the LORD your God will gather you and bring you back." (Emphasis added)

That passage is not the only prophetic warning God gave to His people in the book of Deuteronomy. Here are some others dealing with this theme:

4:25–27—God would scatter Israel to the nations and into exile when they became disobedient.

8:19–20—God would destroy Israel as a nation when they became rebellious.

28:62–66—God would scatter Israel among the nations when disobedient.

29:24–29—God would uproot Israel from their land for abandoning His covenant.

31:14—Israel's future rebellion is predicted.

In addition to the prophecies concerning Israel's protracted future, God added an identifying hint, specifically for the last-days generation. The clue would be so obvious and easily verifiable that the world would be without excuse.

He will bring you to the land that belonged to your ancestors, and you will take possession of it. He will make you [the returned Israel of the last days] *more prosperous and numerous than your ancestors*. (Deut. 30:5, emphasis added)

Today, the tiny nation of Israel is situated squarely in the land of their ancestors. It is among the most prosperous, powerful, intellectually advanced, and technologically superior nations on the planet. Its distinctly Jewish citizenry approaches seven million. Their population is now greater than the number of those killed by the Nazis in the Holocaust, and certainly more than existed in its ancient unified kingdom at any time in history, even under King David. When examining current population trends, some experts predict the population of Israel will reach ten million by 2025, perhaps sooner.[1]

A number of great minds have pondered the miracle of the continued existence of the Jewish race. Historian Arnold Toynbee (not a friend to the Jewish people) completed his classic twelve-volume investigation of the rise and fall of human civilizations in 1961. The work was titled *A Study of History*.

In his comprehensive analysis, Toynbee reported that he was disturbed by only one seeming negation of his understanding of the universal rules governing the inevitable decline of every people on earth. He had bumped, unexpectedly, into an inescapable truth of history—*only the Jews had survived*. Toynbee proclaimed the Jews to be nothing more than a historical oddity, "a vestigial remnant." He predicted that they were a people soon destined to perish.[2]

Toynbee could not have been more mistaken. The words of the prophet Jeremiah not only give the answer to Toynbee's dilemma, but they also strike a serious blow to his grim prediction: "Hear the word of the LORD, you nations; proclaim it in distant coastlands: 'He who scattered Israel will gather them and will watch over his flock like a shepherd'" (Jer. 31:10).

Samuel Clemens (Mark Twain), the famous author and

agnostic, apparently was also overwhelmed by the unexplainable phenomenon of the Jewish people. In 1899 he wrote:

The Egyptian, the Babylonian, and the Persian rose, filled the planet with sound and splendor, then faded to dream-stuff and passed away. The Greek and Roman followed, made a vast noise and they are gone; other peoples have sprung up and held their torch high for a time, but it burned out, and they sit in twilight now, or have vanished. The Jew saw them all, beat them all, and is now what he always was, exhibiting no decadence, no infirmities of age, no weakening of his parts, no slowing of his energies, no dulling of his alert and aggressive mind. All things are mortal but the Jew. All other forces pass, but he remains. What is the secret of his immortality?[3]

Just a few years earlier, in 1891, Leo Nikolaivitch Tolstoy, a Russian Orthodox Christian best known for his novel *War and Peace*, had written an article titled "What Is a Jew?" In that reflective piece Tolstoy observed:

The Jew is the emblem of eternity. He who neither slaughter nor torture of thousands of years could destroy, he who neither fire, nor sword, nor Inquisition was able to wipe off the face of the earth. He who was the first to produce the Oracles of God. He who has been for so long the Guardian of Prophecy and has transmitted it to the rest of the world. Such a nation cannot be destroyed. The Jew is as everlasting as Eternity itself.[4]

In August 2015, CBN's Scott Ross interviewed author and analyst Caroline Glick regarding the current trends in Israel and the Middle East. Glick observed, "The one island of safety and tranquility and peace is Israel . . . The only country that's a coherent nation state, an organic nation state in this region is the Jewish state. Every other state you see is either collapsing or on the verge of collapse and struggling in order to survive.[5]

Tolstoy's discerning words of the late nineteenth century continue to ring with prophetic fulfillment today. Amazingly, the "nation" Israel of which Tolstoy spoke was not yet a recognized political state. That miraculous geopolitical fact would not come to fruition for another fifty-six years after he first penned his reflection.

Yet, the nation of Israel is here today, and for now it certainly is an island of tranquility in the Middle East. It is powerful, prosperous, and one of the world's premier leaders in technology and sheer brainpower. The Jewish people and the returned Israel are indeed "as everlasting as Eternity itself." How could Israel's current existence in the land of promise not be a definitive sign that we are in the "last days"?

Yahweh is on His throne, and His Word is true.

ADDITIONAL SCRIPTURES PREDICTING THE RETURN OF ISRAEL

Isaiah 11:11–12	Ezekiel 39:27–29
Isaiah 43:5–6	Jeremiah 16:14–15
Isaiah 66:7–8	Jeremiah 23:3–6
Ezekiel 34:13	Amos 9:14–15
Ezekiel 37:11–12, 14,	Hosea 3:4–5
21–22, 25	Zechariah 10:8–10
Ezekiel 38:7–8	Luke 21:24

16

THE BLESSING

Why will you ask proof of the veracity of One who cannot lie?
—CHARLES HADDON SPURGEON

FROM THE INCEPTION OF the Nobel Prize in 1901 until 2013, there had been a total of 855 Nobel laureates. Almost one-quarter of those prizes (193) were awarded to Jewish recipients, most of them hailing from the land of the prophetically restored Israel.[1]

By 2013, the tiny nation had fewer than five million Jews in the total population, yet had won more Nobel Prizes per capita than the United States, France, or Germany, producing multiple winners in all six of the Nobel categories.[2]

Although Jews comprise less than 0.2 percent of the world's population, overall they have been awarded 41 percent of all the Nobel Prizes in economics, 28 percent in medicine, 26 percent in physics, 19 percent in chemistry, 13 percent in literature, and 9 percent of all the peace awards.[3]

Israeli science has catapulted in the past decade of Nobel

Prize awards, with 0.77 laureates per million people, compared with 0.2 for the United States. Despite its international hardships, Israel is still the world's leading exporter of brainpower. One-quarter of Israel's academic scholars work at leading academic institutions in the United States, five times more than from any other nation except Canada.[4]

To this day, Israel leads the world in the proportion of scientists and technicians in the workforce with 145 people per 10,000. By comparison, the United States only has 85 per 10,000. Japan boasts 70, while Germany registers just 60. More than 25 percent of Israel's total workforce is employed in technical professions, making it the world's leader in this category as well.[5]

As of this writing, Israel has been in existence for fewer than seventy-five years. Yet, this diminutive, war-torn, isolated nation manages to impress:

- Israel has the eighth longest life expectancy in the world: 82.0 years—more than the United Kingdom, the United States, and Germany.
- Israeli scientific research institutions are ranked third in the world.
- Israel is ranked second in space sciences.
- Israel is one of the ten countries in the world capable of launching its own satellites.
- Israel produces more scientific papers per capita than any other nation by a large margin—109 per 10,000 people—as well as one of the highest per capita rates of patents filed.
- Israel leads the world in patents for medical equipment.
- Israel has more NASDAQ-listed companies than any other country, besides the United States, and more than all of Europe, India, China, and Japan combined.

- Israel is among the top three countries in cyberattack defense.
- Israel has the highest ratio of university degrees to population in the world.
- Israeli universities are among the best of the world.
- Israel is the second-most educated country after Canada.
- Israel's $300 billion economy is larger than all of its immediate neighbors combined.
- Israel's military is ranked the eleventh most powerful military in the world, and without question the most powerful military in the Middle East.[6]

Israel is one of the world's foremost military nuclear powers. Some sources have it listed as the third-ranking nuclear power, with an arsenal approximating four hundred warheads, only trailing the United States and Russia in total nuclear armament. It is difficult to determine the exact number of nuclear weapons that Israel possesses since its government engages in strategic ambiguity.[7]

By 2013, Israel was also leading the way in futuristic technologies. The fledgling nation was already famed for having the highest concentration of startups in the world. Thousands of Israeli technology startups have given rise to advances in fields as varied as irrigation, GPS navigation, and cherry tomatoes. The quantity of computer, cell phone, and medical technologies invented by Israel are too numerous to list.

Israel is also responsible for the world-changing technologies of 3-D printing, human brain hacking, and software that can predict pandemics and genocides several months before they happen, a technology used with success in 2012.[8]

Given what we now know about the necessity of the

computer, biometrics, medical, and communications technology needed to implement the end-time technology spoken of in the Bible, isn't it interesting that a startling amount of that technology is coming straight out of the prophetically reborn nation of Israel?

HOW JEWS HELPED SAVE AMERICA

Most people understand the special relationship that Israel and the United States have enjoyed throughout much of Israel's limited existence. A total of sixteen countries host 98 percent of the world's Jewish population. Of those sixteen, Israel and the United States together account for 83 percent of the total global Jewish population.[9]

The United States traditionally has been a great ally of the young nation of Israel. However, even as closely as the United States and Israel are tied, apparently few people know of the important role of the Jewish people in American history.

Following is an excerpt from an amazing historical overview outlining the Jewish contribution to America's history. The article, written by best-selling author Bill Federer, is titled "How Jews Helped Save the United States":

> The American Revolutionary War was the first time since being exiled from Jerusalem that Jews fought alongside Christian neighbors as equals in the fight for freedom. Jewish merchants . . . [provided] clothing, guns, powder and food to the needy Revolutionary soldiers. Some merchants lost everything. . . .
>
> President Calvin Coolidge recounted, May 3, 1925: "Haym Solomon, Polish Jew financier of the Revolution. . . [Solomon] pledged his personal faith and fortune for enormous amounts, and

personally advanced large sums to such men as James Madison, Thomas Jefferson, Baron Steuben, General St. Clair, and many other patriot leaders who testified that without his aid they could not have carried on in the cause."

In 1975, a U.S. postage stamp honored Haym Solomon, with printing on the back: "Financial hero-businessman and broker Haym Solomon was responsible for raising most of the money needed to finance the American Revolution and later saved the new nation from collapse."

George Washington sent a letter to the Jewish Congregation in Newport, Rhode Island, and in Savannah, Georgia, stating: "May the same wonder-working Deity, who long since delivered the Hebrews from their Egyptian oppressors, planted them in a promised land, whose providential agency has lately been conspicuous in establishing these United States as an independent nation, still continue to water them with the dews of heaven."[10]

And of course, it was J. Robert Oppenheimer, probably the best-known Jewish scientist born in the United States, who worked on the Manhattan Project, the program that produced the atomic bombs that ended World War II in August 1945, potentially saving millions more lives. And, of course, we now know that ending World War II actually paved the way for the rebirth of Israel.

There were no fewer than a dozen more American-born Jewish scientists who worked with Oppenheimer. There were another dozen foreign-born Jewish scientists assisting in the undertaking as well.[11]

SOME PEOPLE LIKE THE JEWS, AND SOME DO NOT. BUT NO THOUGHTFUL MAN CAN DENY THE FACT THAT THEY ARE, BEYOND ANY QUESTION, THE MOST FORMIDABLE AND MOST REMARKABLE RACE WHICH HAS APPEARED IN THE WORLD. —WINSTON S. CHURCHILL

From Oppenheimer's initial technology development sprang most of the nuclear technology the world possesses today. And without nuclear technology, many Bible scholars believe other important end-time prophecies could not be fulfilled.

How is it that the world's Jewish populace, even before they were reassembled into a new nation, could have had such a disproportionate impact on world history, including an indelible mark on United States history? After all, the entire global population of Jewish people as of 2014 was only fourteen million people, markedly less than the total population of the state of Florida?[12]

And how is it that the miniscule country of modern-day Israel, with a 2016 population of less than that of the state of New Jersey, can currently lead the world in so many innovations and in so much total intelligence, military might, and amazing historical achievements? And how in the world could Israel have possibly achieved all this in fewer than seventy years of its current total existence?

Is this merely a historical mishap? Or, is something suspiciously miraculous involved? Could the phenomenon, which only our generation has experienced, be an end-time signal from Yahweh?

But what could the return of Israel and the regathering of a

diminutive, ancient people group called the Jews possibly have
to do with the end-times?

Yes, indeed, what?

17

JEWISH BELIEVERS IN THE TIME OF THE END

All of a sudden it clicked, that . . . Jesus died for me, too.[1]
—LAWRENCE KUDLOW

THE SCRIPTURES FORETOLD THAT in the very last days, before the return of Yeshua, at least some in God's revenant nation would turn their hearts toward Him; they would receive Yeshua (Jesus) as Messiah. That biblical prediction is occurring now, in ever-increasing numbers.

In the eleventh chapter of the New Testament book of Romans, we find the apostle Paul's discourse concerning the Jewish rejection of the gospel. However, Paul made it abundantly clear that in the future (in the last days) a "remnant" of the Jews would indeed accept the gospel and turn to Yeshua as Messiah. *Barnes' Notes on the Bible* interprets the passage:

> It is clear here that the apostle fixed his eye on a *future conversion of the Jews* to the gospel, and expected that their conversion would precede the universal conversion of the Gentiles to the Christian faith,

there could be no event that would make so immediate and decided an impression on the pagan world as the conversion of the Jews. *They are scattered everywhere* [when Barnes wrote this, the nation of Israel had not yet been resurrected!]; they have *access to all people; they understand all languages; and their conversion would be like kindling up thousands of lights* at once in the darkness of the pagan world.[2]

When the State of Israel was established in 1948, only a handful of Israeli Jews believed that Yeshua is Messiah. However, from 1998 to 2013, the number of Jews living in Israel who profess Yeshua as Messiah tripled. The number of Messianic congregations also tripled during that time. Today in Israel, there are more than twenty thousand Jews acknowledging Yeshua as Messiah, with over 150 congregations of Jewish believers worshipping alongside their Gentile Christian brothers and sisters.[3] And these staggering numbers do not even count the many hundreds of thousands living throughout the world who now claim Jesus as Messiah.[4]

AND THIS GOSPEL OF THE KINGDOM WILL BE PREACHED IN THE WHOLE WORLD AS A TESTIMONY TO ALL NATIONS, AND THEN THE END WILL COME. —JESUS CHRIST (MATTHEW 24:14)

The count of the *last-days* Jewish ingathering is only expected to multiply, aided in part by a number of renowned Orthodox Jewish rabbis who have recently begun pointing other Jews toward Yeshua as Messiah.

THE RABBINIC NOTE THAT SHOOK THE WORLD

Between 2005 and 2007 an unbelievable, yet highly documented, account of Israel's most venerated rabbi, Yitzhak Kaduri, exploded upon the world scene.

The 108-year-old rabbi told his followers that he was leaving behind a handwritten note, to be shared after his death. He insisted the note would reveal the name of the "real" Messiah, whom he claimed to have met in a vision.

At his death in January 2006, Kaduri's funeral drew over 250,000 people. The president of Israel delivered the eulogy. Kaduri's death note was posted one year later, at his official instruction, on his ministry website. The posting of Kaduri's Messiah note was reported by several Israeli-based media sources.

When the message was finally decoded, several months after its posting, the note disclosed the name of the "real" Messiah. The name was revealed as Yehoshua—the Hebrew long form of *Yeshua* . . . or Jesus.

The Kaduri story is an extremely complex one, and highly controversial among Orthodox Jews. Many reject the account flat out and say it is bogus. But since a number of Kaduri disciples—now believers in Yeshua as Messiah—claim they were taught by Kaduri himself in his yeshiva in Jerusalem, the account has become increasingly difficult to convincingly refute.

To this day, Kaduri's Yeshua legacy continues to spark a number of Israeli Jews to acknowledge Yeshua as Messiah. Many now believe the Kaduri event to be a definitive and exciting end-time marker.[5]

But Rabbi Kaduri was not the only rabbi who insisted his fellow Jews "take a closer look" at Yeshua as Messiah.

A COALITION OF RABBIS WANT ANOTHER LOOK

On the day before Christmas in 2015, more than twenty-five prominent rabbis from Israel and abroad issued a declaration calling for a "renewed look" at Jesus. They also called for a closer investigation of Christianity and the New Testament documents. This shocking declaration was an enormous eye-opener, for Christians and Jews alike.[6]

The Israeli-based news agency Israel Today reported:

What we are now witnessing is the undoing of 2,000 years of Jewish rejection and animosity towards Jesus, a miracle by any estimation. For the out-and-out refusal by Jews to accept Jesus is slowly, but surely, coming to an end, as growing numbers of prestigious Orthodox rabbis welcome Jesus back. And there is more. "After nearly two millennia of mutual hostility and alienation, we Orthodox Rabbis who lead communities, institutions and seminaries in Israel, the United States and Europe . . . seek to do the will of our Father in Heaven by accepting the hand offered to us by our Christian brothers and sisters."[7]

For a group of Orthodox Jewish Rabbis to "accept the hand" of Christians and then call them "our Christian brothers and sisters," is simply astounding. It is nothing short of supernatural! For more than two thousand years, Orthodox Jews, by and large, have taught their children and synagogue congregations that there is a gulf of separation between Jews and Christians—a chasm they are forbidden to cross over. Obviously Yahweh is doing a new work in these prophetic last days.

"AND I WILL POUR OUT ON THE HOUSE OF DAVID AND THE INHABITANTS OF JERUSALEM A SPIRIT OF GRACE AND SUPPLICATION. THEY WILL LOOK ON ME, THE ONE THEY HAVE PIERCED, AND THEY WILL MOURN FOR HIM AS ONE MOURNS FOR AN ONLY CHILD, AND GRIEVE BITTERLY FOR HIM AS ONE GRIEVES FOR A FIRSTBORN SON."

—ZECHARIAH 12:10

INSIDE ISRAEL AND AROUND THE WORLD

I am blessed to have several reliable connections within the Messianic community of Israel. Those sources consistently relate the same information regarding the increasing number of Jews who are coming to Yeshua as Messiah. They also claim that a large number of Israeli Jews are already believers in Yeshua. However, most do not speak publicly of their belief in Yeshua for fear of intense persecution from other Jews, or even from members of their own family. Many of these Jewish believers, at their own request, are being covertly discipled in the gospel of Yeshua by several ministries established in Israel for this very purpose.

Presently there are "underground" meeting rooms established throughout the country where Orthodox Jews who seek more information about Yeshua can congregate to be discipled. There they have access to articles, books, and movies to answer their many biblical questions. There truly is a strong movement of "Yeshua seekers" in Israel, and my contacts insist this growing phenomenon is relatively recent and absolutely unprecedented.

One such source is Israeli Messianic rabbi Zev Porat. Rabbi Porat is the founder of Messiah of Israel Ministries.[8]

Zev was born in Israel and has lived there most of his life. His father was a rabbi. Both of his grandfathers, and his great-grandfathers, were also rabbis. One of his great grandfathers knew Rabbi Yitzhak Kaduri personally. As a result of his personal connections with the Kaduri story, Zev has conducted many video interviews (currently posted all over the Internet) with Kaduri's yeshiva students. These are former rabbinical students who are believers in Yeshua today because of Rabbi Kaduri's teachings and Kaduri's Yeshua death-note.

Additionally, Rabbi Porat has led numerous Jews to Yeshua as Savior and Messiah through his in-the-street witnessing and follow-up discipling approach. Much of Rabbi Porat's methodology involves using the book *The Rabbi Who Found Messiah* and the documentary movie by the same title. Both resources are being widely distributed throughout Israel.[9]

IT MIGHT SEEM STRANGE TO SOME THAT A SCIENTIST AND A JEW COULD COME TO FAITH IN JESUS. BUT FAITH IS NEVER A LEAP INTO THE DARK. IT IS ALWAYS BASED ON EVIDENCE. THAT WAS HOW MY WHOLE SEARCH FOR GOD BEGAN. —DR. DAVID BLOCK, PROFESSOR OF APPLIED MATHEMATICS AND ASTRONOMY[10]

History is replete with records of prominent Jewish men and women who have come to Yeshua as Savior and Messiah. One such list is found at the website of the Association of Messianic Congregations.[11]

A prominent name appearing on that roll of Messianic Jewish believers is Jay Sekulow, attorney and chief counsel for the American Center for Law and Justice. Sekulow is often involved in defending the First Amendment freedom-of-faith rights of American citizens. On numerous occasions Sekulow has successfully argued before the Supreme Court of the United States in matters of religious freedoms.

After Sekulow became a believer in Yeshua, he testified that he attempted for years to understand Isaiah 53, the "suffering servant" passage of the Old Testament. Sekulow says of his journey:

> I kept looking for a traditional Jewish explanation that would satisfy, but found none. The only plausible explanation seemed to be Jesus. My Christian friends were suggesting other passages for me to read, such as Daniel 9. As I read, my suspicion that Jesus might really be the Messiah was confirmed. . . . I'd always thought my cultural Judaism was sufficient, but in the course of studying about the Messiah who would die as a sin bearer, I realized that I needed a Messiah to do that for me.[12]

The astounding reports of Jewish conversions, both in the land of Israel and around the world, continue to bloom. How could today's born-again believer not see what is happening in our midst? How could we miss the "blossoming of the fig tree" (see Matthew 24:32)?

And how can we not be passionately moved to understand that the return of the Lion of Judah is drawing nigh?

18

THE WORLD WAR III ZEITGEIST

I know not with what weapons World War III will be fought, but World War IV will be fought with sticks and stones.

—ALBERT EINSTEIN

"THERE ARE MUSLIMS THAT have access to [President Obama] in the White House. Our foreign policy has a lot of influence now, from Muslims. We see the prime minister of Israel being snubbed by the president and by the White House and by the Democrats, and it's because of the influence of Islam. They hate Israel, and they hate Christians. And so, the storm is coming." So said the Reverend Franklin Graham on March 2015 on CBN's *The 700 Club*.

"Can you imagine the outcry if 21 Muslims had been beheaded by Christians?" he asked in response to ISIS' video portraying the beheading of that same number of Coptic Christians. "Where is the universal condemnation by Muslim leaders around the world? As we mourn with the families of those 21 martyrs, we'd better take this warning seriously as these acts of terror will only spread throughout Europe and the United States."

"Why?" you ask. Reverend Graham has the answer: "The Bible tells us that in the end-times there will be 'distress of nations with perplexity,'" he posted on Facebook.[1]

THE CENTURY OF WAR

The world has suffered two devastating global wars in the last century. In World War II alone, estimates indicate that more than forty million civilians perished, along with more than twenty million soldiers. Some estimates put the figures significantly higher. From that war emerged international atomic technologies and the beginning of the nuclear arms race.

Today, the world's nine nuclear powers are sitting atop approximately sixteen thousand deliverable nuclear warheads. The United States and Russia, the two undisputed nuclear superpowers, account for 93 percent of all the nuclear weaponry. These two nations alone possess enough nuclear firepower to destroy all the inhabitants of the earth several times over. This prophetic potential has existed fewer than seventy years.[2]

Grant Jeffrey, PhD (1948–2012), was a Canadian teacher of biblical prophecy and archaeology. In chapter 15 of his book *Armageddon: An Appointment with Destiny*, he wrote:

> Jesus Christ said, "And ye shall hear of wars and rumours of wars: see that ye be not troubled: for all these things must come to pass, but the end is not yet. For nation shall rise against nation, and kingdom against kingdom . . ." (Matthew 24:6–7). . . .
>
> Throughout history mankind has endured thirteen years of war for every single year of peace. However, since 1945 the number of wars has increased tremendously. As dozens of new nations

demanded independence and old empires disintegrated, more than three hundred wars were fought since World War II. A military study, *The War Atlas*, concluded that the world has not known a single day since World War II without some nation waging a war or conflict somewhere on earth. Despite thousands of peace treaties, the last one hundred years has truly become "the century of war."[3]

ZEITGEIST

Zeitgeist is a German word translated "the spirit of the times." In April 2015, WND featured a headline article titled "Is World War III Coming Soon?"

The prestigious roll call of World War III watchers listed in the piece included: Pope Francis, former congresswoman Michelle Bachman, former Soviet leader Mikhail Gorbachev, former Ukrainian ambassador Yuri Shcherbak, news mogul Glenn Beck, syndicated radio host Mark Levin, the King of Jordan, Brig. Gen. Masoud Jazayeri (Iran's deputy chief of staff), and an assortment of internationally known authors.[4]

Since that time, many other influential people have joined the growing list. The inventory includes various global media sources, as well as Jack Ma, founder and executive chairman of Alibaba Group; Manuel Valls, prime minister of France; Dmitry Medvedev, Russia's prime minister; a variety of international financial experts; Sirajul Haq, a renowned Pakistani Muslim cleric; and Russia's president, Vladimir Putin.

"FRENCH PM: TERROR ATTACKS IN FRANCE, ISRAEL SHOW WE ARE 'IN WORLD WAR.'" —*THE TIMES OF ISRAEL*, JANUARY 19, 2016[5]

WARS AND RUMORS OF WARS

Even China joined the rhetoric of a looming global war by threatening that "World War III was inevitable" if the United States did not capitulate to specific geopolitical demands.[6]

In September 2015, both China and Russia arrived in Syria with troops, naval ships, and fighter jets. ISIS had been relentlessly wreaking havoc in the Middle East, particularly along the Euphrates River area from Syria through Iraq, as well as directly threatening the United States and Israel. Consequently, an ever-growing number of media pundits were eyeing the explosive situation as the groundwork for a potential world war.[7] Joel Richardson, *New York Times* best-selling author of *Islamic Antichrist*, wrote, "The world is presently teetering on the edge of World War III. This is not an overly sensationalized statement."[8]

Of course, there is always the continual concern of the rogue nation of North Korea. In early February 2016, a former director of the U.S. Strategic Defense Initiative, Henry Cooper, claimed North Korea was treading on very dangerous ground—yet again. Cooper was a former ambassador and served as President Ronald Reagan's chief representative in the "Star Wars" defense initiative negotiations with the Soviet Union. He also was SDI director under President George H. W. Bush.

Cooper revealed that North Korea was preparing its Sohae satellite complex for launch within days. The announced southern trajectory, Cooper said, could prove to be threatening to the United States. North Korea was claiming the launch was simply a "test."

Cooper's analysis of that claim was that it would be difficult to distinguish a test from an actual attack, and the best way to counter such a threat to the U.S. homeland would be to knock out the missile at the moment it began its trajectory over a southern polar route.

Cooper insisted that if the North Korean satellite turned out to be a nuclear device (at that time, or with another similar launch in the future) and if it was detonated over one hundred miles above the United States, it could destroy all life-sustaining critical infrastructures that rely on the national grid. A direct strike by such an electromagnetic pulse (EMP), he predicted, could lead to the death of most Americans within the following year.[9]

In spite of warnings from an assortment of world leaders, North Korea launched their satellite-missile just a few days later. On February 7, 2016, the Agence France-Presse (AFP) published an article titled "Global outrage over North Korea rocket launch." The AFP reported, "The international community is still struggling to reach agreement on how to respond to Pyongyang's latest nuclear test—of what it claimed was a hydrogen bomb—on January 6."[10]

A February 6 Fox News report revealed the United States, Japan, and South Korea had requested an emergency meeting of the United Nations Security Council, in response to North Korea's long-range rocket launch. Fox noted, "The January nuclear test was North Korea's fourth. The other tests took place in 2006, 2009, and 2013. Each test was followed by long-range rocket launches, raising concerns that North Korea is perfecting its military arsenal with the intention of producing warheads for intercontinental ballistic missiles that can reach the United States."[11]

Stoking the World War III zeitgeist fires even higher, February 12, 2016, came with Russia's warnings of the possibility of a coming "world war." Both Russia and the United

States demanded ceasefires in the long-running civil war in Syria. They each wanted the ongoing battle to be concentrated against the Islamic State of Iraq and the Levant (ISIL)—but each demanded conflicting terms.

The Gulf States, led by Saudi Arabia, staged their own involvement. Those nations said they were committed to sending ground troops to Syria. Their favored rebel groups had been pulverized by Russian air raids and driven back on the ground by Iranian-supplied pro-regime troops. This turn of events led Russia to issue its warning of a "new world war."[12]

Certainly there are many factors in today's fragile world easily capable of touching off a conflict of World War III proportions. The persistent global war-atmosphere talk sounds ominously like the last-days spirit of "wars and rumors of wars," and nations rising against nations, of which Jesus spoke in Matthew 24:6–7.

PROPHETIC WORLD WAR III FACTORS

The FBI currently reports an ISIS presence in all fifty of the United States, at the same time that Islamic jihadists beckon for a World War III scenario—especially targeting Israel and the West.[13]

The Islamic theology of ISIS *demands* an apocalyptic war. They believe that their Mahdi (Islamic savior and world ruler) will not come to rule the planet until the earth has been cleansed of infidels through a decisive Islamic victory, resulting from a global war. They fervently push toward that goal.

Moreover, Iran has made clear its intention of possessing nuclear weapons—soon! On a number of highly publicized occasions, several of Iran's leaders have openly expressed their desire to "eliminate" the United States and Israel, further increasing the level of world war anxiety.[14]

In addition, Iran is funding proxy terrorist groups, like Hezbollah and Hamas, specifically to engage in targeted acts of terrorism. Iran and Russia are presently in close alliance, especially in the area of nuclear proliferation.

Added to the developments of China's and Russia's growing aggression in the Middle East, numerous experts predict a global economic collapse is on the horizon. A good portion of this concern is tied to the current unstable geopolitical atmosphere.

THE WORLD HAS NOT KNOWN A SINGLE DAY SINCE WORLD WAR II WITHOUT SOME NATION WAGING A WAR OR CONFLICT SOMEWHERE ON EARTH. —DR. GRANT JEFFREY

Adding even more fuel to the fires of aggression, Pope Francis is, at the same time, calling for the establishment of a new, one-world government organization (to combat man-made global warming), and insisting on the official establishment of a legitimate state of Palestine.[15]

And the "wars and rumors of wars" spirit continues to ooze around the world, fanning the flames of global anxiety. All the while, much of the world appears to be hoping for a strong and world-impacting leader to arise to save the world from certain destruction. Thus, without realizing it, many are actually promoting the rise of the biblically prophesied Antichrist, the one who will promise supernatural deliverance. The Bible declares such a one will eventually affect a covenant with many—actually bringing a perceptible measure of long-desired peace to the world . . . but only temporarily.

Not surprisingly, every one of the aforementioned elements—from the return of Israel, the explosion of Middle East unrest, the rise of the spirit of global war, to the appearing of the Antichrist—are mentioned in the pages of biblical prophecy. We are the first generation to see all these things converging, starting fewer than one hundred years ago.

The convergences continue to advance at an alarming pace, and so does the World War III zeitgeist.

19

ADVANCING LIKE A STORM

People who call themselves supporters of Israel are actually supporters of its moral degeneration and ultimate destruction.[1]

—NOAM CHOMSKY

AND THE SPIRIT OF the living Word of Yahweh came unto the prophet Ezekiel and said, "O Son of man, declare unto the nations; to Gog of Magog and all the rebellious ones who string along with you . . . Behold, many years from now—*in the time of the end*—you will come against My people. They will be a land that has recovered from devastation, whose people I have gathered from among the many nations of the world and brought to the mountains of Israel.

> I will bring them out from all the peoples, and I will settle them in
> the Beautiful Land, and at that time they will dwell in what they
> will call "safety," saying, "See how strong we have become." But
> you, Magog, and all your troops, and the many nations with you,
> will go up against them, advancing like a storm; you will be like a

cloud of locusts, completely covering the land. The world will stand in amazement as they watch what I the LORD am doing. See, I am telling you this now, so that when I cause it to come to pass—you and all the nations will know that I am the LORD, and beside me there is no other." (Eze. 37–39, paraphrased)[2]

PROPHECY ON THE BRINK . . .

Messianic Christian scholar Dr. Arnold Frutchenbaum (who has written ten books and three sets of biblical commentaries) believes the world might be on the brink of watching the prophecies of Ezekiel 38–39 come to pass. His assessment is based, in part, on the important language nuance concerning the word translated "safety" in Ezekiel 38. The Hebrew word is *betachm*, he explains, which can also be translated as a "*false* confidence and security," an apt description of the attitude of our day.[3]

The *NAS Exhaustive Concordance* affirms that *betachm* can mean "without care," and living "unawares." Certainly, these definitions match Dr. Frutchenbaum's scholarly observations.[4]

Ezekiel 38:11 predicts the last-days Israel will be living in a land of "unwalled villages" without "bars or gates." In the days during which Ezekiel lived, practically all the cities were fortified with walls to protect from marauding invaders. But the Israel of today dwells in the land primarily without these defenses, just as the prophecy declared they would.[5]

Joel C. Rosenberg is the *New York Times* best-selling author of *The Ezekiel Option: The Last Jihad*, a prophetic novel based on Ezekiel's end-time prophecies. When addressing the question of whether or not Ezekiel 38's war of Gog and Magog would occur before or after the rapture, Rosenberg responded, "The truth is we simply do not know the answer for certain, because

Ezekiel does not say. Many of the theologians I have cited in this book believe the war will occur after the Rapture. In the novel *Left Behind*, Tim LaHaye and Jerry B. Jenkins describe the War of Gog and Magog as having already happened before the Rapture takes place. In *The Ezekiel Option*, I also chose to portray the war occurring before the Rapture."[6]

Regardless of the various eschatological interpretations, in Ezekiel 38–39 we discover that after a politically viable Israel is "resurrected" to new existence (in the very last days), there will eventually arise a coalition of nations whose purpose will be to wipe the returned Israel from the face of the map. Nothing short of Israel's annihilation will satisfy them.

Psalm 83, written a thousand years before the time of Christ, also speaks of the supernaturally returned Israel being attacked by a coalition of nations. The Psalm 83 nations are predicted by many to eventually join up with the Ezekiel 38 entities. A good number of Bible scholars believe they now see these prophecies developing.

Furthermore, the world has witnessed the tide slowly turning against Israel for years—at least at political levels. And sadly, Ezekiel's prophecy is unambiguous—no one comes to Israel's defense in the final days. By definition, that state of affairs would also have to include the United States.

WHO STANDS WITH WHOM?

Even as relations between the leaders of Israel and the United States seemingly deteriorate, especially over contentious geopolitical ideologies, Israel still maintains its broadly favorable image among the general population of the United States, though decreasingly so.

As an example of the documented trends toward Israel versus the Palestinian Arabs, consider the period of the Six-Day War in June 1967. During that time, 56 percent of Americans, responding to a Gallup poll, indicated their support lay with Israel. Only 3 percent sided with the Arab states. But the number of Americans siding with the Palestinians went from single to double digits in the years 1977–78 (beginning of the Jimmy Carter administration), and have remained in double digits, trending slightly upward ever since.[7]

Further magnifying the pro-Arab trend was the alarming 2014 Gallup survey claiming: "Latest Gallup Poll Shows Young Americans Overwhelmingly Support Palestine."[8]

Also in 2014, The European Council on Foreign Relations reported that 18 percent of respondents in France and 27 percent in the UK sympathized with the Palestinians, while only 11 percent of French respondents and 12 percent of British sympathized with the Israelis.[9]

Some interpret the statistics to signify that the world is growing increasingly divided over the issue of Israel and the Palestinian Arabs, especially among the younger generations. Ezekiel 38 appears to predict just such an eventual shift in "public opinion," followed by the development of an anti-Israel alliance formed for the purpose of Israel's demise.

WHO ARE THESE NATIONS?

The terms used to identify the Ezekiel 38 nations are a bit difficult to translate into modern nation/state identifications. Consequently, there are several schools of thought concerning those readings.

In the King James Version, the nations are listed as: Gog,

Magog, Meshech, Tubal, Persia, Ethiopia, Libya, Gomer, and Togarmah, and "many people with thee" (vv. 2–3, 5–6). The New International Version lists them as: Gog, Magog, Meshek, Tubal, Persia, Cush, Put, Gomer, and Beth Togarmah from the far north, and "the many nations with you." (Two footnotes in this passage also identify a "Rosh.")

From these lists, we immediately recognize the names of the modern nations of Libya and Ethiopia, and of course we know the nation listed as Persia is modern Iran. The other names in Ezekiel's list are ancient tribal names originating from the Genesis 10 Table of Nations.

Most schools of interpretation agree that at least these modern nations are represented in Ezekiel 38: Russia, Turkey, Libya, Ethiopia, Sudan, Syria, Lebanon, Jordan, and Iraq. Some include Afghanistan, Germany, and southeastern Europe in the list as well.

Our historical generation is the first to witness Israel's return, foretold in Ezekiel 37. But we are also eyewitnesses to the prophesied coalition of Ezekiel 38, forming even now.

COMMONLY PROPOSED EZEKIEL 38 NATIONS (NIV AND KJV)

Ancient Nations	Modern Nations
Magog	Russia and/or Turkey
Meshech and Tubal	Russia and/or Turkey
Persia	Iran, Iraq, Afghanistan
Cush	Ethiopia and Sudan
Put	Libya
Gomer	Eastern Europe
Togarmah	Southeastern Europe
"Many people with thee"	Various other nations

ISLAM—THE COMMON DENOMINATOR

Another prominent feature of the nations of Ezekiel 38 is the fact that today, most of them are thoroughly Islamic.

Although Russia is not a majority Islamic nation, it is in strong alliance with Iran, which is majority Islamic, and is currently building alliances with other Islamic nations on this list. Moreover, Islam is the second most widely professed religion in Russia. It is considered to be one of Russia's traditional religions and is declared by law to be a part of Russia's historical heritage.[10]

Islam would not be born until the AD 600s. So, when Ezekiel was given this particular end-times list of nations, he could not have known of Muhammad and Islam, or the resulting vitriolic hatred of Israel and the modern-day Western powers.

Yet, Islam is now an authoritative, unifying, and spiritually motivating force in bringing together these aggressive nations for the expressed purpose of destroying Israel.

HOW WORLD WAR BEGINS

History has yet to give us a global war in one single, overnight, and unexpected occurrence. Rather, there has always been a lengthy buildup process. Of course, there have only been two world wars from which we can draw these conclusions, but even from them we can detect a pattern in the events that lead to global war. It appears a similar pattern may be developing right under our collective noses.

World War I actually escalated over *four decades* and out of a protracted series of conflicts in the Balkans. The international matters of continually heated discord were political, economic, and territorial. Sound familiar?

"DO YOU KNOW HOW MANY TIMES WE'VE COME CLOSE TO WWIII OVER A FLOCK OF GEESE ON A COMPUTER SCREEN?" —ALAN MOORE[11]

World War II, the deadliest and largest international conflict in history, was birthed out of a long process of "wars and rumors of wars" involving many nations and complex geopolitical issues. However, practically every historian agrees that World War II actually grew out of World War I. The end of the First World War and the beginning of the Second World War was only separated by about twenty-one years.

World War I vastly altered the map of Europe and proved to be devastating, especially to Germany. Under the Treaty of Versailles, Germany lost a sizable percentage (about 13 percent) of its home territory and forfeited all of its overseas colonies. German annexation of other territory was prohibited, massive reparations were forced upon them, and limits were placed on the size and capacity of the country's military forces.[12]

A charismatic revolutionary by the name of Adolf Hitler became the chancellor of Germany in 1933. He abolished Germany's democracy and demanded a radically and racially motivated *new world order*. Hitler instituted an immense campaign of Germany's rearmament and a reestablishment of national Germanic pride. Leading political scientists of the day predicted that a second great war was on the brink. Numerous pundits mocked their gloomy predictions.

Through several more years of complex geopolitical maneuverings by a number of world powers of the day, Hitler invaded Poland—sparking the deadliest world war humankind has known to date—killing more than sixty million people.

Numerous historians, military analysts, major media outlets, and a growing number of Bible scholars believe they see an analogous process in the making. They propose that the last several decades have witnessed a similar buildup of "little things," contributing to the current geopolitical melting pot necessary for the emergence of World War III. It appears it is no longer a matter of *if*—but *when*.

> "WE CANNOT HAVE ANOTHER WORLD WAR. WAR IS THE WRONG WORD. WE SHOULD BAN THE TERM 'WORLD WAR III' AND SAY INSTEAD APOCALYPSE OR HOLOCAUST." —GOLO MANN[13]

Meanwhile, the world is also witnessing a modern resurgence of the ancient Ottoman Empire. The feverish revival is once again stoking the fires of radical Islam, especially centered within the nation of Turkey, a nation that was once touted as the region's foremost democracy. Today, Turkey boasts almost a 99 percent Islamic population.[14]

Numerous students of the Word of God see this recent turn of events in Turkey, especially when added to the elements previously discussed, as an ominous marker of the end-times. And only our generation has seen it happen.

20

PASS THE TURKEY, PLEASE

Several experts on the Middle East concur that the Middle East cannot be democratized.[1]

—RECEP TAYYIP ERDOGAN, PRIME MINISTER OF TURKEY

"LOOK AT HITLER'S GERMANY, you can see it," said Turkish president Recep Tayyip Erdogan in December 2015. He was speaking of his desire to switch Turkey from a constitutional parliamentary republic rule to a "presidential rule." Some say Erdogan's shocking comparison to "Hitler's Germany" and his meaning of *presidential rule* is something more akin to Vladimir Putin's "legal" dictatorship.[2]

Turkey has had some form of constitutional rule since the foundation of the Ottoman Constitution and parliamentary system in 1876. Those ideals have been the central features of all subsequent Turkish constitutions. Erdogan wants to change all that, and he has enormous public backing.

THE ANCIENT HISTORY OF TURKEY[3]

Turkey's initial stages of population date back to the day when Noah and his family landed on the Turkish mountains of Ararat and departed the ark. From there, according to the Word of God, all the peoples of the earth were repopulated. Because of this fact, many people groups who conquered and settled the ancient land often trace their heritage back to the biblical record of nations found in Genesis 10.

There are historical references to ancient people groups whose names could be the original form of *Turk*, such as Togarmah, the grandson of Japheth and the son of Noah.[4] Tenth-century Jewish sources also list Togarmah (mentioned in Ezekiel 38) as the father of the Turkic peoples.[5]

The term *Turk* is most likely derived from the Old-Turkic migration term *turuk* or *toruk*, which means "created," or "born." This is certainly a startling revelation given what we know about the Noah account and the rebirth, or re-creation, of the world in that region.[6]

The history of the Turks envelops a period of more than four thousand years. A primeval people known as the Turuks first lived in central Asia around 2000 BC, eventually branching out and establishing numerous independent empires throughout Asia and Europe. These empires (among several others) included the Great Hun Empire (established during the third century BC), as well as the Seljuk Empire (1040–1157). Consequently, the Turks have deep ancestral ties to China, Russia, and eastern Europe.

THE SETTLING OF ANATOLIA—THE SELJUK EMPIRE

The earliest records indicate the Turks began their heaviest settlement efforts in the region of Anatolia (roughly the area of modern Turkey, also known as Asia Minor) in the early eleventh century by way of continual migrations and often-brutal incursions. The Seljuk dominion was established over the regions of primeval Iran and Iraq, and included Anatolia as well as parts of central Asia and modern Afghanistan.

THE OTTOMAN EMPIRE

The Seljuk state began its deterioration with the Mongol invasion of Anatolia in 1243. From the reconstruction efforts following this attack eventually arose the Ottoman Empire, named after its Turkish founder, Osman, in 1299. The Ottomans finally ruled over a massive domain stretching across three continents. The Ottoman conquest of Constantinople in 1453 marked the end of the Middle Ages.

The Turkic peoples ultimately came into contact with the Muslims of the region. Most of them gradually adopted Islam as their preferred faith system, but small groups of Turkic people practiced other religions, including Christianity, Judaism (Khazars), Buddhism, and Zoroastrianism. The vast majority of Turkic people today are Sunni Muslims, with a smaller population of Shia Muslims.

As Islam became the official religion of the ancient Ottoman Empire, the jihad (Islamic holy war) became the fuel of the empire's conquests of the region, including the defeat of the Arab regions of the Middle East. The Islamic caliphate became the government/religious system. The caliph was the highest position in the Ottoman government. (The caliph was defined as the designated successor to the prophet Muhammad (570–632). Thus Turkey became the central home to the original Islamic caliphate. This fact has become the impetus for today's Sunni

Islamic attempt to revive that caliphate and to once again implement Muslim supremacy throughout the Middle East, including the Levant (Syria, Lebanon, Israel, Jordan, and Cyprus).

ISLAM—THE RELIGION OF "PEACE"

Under the Ottomans, Islam launched wave after wave of brutal and devastating jihads in their zealous attempt to dominate the world. In reality, Islam was practicing regional jihad long before the Christian crusades were commenced to put a halt to the quickly spreading Islamic conquest efforts.[7]

At its height, the Ottoman, jihadi-born empire extended over what is today Greece, Bulgaria, Yugoslavia, Albania, and Romania in the Balkans, over all the islands in the Eastern Mediterranean, and over what is now known as the Middle East. The borders of the empire extended from the Crimea in the north to Yemen and Sudan in the south and from Iran and the Caspian Sea in the east to Vienna in the northwest and Spain in the southwest. The Islamic Ottomans attempted to cleanse its empire of Christian minorities—Armenians, Assyrians, and Greeks—by conducting several barbaric genocide campaigns.

The Ottoman caliphate crucified, beheaded, tortured, mutilated, raped, enslaved, and otherwise massacred countless "infidel" Christians. The official number of Armenians killed in the genocide is 1.5 million; hundreds of thousands of Greeks and Assyrians were also systematically slaughtered, bringing the total massacred to close to 2 million people—most of them Christians.[8]

The Ottoman Empire lasted for 623 years, until the end of World War I.

DECLINE OF THE EMPIRE

Starting in the sixteenth century, the Ottoman Empire incrementally lost its economic and military superiority to the nations of the technologically and educationally advancing European states. As a result, the balance of power shifted in favor of the Europeans.

The Ottoman Constitution (1876) was introduced in an effort to reform the Ottoman Empire under the guidance of European Westernization. Western-educated Ottomans drafted the constitution themselves. But prior to the Ottoman Constitution, the newly formed United States of America would fight its first foreign wars—the Barbary Wars—against marauding Islamic pirates of the North African coast.

THE OTTOMANS AND THE UNITED STATES

Between the 1500s and 1800s, more than a million Europeans, most of them white Christians, were captured and enslaved by the Islamic Barbary pirates of the North African coastal regions.[9]

Back on the American continent, the very first overseas war to be fought by the newly liberated United States of America would be engaged against a part of the Islamic Ottoman Empire. That war occurred during the presidency of Thomas Jefferson.

Pirates from the region of the Barbary Coast of North Africa (Tripoli, Algiers, Benghazi) began seizing American merchant ships and holding the crews for ransom. The first piracy of a U.S. ship occurred in 1784. The Muslim pirates demanded that the nascent United States pay tribute to the Barbary rulers. Jefferson refused to pay the ransoms. Congress authorized construction of the first six ships of the U.S. Navy.

In March 1786, Thomas Jefferson and John Adams went to

London to negotiate with Tripoli's envoy, ambassador Sidi Haji Abdrahaman. When the American diplomatic duo inquired "concerning the ground of the pretensions to make war upon nations who had done them no injury," the ambassador replied, "It was written in their Koran, that all nations which had not acknowledged the Prophet were sinners, whom it was the right and duty of the faithful to plunder and enslave; and that every mussulman [Muslim] who was slain in this warfare was sure to go to paradise."[10]

It would appear the Islamic jihad "reasoning" we hear today is the very same mantra that has been repeated from the beginning—*conquer the infidels and secure a place in paradise*. It would also appear that from an accurate historical perspective, Islam has never been a "religion of peace," nor have Islamic marauders and conquerors (ISIS or ISIL) ever been simply a part of an Islamic extremist faction.

"SO LET'S START WITH THIS FACT: FOR MORE THAN A THOUSAND YEARS, PEOPLE HAVE BEEN DRAWN TO ISLAM'S MESSAGE OF PEACE. AND THE VERY WORD ITSELF, ISLAM, COMES FROM *SALAM*—PEACE."

—BARACK OBAMA[11]

The Barbary Wars ended in 1805 with Islam in defeat and the United States victorious. Thus the U.S. legacy with the "peaceful religion of Islam" began. To this day, few in America appear to remember our history with our very first foreign enemy, an enemy that still assaults us to this day and was directly responsible for the world's worst mainland terrorist attack—September 11, 2001.

WORLD WAR I (1914–1918)

The weakening of the Ottoman Empire continued. The Ottomans entered the First World War in 1914 (after Russia declared war on the region on November 1 of that year) on the side of the Central powers: Germany, Austria-Hungary, and Bulgaria. The Ottomans were defeated in 1918. Under the terms of the resulting treaty, Britain, France, Russia, and Greece took control of the territories previously held by the Ottomans—officially ending the Ottoman Empire and the brutal autocratic Islamic rule.

THE ATATURK REBELLION

A fiercely passionate national liberation movement, led by Ottoman military commander Mustafa Kemal, was born in reaction to the occupation enacted by the treaty. Under Kemal's command the resistance became united, eventually affecting national liberation.

Kemal's last name was changed to *Atatürk* or "Father of Turks" to reflect his stature among the people of the new nation. The signing of the Lausanne Peace Treaty on July 24, 1923, sealed Ataturk's victory. Signed with Great Britain, France, Greece, Italy and others, the treaty recognized the creation and international borders of an independent Turkish state.

THE SECULAR REPUBLIC OF TURKEY

The Republic of Turkey was declared on October 29, 1923. Mustafa Kemal Ataturk was elected as its first president.

Until his death in 1938, Ataturk transformed Turkey into a largely secular democracy, boasting a broad range of reforms that were virtually unparalleled in any other country of its day. Ataturk's societal revolution brought a predominantly Muslim nation in line with Western civilization. For years, Turkey was the United States' principal secular ally in the region. But now, everything is changing. As the *Washington Post* reported in February 2016:

> ISTANBUL—Turkey is confronting what amounts to a strategic nightmare as bombs explode in its cities, its enemies encroach on its borders and its allies seemingly snub its demands.
>
> As recently as four years ago, Turkey appeared poised to become one of the biggest winners of the Arab Spring, an ascendant power hailed by the West as a model and embraced by a region seeking new patrons and new forms of governance.
>
> All that has evaporated since the failure of the Arab revolts, shifts in the geopolitical landscape and the trajectory of the Syrian war.[12]

This brings us to where we are today, and Turkey's astounding place in current end-times prophecy. Prepare for, perhaps, a revelation or two as you turn to the next chapter.

21

CALIPHATE RISING

Fear him, whom you hate.

—UMAR IBN AL-KHATTAB, SECOND CALIPH OF ISLAM

UNDER THE CURRENT LEADERSHIP of Prime Minister Recep Tayyip Erdogan, Turkey is more prosperous than ever. Much of the nation's wealth comes from Middle Eastern oil money. And that capital is reinvested into the Turkish infrastructure, agriculture, housing, military, and education. So, why would anyone think that Erdogan's Turkey is a bad thing? A 2013 article in the *Atlantic* answers that question. The article is titled, "4 Jarring Signs of Turkey's Growing Islamization." Following is an excerpt:

> The Justice and Development Party (AKP) has been in power for more than ten years, with Prime Minister Recep Tayyip Erdogan in charge for most of them. Their goal is change. They want to make Turkey wealthy and Islamic. They have turned from the vaguely socialist policies of their predecessors to crony

capitalism, and from the staunchly secular and pro-western policies established by Ataturk, the Republic's founder, to religious and Muslim-world-centered policies. They have abandoned Ataturk's non-interventionist stance for an active role in Egypt, the Israeli-Palestinian conflict, and now Syria.

Turkey's building boom includes 17,000 new mosques built by the government since 2002. Secularists are outraged, and an opposition leader, Republican People's Party (CHP) MP Mehmet Ali Ediboglu, calls this just another step in a process that, he claims, will end in an Islamic republic.

Obama has called Turkey a critical ally and has spoken of his friendship for the Turkish leader. Yet Erdogan is trying to change the Turkish constitution from a parliamentary to a presidential system—with the hope, of course, that he will be the president. His opponents charge that Erdogan's model is Russia's Putin, a virtual dictator by legal means.[1]

Following are the sentiments among the more radical Muslims of the region as expressed on a 2010 pro-Islamic website: "Now, on the 86th anniversary of this Earth shattering event (the anniversary of the dismantling of the Islamic caliphate of Turkey), the United States of America still has their President, England still has its Queen, the Catholics still have their Pope—but the Muslims are condemned to roam the wilderness leaderless."[2]

However, not all who live in Turkey feel the same. A supporter of the secular state of Turkey had this to say in a 2013 article published by the *Jerusalem Post*, "[A] sense of 'us' and 'them' has become an increasing part of the fabric of Turkish society under Erdogan."

The man went on to accuse Erdogan of alienating anyone who does not live according to the Islamic values he espouses. The article claims there are hundreds of top Turkish generals that have been jailed for plots to overthrow Erdogan's government, prompting accusations of an Islamic political witch hunt. Fears of an emerging neo-Ottoman empire reverberate around the world.[3]

Today, there are 1.57 billion Muslims of all ages living in all five inhabited continents. They represent 23 percent of an estimated 2009 world population of 6.8 billion.[4]

And Turkey aspires to be the reestablished central caliphate of all Islam. Just as Yahweh had His resurrected Israel, it appears to a number of prophecy buffs that Satan might be in the process of establishing his own "resurrected Ottoman Empire."

PROPHETIC CONNECTIONS TO TURKEY

As of this writing, there is no way to know how long Erdogan might succeed in holding power in Turkey, much less whether or not he will succeed at turning Turkey back into an Islamic caliphate. However, a growing number of Bible experts agree: regardless of what transpires with Erdogan, the world must keep an eye on Turkey in order to fully understand what is happening with overall end-time prophecy fulfillment. Reflect on the following seven reasons for this line of thinking:

- Noah's ark came to rest in the mountains of northern Turkey (Mount Ararat). It was from the area of modern Turkey where the earth was eventually repopulated and thus "reborn."
- The geographical locations of the seven churches to which the seven letters of the book of Revelation were written are all located in modern-day Turkey. All of those letters are obviously connected with end-time prophecy interpretation (Rev. 1:4).

- The book of Revelation declares the earthly throne of Satan is located in modern Turkey, in the region of the ancient city of Pergamum (Rev. 2:12–13). Thus, it makes sense to many that the last days out-pouring of evil against Israel, and the ushering in of Jacob's Trouble, might emanate from the place biblically designated as Satan's earthly headquarters and domain.

- The Euphrates River originates in the mountains of northern Turkey and runs through Syria and Iraq, eventually emptying into the Persian Gulf. The Euphrates River figures prominently into end-time Bible prophecy. The Euphrates is the featured landmark location of a possible World War III event foretold in Revelation 9:13–19. Additionally, the vast majority of the ISIS strongholds are currently located along the Euphrates River.

- The Scriptures speak of Israel being attacked from the "north" (Ezekiel 38:6, 15 and 39:2) in the last days. While many prophecy experts believe this to be a likely reference to Russia, others have noted that Turkey is exactly due north of Israel and may be the more likely candidate. For this reason, some prophecy experts believe that Ezekiel's Gog and Magog references speak directly to Turkey and not to Russia. This assertion is based upon the fact that the ancient Scythians (as the Greeks called the Magogites) were known to have originated in the area of modern-day Turkey. This would have been familiar information to Ezekiel. The Scythians did not move into the more recent Russian areas until hundreds of years after Ezekiel's time and prophecy. It is also being discussed that the Magog reference in Ezekiel may well apply to a combined force of Turks and Russians—especially since they originated from the same people groups.[5]

- All of the seven "stan" countries of modern Asia (Afghanistan, Kazakhstan, Kyrgyzstan, Pakistan, Tajikistan, Turkmenistan, and Uzbekistan) originated from Turkey. This is also true of modern

Russia. These nations may prove to be monumentally important to the ultimate fulfillment of Ezekiel 38.

- Modern Islam, the driving force behind the majority of the world's hatred for Israel and Christians, still looks to Turkey as the central leading caliphate of the Muslim world. Turkey was home to the fourth and last caliphate, which was abolished in 1924, and under Prime Minister Erdogan, seeks to become that caliphate once again.[6]

THEREFORE, THE OBSERVATION MUST BE EXPLICITLY MADE: IN THE MIDDLE EAST AND IN THE MUSLIM WORLD, SUSPICIONS LINGER CONCERNING THE OBJECTIVES OF THE WEST AND NOTABLY THE US. —RECEP TAYYIP ERDOGAN, PRIME MINISTER OF TURKEY[7]

What you have read in these last two chapters is only a sampling of the many considerations causing modern prophecy experts to ask, "Could the recent re-Islamization process of Turkey, a clearly biblical nation of great importance, be significant in discerning the signs of the times? Are we presently witnessing a last-days resurrection of the ancient Ottoman Empire, determined to dominate the world through Islamic jihad—and to destroy Israel . . . *from the north?*"

Numerous scholars answer with a resounding, "Yes."

What say you?

22

THE DAMASCUS DILEMMA

This is not a conflict that we are involved in. It is an internal conflict. However, we need to be prepared, and we are not willing to have the fighting spill over into Israel.[1]

—LT. COL. PETER LERNER, ISRAELI ARMY SPOKESMAN

"THE SYRIAN CIVIL WAR has turned into a conflict so complicated, even the experts admit it almost defies description. It's also a war no one is really winning or can win."[2]

Those are the doleful words of an Australian news source attempting to explain the complexities of the horror that erupted in Syria after the advent of the 2011 Arab Spring uprisings.

Perhaps conditions inside Syria can best be summed up by the words of Syrian widow Mariam Akash. A sniper had just killed her husband, leaving her to survive alone while attempting to provide for her nine children, "We're just living on the edge of life. We're always nervous, we're always afraid."[3]

HOW IT BEGAN[4]

The complexity of the 2011 Syrian civil war can be summarized in a single sentence: angered by broken promises of economic and political reforms, and encouraged by the recent Arab Spring uprisings in other Middle Eastern locations, irate Syrian citizens initiated a sequence of antigovernment protests.

Syria, and its capital of Damascus (one of the oldest cities in the Middle East), were soon embroiled in an almost impossible-to-explain civil war. Numerous variables resulted in the initial protests turning deadly, but the vital spillover point was the death of a group of children who had been rounded up and held in detention by government forces. The children had been accused of painting anti-Assad regime graffiti. A throng of incensed protestors began to form.

Adding fuel to the expanding fire of outrage, Syrian government forces attacked the mobs by firing into their crowds. Very quickly, throngs of everyday citizens took up arms against the government. Some were reported to be former Syrian military members.

As the escalation continued, the initial rebels were soon joined and/or infiltrated by Islamic jihadists and other independent groups with their own agendas. Thus, according to many analysts, the situation in Syria soon became unwinnable by anyone.

By February 2016, at least 250,000 people had died in Syria's four-and-a-half-year war, and more than 5 million had fled the country. Additionally, 7.6 million were displaced inside Syria, more than half of Syria's prewar population.[5]

THE PERPLEXING COMPLEXITY—EXPLAINED

Taking advantage of the growing Syrian civil war, ISIS saw an opportunity to expand, into Syria, their dreams of a caliphate. They began their march toward Damascus.

Not to be outdone, different Islamic factions also envisioned an occasion to seize control of the region. Soon there was infighting among the various Muslim groups, bringing even more bloodshed to the already perplexing situation.

The Islamic nation of Turkey looked the other way when it came to the emerging Syrian civil war. They especially ignored the ISIS encroachment on the area. Various news agencies reported that Turkey was actually assisting and funding ISIS in their involvement in Syria.[6]

Added to the unholy mix, strong evidence suggested that the Saudis were also funding ISIS. This allegation was believable to many because the Syrian regime is of the Shia Islamic sect, while the Saudi rulers and the majority of Saudi citizens are Sunni Muslims. The Saudis desired to replace the Syrian Shiite regime with Sunnis.[7]

HERE COMES "THE BEAR"

In October 2015, in the middle of the escalation, Russia joined the fray. Russia has a base in the Syrian port of Tartus; it is the nation's sole naval base in the Middle East. This port on the Syrian coastline is only a thousand nautical miles to Russia's naval bases on the Black Sea.

Additionally, Syria is a major customer of Russia's arms sales. Despite much of the rest of the world imposing an arms embargo upon Syria, Russia and Iran still provide the country with military weapons. For this reason, and the fact that Putin appears to be genuinely concerned about the proliferation of Islamic terrorism, Russia supports the Assad regime.[8]

In February 2016, a top European analyst suggested that Russian president Vladimir Putin's foremost goal in Syria is not only to keep President Bashar al-Assad in power but to weaken Chancellor Angela Merkel in Germany. Putin intends to do this by flooding Germany and the rest of the European Union with millions more migrants and refugees during 2016. His ultimate objective of Russia's presence in the Middle East, the analyst claimed, is to destroy the European Union.[9]

The West, however, does not support Assad. And since the West was doing little to affect a real change among the chaos, Putin formed a military alliance with Iran in order to prop up the struggling Assad. All of that happened at the same time the United States and a coalition of other nations were engaged in talks with Iran over a nuclear limitation agreement. This was the agreement about which Israel's Netanyahu warned Congress in 2015.

To further complicate the matter, the West is not a great friend to Russia or Iran, but neither are they friends to the rebels—which now includes ISIS among their mixed membership. Consequently, as the West began its ISIS bombing campaign and Russia began its own ISIS bombing campaign, accusations abounded as to who was bombing whom—and why. To a number of observers, it appeared that a "war within a war" might ensue unless cooler heads prevailed.

HERE COMES "THE DRAGON"

Then, as if the matter could not become any more complex, the emerging world military power of China decided to flex its international muscle. China established its first overseas military outpost in one of the world's most troubled hotspots—the

North African nation of Djibouti.

Djibouti is bordered by Ethiopia, an Ezekiel 38 nation. It is home to Camp Lemonnier, the Pentagon's main intelligence-gathering post for the Arab world. The base holds close to forty-five hundred U.S. military personnel, including Special Forces. Djibouti is also the site of the world's most strategically important and busiest shipping lanes.

In so situating itself, China landed its military forces very near the region of heated turmoil, along with Russia and the United States—the world's most formidable nuclear super-powers. Then, in December 2015, the Kremlin announced that China was prepared to deploy as many as five thousand of its troops into the Syrian war zone to help Russia in the fight against ISIS.[10]

The world watched as Russia, China, and Iran came together in military compacts to prop up the Syrian regime of Bashar al-Assad. How could the presence of these three nations, forming up before the eyes of the world in the heart of the Middle East, not be considered an unprecedented connection to biblical end-time prophecy?

In February 2016, Russia's prime minister, Dmitry Medvedev, warned that if a peace deal was not soon reached in Syria, an extended global war scenario might develop. Medvedev said, "All sides must be forced to the negotiating table instead of sparking a new world war."[11]

SYRIA IN BIBLE PROPHECY

There are two biblical passages that appear to point directly to Syria, and specifically to the utter destruction of Damascus as being a signal of last-days: Isaiah 17:1–3 and, what many believe to be a companion passage, Jeremiah 49:23–27.

There are differing schools of thought regarding these two passages. Some believe the events of which they speak will occur in the last days. Others, however, claim the passages were already fulfilled, in ancient wars in and around the land of Syria, during the historical time frame in which the prophecies were originally given.

The centerpiece verses (only parts of much larger sections of prophetic scripture) are these:

> "See, Damascus will no longer be a city but will become a heap of ruins." (Isa. 17:1)

> "I [the LORD] will set fire to the walls of Damascus; it will consume the fortresses of Ben-Hadad." (Jer. 49:27)

In the summer of 2013, on his radio show, "Bible Answer Man" Hank Hanegraaff took a call from a man who said he had heard pastors claim that the book of Isaiah details the future destruction of Damascus.

"So, what you're saying is they're tying in the passages in Isaiah to what is currently happening in Syria," Hanegraaff responded. "This is just a classic example of newspaper eschatology and shame on the pastors that are doing this, because it either is a case of them not knowing the word of God, which seems unlikely to me, or simply wanting to invite sensationalism and sophistry.

"If you look at what the Bible actually says," he continued, "it is very clear that the fulfillment comes in the biblical text as well."[12]

New York Times best-selling author and Middle East expert Joel Richardson disagrees with Hanegraaff. He says of the theological dispute over Damascus, "If one examines this larger portion of Isaiah's prophecy in its proper context, rather than pulling out a single verse here or there, then it is clear that its ultimate context is the Day of the LORD, the judgment against the nations and the return of Jesus.[13]

Joel C. Rosenberg, another *New York Times* best-selling author and prophecy expert, agrees with Richardson. "There's no question that Damascus has been attacked and conquered numerous times through history. Nobody is debating that," he wrote. "The question is whether the actual text has come to fulfillment."

Rosenberg went on to say, "It's true that Isaiah prophesied about the conquering of Damascus—that happens in chapter 7 and 8—and that is exactly what came to fulfillment in 732 B.C., but in chapter 14, in verse 28, Isaiah says something that's fascinating and relevant . . . "'This prophecy came in the year King Ahaz died.'

"This means that the prophesies of Isaiah 17 were not given to the prophet until 715 B.C.," he concluded "which is nearly two decades after the conquering of Damascus [in 732], so this gives us assurance that Isaiah 17 wasn't fulfilled in 732." Rosenberg believes the Damascus prophecies of Isaiah 17 are meant for the very last days—after Israel returned to the promised land.[14]

Responding to an August 2013 media interview request regarding the crisis in Syria, I expressed my view of the matter as being most similar to Richardson's and Rosenberg's.[15]

I also understand Isaiah 17 as one important part of the larger prophecy the prophet Isaiah was setting forth in chapters

13–23. Those chapters speak of judgments not only against Israel, but also against all of the surrounding Gentile nations—most of which are now Muslim dominated.

Isaiah 17 indicates Damascus will be utterly leveled and in ruin. Aram (the southern region of Syria) will fall as well, and Aroer (the northern region of Jordan) will also be greatly affected.

According to the prophecy, entire regions of northern Israel will become virtually desolate, and the nation of Israel will be adversely affected for a long time as well. Given the devastating military capabilities of Israel, and the chemical artillery cache of Syria, as well as the presence of major nuclear superpowers in the region, one can easily see how an escalated Syrian conflict could hasten these prophecies to fruition.

Additionally, Psalm 83 appears to declare that Arab (Muslim) nations surrounding Israel will attack the nation in its perceived weakness, yet Israel will prevail. And in Ezekiel 38–39, another alliance of additional, outlying nations (mostly Muslim) is also predicted to attack Israel. However, according to both passages, God intervenes supernaturally, and Israel is ultimately spared.

NORTH THUNDER

On February 14, 2016, the Saudi Press Agency reported that Saudi Arabia was ready to participate in any ground incursion proceeding in Syria, especially if the U.S.-led coalition decided to commence a Syrian theater of operation.[16]

While the Middle East was increasingly becoming a potential world war powder keg, President Barack Obama blamed climate change for the problems of terrorism.

"[ISIS] will be defeated. There will be ongoing efforts to— disrupt the world order from terrorists . . . There's always some bad people out there tryin' to do bad things. And we have to be vigilant in going after them . . . But, if you start seeing the oceans rise by five, six, seven feet—if—you see major shifts in weather patterns [because of "manmade global warming"] so that what have been previously—bread baskets to the world suddenly can no longer grow food, then you're seeing the kind of crisis that we can't deal with through the deployment of the Marines . . . And, you know, if you look at world history, whenever people are desperate, when people start lacking food, [because of global warming] when people—are not able to make a living or take care of their families—that's when ideologies [ISIS] arise that are dangerous." —Barack Obama[17]

The Saudi Press Agency report also claimed that 350,000 troops from the Persian Gulf Arab states, along with a large coalition of other nations, would take part in the Saudi-led military exercise. They further asserted that 2,540 warplanes, 20,000 tanks and 460 helicopters would be a part of the massive military practice—dubbed "North Thunder." Media reports said the massive Saudi-led maneuver would be unprecedented in the history of the region. They claimed that Egypt, Sudan, Pakistan, and Persian Gulf Arab states were among the twenty-five countries taking part in the military exercises.

Reacting to the threat of a potential troop deployment, Syrian foreign minister Walid al-Muallem said, "Let no one think they can attack Syria or violate its sovereignty because I assure you any aggressor will return to their country in a wooden coffin."[18]

Given the headlines regarding the current Middle East upheaval, Syria at the epicenter of a major war in the region, the China/Russia/Iran coalition, the explosion of ISIS in the region, and the current re-Islamization efforts of Turkey, it is difficult to understand how any serious student of the Word could not see the developing prophetic scenario.

But, where did today's Middle East crisis begin? Is there a documented, and perhaps prophetic, tie-in indicating the sparks that ignited the whole thing?

Read on—you may be in for a shock.

23

DEADLY CONNECTIONS

A thousand fibers connect us with our fellow men; and along those fibers, as sympathetic threads, our actions run as causes, and they come back to us as effects.

—ATTRIBUTED TO HERMAN MELVILLE

WITH SADDAM HUSSEIN'S INVASION of Kuwait in January 1991, there appeared to be a deepening awareness that something intensely spiritual was awakening in the world. People who had not set foot in a church in years suddenly drifted toward worship services and/or pastoral counseling. Numerous churches across America swelled to capacity crowds.

There was something about Saddam Hussein, with his history of butchery, blasphemous declarations, and continual threats to bring the world the mother of all battles that felt absolutely supernatural.

In August 1990, the Iraqi dictator-madman executed a massive five-month attack on Iraq's tiny, oil-rich neighbor, Kuwait. As United States troops gathered in the Middle East, and coalition forces were being built by the George H. W. Bush administration, horrifyingly high U.S. military casualty estimates were broadcast on the evening news.

The United States, and twenty-seven coalition allies, finally launched their offensive against Hussein's Iraqi forces on January 16, 1991. Operation Desert Storm was under way.

In the final moments leading up to the Gulf War, around the globe people asked: "Does the possibility of this looming and potentially devastating war carry any biblical significance—could this be the beginning of a soon-coming World War III?"

I remember assuring my congregants that although I was not prepared to make an authoritative statement about the event's particular biblical place, I could only believe it must carry at least some manner of biblical importance. How could it not?

Hundreds of thousands of troops from a huge, multinational coalition were gathering along the area of the famed and biblical Euphrates River. Several passages clearly predict an end-time war in that precise location. In addition, the Muslim world was being stirred into unprecedented fury. The entire Middle East was on high alert.

While Iraqi-launched Scud missiles rained down upon Israel, the powerful nation of God's promise sat atop the largest nuclear arsenal in the Middle East. Israel made it known they were prepared to unleash the power of their legendary "Samson Option"—a massive nuclear retaliation of last resort that would be leveled against any country that launched a devastating attack upon them.

However, with the coalition's overwhelming defeat of Iraq, Americans quickly went back to their mundane routine of life—giving little thought to the potentially prophetic implications of what they had just witnessed; if we had only known then what we know now.

CONNECTING THE DOTS . . .

Without a doubt, the Gulf War, or Operation Desert Storm, was the primary factor that led to al-Qaida's eventual terror attacks against the United States ten years later, on September 11, 2001. Osama bin Laden made that crystal clear. Even the left-leaning NPR reported the connection in a 2011 report:

> But the first Gulf War did lead to further confrontations and its reverberations are still felt today. Most obviously, it helped set the stage for the U.S.-led invasion of Iraq in 2003. It also became a cause celebre for Osama bin Laden and one of the factors that led to al-Qaida's attacks against the U.S. on Sept. 11, 2001.
>
> Bin Laden was incensed that "filthy, infidel crusaders," as he called American troops, were based in his homeland of Saudi Arabia, home to Islam's two holiest sites. Bin Laden has repeatedly referred to the U.S. going into Saudi Arabia as a key reason for Sept. 11," says [political scientist Steve] Yetiv, who has just published a history of U.S. policy toward Iraq."[1]

Following the September 11, 2001, terrorist attacks, the 2003 Iraq and Afghanistan wars ensued, resulting in the toppling of the regime of Saddam Hussein and a protracted war in Afghanistan.

SADDAM PLANTS THE SEEDS OF ARAB SPRING

In 2013, the *New York Times* recognized a link between Saddam's invasion of Kuwait in 1990 and the beginning of the infamous 2011 Arab Spring uprisings in the Middle East:

> Few of the brave young men and women behind the Arab Spring
> have been willing to publicly admit the possibility of a link between
> their revolutions and the end of Mr. Hussein's bloody reign 10
> years ago.
>
> To see the connection between the overthrow of Mr. Hussein
> in 2003 and the overthrow of Hosni Mubarak in 2011 [begin-
> ning of Arab Spring], one must go back to 1990, when Iraq's
> army marched into Kuwait. The first gulf war—in which an
> American-led coalition ousted Iraq's occupying army—enjoyed the
> support of most Arab governments, but not of their populations.
> Mr. Hussein's invasion of Kuwait threatened the order that had
> kept authoritarian regimes in power for decades and Arab leaders
> were willing to fight to restore it.[2]

Soon after the advent of the Arab Spring, President Barack
Obama gave a glowing speech extolling the virtues of the revolt.
Over the next months, he and Secretary of State Hillary Clinton
would boast about their part in helping to bring about Arab Spring.

The following are telling excerpts taken from Obama's
White House speech on May 19, 2011:

> For six months, we have witnessed an extraordinary change taking
> place in the Middle East and North Africa. Two leaders [Egypt
> and Libya] have stepped aside. More may follow. And though these
> countries may be a great distance from our shores, we know that
> our own future is bound to this region by the forces of economics
> and security, by history and by faith. . . . There must be no doubt
> that the United States of America welcomes change [in the Middle

East] that advances self-determination and opportunity [Arab Spring]. Yes, there will be perils that accompany this moment of promise [Arab Spring]. But after decades of accepting the world as it is in the region, we have a chance to pursue the world as it should be. . . . Today I want to make it clear that it [Arab Spring] is a top priority that must be translated into concrete actions, and supported by all of the diplomatic, economic and strategic tools at our disposal. . . . But our support must also extend to nations where transitions have yet to take place.[3]

There was never a doubt that Obama's administration was in full support of Arab Spring and actually helped move it along and even expand its efforts. By 2016, even the European media recognized as much:

In Washington President Barack Obama has sought, from the start of his presidency, a "new beginning" for America's problematic relationship with the Muslim world. He has given unqualified support to those campaigning for change in the major Arab capitals, actively encouraging the overthrow of one of Washington's longest-serving allies, Egypt's President Hosni Mubarak, and backing the military campaign to overthrow Libya's Colonel Muammar Gaddafi.[4]

In the early days of the Arab uprisings, the sycophantic mainstream media sang Obama's praises and backed his plan to prop up the rebellion. They also praised the White House prediction that the uprising would bring wondrous benefits to the Middle East. That is, until ISIS came along and woke everyone from their dreams of unicorns, daffodils, and rainbows.

FROM ARAB SPRING TO THE WINTER OF DEATH

The Arab Spring honeymoon quickly turned sour. By early 2016, nearly 250,000 people had died in Syria alone since the bloody uprising began and ISIS arose from the turmoil.[5]

The UK's *Telegraph* opined:

> The murder of the US ambassador to Libya is a shocking reminder to Barack Obama that helping to overthrow dictators [Arab Spring] does not guarantee stability in the region. . . .
>
> For more than a year, politicians on both sides of the Atlantic have given their enthusiastic backing to the seismic changes taking place among the ruling elites who have dominated the region for decades. As dictator after dictator has been removed from power, either through force of arms or the overwhelming strength of popular discontent, Western leaders have universally given their support to what they mistakenly identified as an "Arab Spring" of Western-style pro-democracy movements sweeping aside despotism.[6]

Sharyl Attkisson, investigative correspondent for CBS news, commenting in the *Daily Signal* in 2015, said of the Arab Spring/ISIS connection:

> "Arab Spring" is the popular name given to the democratic wave of civil unrest in the Arab world that began in December 2010 and lasted through mid-2012. It turns out the revolutionary movement created an ideal environment for terrorism [ISIS] to grow and thrive.[7]

Author and Middle East analyst Caroline Glick commented in a 2015 CBN interview that the recent breakdown of regional regimes ultimately led to a dangerous Middle Eastern power vacuum. ISIS and its radical Islamic agenda, she said, are now filling those voids of supremacy, "You have spoilers coming in and taking advantage of the power vacuum [left by Arab Spring], whether it's ISIS on the Sunni side or it's the Iranians on the Shiite side with Hezbollah as their strike force. . . . There is no balance of power," she claimed. "What there is—is a nuclear arms race now ensuing because of America's nuclear policy towards Iran."[8]

TYING IT ALL TOGETHER

Let's review the amazing connections we have documented in this chapter: The Persian Gulf War, involving Saddam Hussein's invasion of Kuwait, undeniably instigated the unprecedented September 11, 2001, terrorist attacks. From there we clearly see the connections to the second war in Iraq, as well as our presence in Afghanistan and the Middle East in general. We have also documented the fact that Arab Spring was eventually brought about through the subsequent war in Iraq.

Then, Arab Spring fueled the fire for the rise of ISIS and the very real possibility of the abject extermination of Christians in the Middle East.[9]

Now, because of the unspeakable horrors of ISIS, a refugee crisis of monumental proportions has erupted. That disaster already threatens Europe with untold misery and is quickly making its way to the United States.

All the while ISIS boasts that it is using the crisis as a Trojan horse to implement future terror attacks upon Europe and America.[10]

WE WILL CONVEY OUR DEEP APPRECIATION FOR THE ISLAMIC FAITH,
WHICH HAS DONE SO MUCH OVER THE CENTURIES TO SHAPE THE
WORLD—INCLUDING IN MY OWN COUNTRY. —BARACK OBAMA[11]

And finally, but certainly not the end of the matter, the cata-strophic rise of ISIS brought China and Russia to the Middle East. Their arrival opened a prophetic focus on Syria. Then the two superpowers began making military pacts with each other, as well as with Iran (ancient Persia).

What do you think? Is there anything prophetic in this outlay? Is there anything "Ezekiel 38" about the situation? Could it be that an Islamic-led, multination coalition attack on Israel is imminent?

Military, historical, and biblical analysts are watching the events as they continue to unfold . . . waiting for the next shoe to drop.

MERE COINCIDENCE, OR THE LION'S ROAR?

Perhaps the greatest surprise of all is the amazing word connec-tion of the one with whom today's Middle East scenario first started. From Saddam Hussein to ISIS, to the extermination of Christians in the Middle East and continual threats toward Israel—every bit of it has been a consistent tale of terror, death, and utter *destruction*.

And, as it turns out, the name Saddam, in the ancient Persian language, translates into English as "Destroyer." Reported at Slate.com in November 1998, the word connection was confirmed by Harvard University Persian language expert Dr. Wheeler Thackston:

> Saddam Hussein has no family name. Rather "Hussein" is the name his parents gave the nascent dictator, and "Saddam" is an epithet he adopted before he grabbed power, and is derived from the Persian word meaning, "crush." "Saddam Hussein" is best translated as Hussein-Who-Crushes-Obstacles or Hussein-the-Destroyer.[12]

Additionally, it turns out that the name Saddam was not even the former dictator's given name. It was a nickname bestowed upon him at birth by his mother—commemorating the difficult pregnancy and delivery she had endured.[13]

Even Saddam Hussein's enemies knew exactly what his name meant. Shiite Muslim cleric Muqtada-Al-Sadr leveled a heated tirade against Saddam in November 2003, declaring, "There is no enemy of Iraq but Saddam the destroyer and his cronies, whom we denounce until Judgment Day and they are in immortal hell."[14]

In 2004, the *Guardian* asked, "So why is it that so many Iraqis, even those who suffered most seriously at his hands, remain so ambivalent about the process against Saddam, whom they nicknamed the Destroyer?"[15]

THEY HAD AS KING OVER THEM THE ANGEL OF THE ABYSS, WHOSE NAME IN HEBREW IS ABADDON AND IN GREEK IS APOLLYON (THAT IS, DESTROYER). —REVELATION 9:11

Regardless of how one might wish to biblically interpret this undeniable word connection, the documented fact remains— the present condition of the Middle East can be traced back to the days of the Persian Gulf War, initiated by a despotic and ruthless Islamic ruler named Saddam "the Destroyer"—who may very well have opened up the pit of the demonic Middle East Abyss—ultimately resulting in World War III.

Gee, I don't know.

Probably nothing prophetic to see here—right?

24

HATED BY ALL NATIONS

Then you will be handed over to be persecuted and put to death, and you will be hated by all nations because of me.

—JESUS, MATTHEW 24:9

"IT'S NOT YOUR IMAGINATION . . .

Global terrorism, dominated by Muslim extremist groups, is by far the worst it's been in modern times. It turns out the revolutionary movement [Arab Spring] created an ideal environment for terrorism to grow and thrive."

CBS News investigative correspondent Sharyl Attkisson penned those sobering words in the *Daily Signal* in March 2015.[1]

By November of that same year, the Daily Mail and Fox News were reporting:

Christians face being wiped out from the Middle East within ten years as increasing numbers are killed by Muslim extremists or forced to flee persecution . . .

The alarming rate of decline means [Christianity] could vanish in some areas in just five years unless the world steps in . . .

In Iraq, where Christians are being butchered in mass executions by the Islamic State, their number has plunged from one million to just 275,000 in the last 12 years alone . . .

[Christianity] is also facing increasing pressure in Saudi Arabia, Iran and other Gulf nations . . . The Church is being 'silenced and driven out of its ancient biblical heartland."[2]

Executive vice president for the nonprofit religious-rights group 21st Century Wilberforce, Elijah Brown, told Fox News: "Last Christmas [2015] was the first time that bells did not ring out in the city of Mosul in 2,000 years. I think that speaks to the reality that hundreds of thousands of Christian families are living on the edge of extinction."[3]

Unable to ignore the obvious, in July 2015 the *New York Times Magazine* ran a special story dedicated to the unspeakable Christian genocide occurring in the Middle East at the hands of ISIS. Titled "Is This the End of Christianity in The Middle East?" the article succinctly sized up the situation:

Qaraqosh is on the Nineveh Plain . . . Until last summer, this was a flourishing city of 50,000, in Iraq's breadbasket. Wheat fields and chicken and cattle farms surrounded a town filled with coffee shops, bars, barbers, gyms and other trappings of modern life.

Then, last June, ISIS took Mosul, less than 20 miles west. The militants painted a red Arabic "n," for Nazrane, a slur, on Christian homes. They took over the municipal water supply, which feeds much of the Nineveh Plain. Many residents who managed to escape fled to Qaraqosh, bringing with them tales of summary executions and mass beheadings. The people of Qaraqosh feared that ISIS would continue to extend the group's self-styled caliphate, which now stretches from Turkey's border with Syria to south of Fallujah in Iraq, an area roughly the size of Indiana.[4]

Prophecy students immediately recognize the biblical significance of what the world is currently watching unfold. In that brief snippet from the *New York Times Magazine* report we see the words: *Nineveh Plain, Iraq* (the center of the ancient Babylonian Empire), *Nazarene, Turkey, Mosul, Qaraqosh,* and *Syria.*

In other words, in the heart of the Middle East—in the embryonic center of the biblical lands of antiquity—today's Christian population is being systematically eradicated . . . to the tune of hundreds of thousands. Because of the "peaceful religion" of Islam, Christians face elimination in the very region in which the Christian faith began.

And since the Word of God and the beginning of humankind originated in this area, and because the Bible is clear that everything will eventually terminate in this same region, what could possibly be the prophetic significance of what is now occurring there?

Speaking to the political/religious quagmire of the current ISIS catastrophe, that same *New York Times Magazine* article stated, "It has been nearly impossible for two U.S. presidents— Bush, a conservative evangelical; and Obama, a progressive liberal—to address the plight of Christians explicitly for fear of appearing to play into the crusader and 'clash of civilizations' narratives the West is accused of embracing."[5]

Indeed, a clash of civilizations truly is under way, on a scale unlike the planet has ever seen. And not only is there a clash of civilizations; there also exists a clash of unseen dimensions in the spiritual realms. This alarming scene is being played out before the eyes of the world, on the stage of ancient biblical lands that possess undeniable roots in deeply spiritual matters.

> FOR OUR STRUGGLE IS NOT AGAINST FLESH AND BLOOD, BUT AGAINST THE RULERS, AGAINST THE AUTHORITIES, AGAINST THE POWERS OF THIS DARK WORLD AND AGAINST THE SPIRITUAL FORCES OF EVIL IN THE HEAVENLY REALMS. —EPHESIANS 6:12

Sadly, many Americans appear to enjoy a false sense of security, believing that because a favorite sitcom is on television tonight, and their kids are playing ball in a tournament this weekend, all is right with the world. But everything certainly is not "right with the world." Indeed, the world is beginning to prophetically unravel at the seams, beginning in the Middle East—just as Jesus said it would.

Unfortunately, there are still many in America's church for which the events in the Middle East are merely an abstraction, something they occasionally see on TV, but having no personal application to their own lives. This will doubtless change— soon— and some of God's people will be ill prepared for the day when it comes.

UNEQUALED FROM THE BEGINNING OF THE WORLD
According to the U.S. Department of State, Christians in more than sixty countries face persecution from their governments

or surrounding neighbors. Open Doors USA, a Christian-persecution relief organization, reports that each month 322 Christians are killed for their faith (an average of 10 each day, every day of the year). They also claim that each month 214 churches and Christian properties are destroyed, and 722 forms of violence (beatings, abductions, rape, arrest) are committed against Christians around the world.[6]

Several reliable studies claim that, worldwide, more than one hundred thousand Christians a year are killed for their faith. This trend has been occurring for over a decade.[7]

The ultimate eschatological fulfillment of Jesus' prophetic words in Matthew 24:21 may be interpreted in different ways depending on the position of eschatology one might hold. But for many millions of Christians in today's Middle East, North Africa, North Korea, China, and many other nations, Jesus' words have already been fulfilled: "For then [in the last days] there will be great distress, unequaled from the beginning of the world until now—and never to be equaled again."

Those persecuted Christians of the world, our brothers and sisters in Christ, live every day of their lives under the threat of imprisonment, loss of employment, torture, or death—simply because they profess Jesus Christ as Lord and Savior. But how could anything like this possibly happen in the United States of America? After all, aren't we the largest Christian nation the planet has ever witnessed? Surely the Lord would not allow "His people" to be overrun or destroyed? Certainly, the Lord would not punish His nation simply because of wicked rulers and the vast number of people that follow them?

Or . . . would He?

"For the LORD will strike Israel [God's chosen people], as a reed is shaken in the water; and He will uproot Israel from this good land which He gave to their fathers, and will scatter them beyond the Euphrates River, because they have made their Asherim, provoking the LORD to anger. He will give up Israel on account of the sins of [King] Jeroboam, which he committed and with which he made Israel to sin" (1 Kings 14:15–16, NASB).

25

THEY'RE COMING TO AMERICA

The future must not belong to those who slander the Prophet of Islam.[1]
—BARACK HUSSEIN OBAMA

"BUT RIGHT NOW WE have to have a border, we have to have strength, we have to have a wall, and we cannot let what's happening in this country happen any longer. . . . We have to stop people from coming into our country illegally. . . . The key is, people can come into the country, but they have to come in legally."[2]

When 2016 Republican presidential candidate, Donald Trump, made these statements, many on the left labeled his comments as "incendiary." Trump laid out his opinion in an interview following a campaign speech. He had been asked about the feasibility of establishing databases to track Muslims who were entering the United States and freely moving about the country.

Candidate Trump, by this time in the campaign, had often commented on America's growing concern with lax border enforcement, a mass of daily illegal crossings, and the alarming influx of Muslim refugees pouring into the United States as a result of the ongoing crises related to Arab Spring and the Middle East ISIS expansion. To the consternation of the Islamic world, and the American leftists, Trump's words were resonating with a huge portion of the electorate.

In their reporting the *Guardian* alleged, "Prominent Muslim Americans have reacted with anger and dismay to the incendiary remarks of Donald Trump, the leading Republican candidate in the 2016 presidential race who called for a database of all Muslims in the country to be set up, in order to track their movements."[3]

Regardless of the reported "anger," Trump's poll numbers continued to climb. It appeared that much of America's heartland was in agreement with Donald Trump. Could it be they also perceived the rising tide of danger being brought about by the seeming insanity of current leadership decisions?

A TROJAN HORSE?

Are concerns regarding the Muslim refugee incursion into the United States simply *ill founded*?

Considering America's very first foreign war was engaged against the Islamic pirates of the Ottoman Empire, probably not. And there is also the fact that we have since been attacked by Islamic terrorists on September 11, 2001, and that America has been engaged in a protracted military operation in the Middle East since that time. Why would we not be concerned?

In December 2015, the U.S. Department of Homeland Security admitted to Fox News that since 2001 the agency had revoked ninety-five hundred visas specifically because of terrorism concerns. Michele Thoren Bond, assistant secretary for the Bureau of Consular Affairs, told a House Oversight

Committee meeting that officials did not know what happened to those individuals.[4]

Even DHS secretary Jeh Johnson confessed, "We do have to be concerned about the possibility that a terrorist organization may seek to exploit our refugee resettlement process. This is true of this country, that's true of every other country that accepts refugees."[5]

Secretary Johnson's words had a terrifying ring to them, particularly in light of the fact that ISIS had already declared they planned to use the Syrian refugee crisis as a Trojan horse in order to plant ISIS fighters within the United States and Europe.[6]

Speaking on the Fox News Channel in December 2015, Rep. Michael McCaul (R-TX), chairman of the House Homeland Security Committee, said that by bringing thousands of Syrian refugees into the country, we are "playing Russian Roulette with national security. . . I will say 2,000 of them have been brought in already, and we don't have the ability to monitor them . . . We're a humanitarian nation, but let's get this thing right before we start bringing in tens of thousands of Syrians."

McCaul continued with his dire warning, "ISIS in their own words has said they want to exploit [the refugee crisis] to infiltrate the West. Now we have our intelligence community reporting to me that specific individuals now are trying to get into the United States through this program. It would be highly irresponsible for me to be complicit with a federal program that could bring terrorists into the United States at this particular time."[7]

Shortly thereafter, President Obama announced his plans to bring into the United States another 10,000 Syrian refugees during 2016.[8]

Added to these concerns were the official FBI reports that the agency was then tracking ISIS terror suspects within all fifty states. FBI director James Comey told a 2015 meeting of the National Association of Attorneys General, "This isn't a New York phenomenon or a Washington phenomenon. This is all 50 states and in ways that are very hard to see. ISIL in particular is putting out a siren song with their slick propaganda through social media."

Comey went on to explain how the Islamic terror leaders were appealing to ISIS operatives in the United States with their polished messaging, "Troubled soul, come to the caliphate, you will live a life of glory, these are the apocalyptic end-times, you will find a life of meaning here, fighting for our so-called caliphate. And if you can't come, kill somebody where you are."[9]

Later, in the same year in which Director Comey had issued his warning, one such attack came to gruesome fruition. On December 2, 2015, in San Bernardino, California, an Islamic married couple slaughtered fourteen people and wounded twenty-two others at an office Christmas party.

Just before the shooting, the killers had gone online and pledged their allegiance to the Islamic State and to Islamic jihad. The woman was confirmed to have direct ties to an Islamic terror group inside Syria. Additionally, law enforcement authorities uncovered information in a subsequent investigation indicating the couple were already in the final stages of a plan to commit an even more heinous attack—"with a lot more people inside"—possibly a nearby school or college.[10]

That is what only two people with ties to Islamic terrorism were able to pull off. And, do not forget, DHS tells us there are at least ninety-five hundred others like them dwelling among us, and the Department of "Homeland Security" does not have a clue where they are.

Shortly after the San Bernardino terror attack, the Obama administration admitted Islamic terrorists might indeed be able to infiltrate the Obama-led Syrian refugee program. However, he assured Americans their concerns about the safety of the program were overblown.[11]

However, in testimony before the Senate Armed Services Committee on March 1, 2016, U.S. Air Force General Philip Breedlove claimed ISIS was "spreading like a cancer" within the mix of [refugees], "taking advantage of paths of least resistance, threatening European nations" and the United States.[12]

I MADE CLEAR THAT AMERICA IS NOT—AND NEVER WILL BE—AT WAR WITH ISLAM. —BARACK OBAMA[13]

JUDGMENT FROM GOD

Numerous Bible experts and prophecy watchers believe the United States may currently be in the throes of a particular type of judgment from God, a judgment not uncommon even to the ancient nation of Israel.

While I am certainly not suggesting the United States of America is equal to God's covenant-established nation of Israel, we still must ask, "Is national sin, of any nation, an insult to the holiness and the clear commands of the Lord? Would He inflict His judgment upon such a rebellious nation?"

English Presbyterian clergyman John Flavel (1627–1691) certainly thought so:

When the same sins are found in one nation, which have brought down the wrath of God upon another nation, it is an evident sign of judgment at the door, for God is unchangeable, just, and holy. He will not favor that in one people which He hath punished in another, nor bless that in one age which He hath punished in another, nor bless that in one age which He hath cursed in another.[14]

Since Flavel's message is so pungent, let us reflect on what Scripture tells us God would do to them if they ever turned their backs on His Word.

The following passage is from Deuteronomy, delivered through Moses to the children of Israel just before they were to enter the land of promise. Note the method by which God would begin His judgment upon Israel—*His chosen ones*:

[Once you have rejected God,] [t]he foreigners who reside among you will rise above you higher and higher, but you will sink lower and lower. They will lend to you, but you will not lend to them. They will be the head, but you will be the tail.

All these curses will come on you. They will pursue you and overtake you until you are destroyed, because you did not obey the LORD your God and observe the commands and decrees he gave you. (Deut. 28:43–45)

Could it be that because America no longer recognizes and sanctifies the "borders" of the womb, the conception of human life, marriage, family, parenthood, sexuality, and gender identity, God has given over our national borders and no longer recognizes them as under His protective domain?

Is it possible that ever since we began to violate the "borders" of our children's hearts, teaching them that they came from an accidental sludge pond and are nothing more than souped-up gorillas, rather than lovingly created by the hand of God—He has given us over to a "depraved mind" (see Romans 1:28)? Might God have executed judgment through broken national borders? The biblical precedent is certainly laid out before us as a distinct possibility.

To further bolster this truth, consider the following passage, also from Deuteronomy:

> See, I set before you today life and prosperity, death and destruction. For I command you today to love the LORD your God, to walk in obedience to him, and to keep his commands, decrees and laws; then you will live and increase, and the LORD your God will bless you in the land you are entering to possess.
>
> But if your heart turns away and you are not obedient, and if you are drawn away to bow down to other gods and worship them, I declare to you this day that you will certainly be destroyed. You will not live long in the land you are crossing the Jordan to enter and possess.
>
> This day I call the heavens and the earth as witnesses against you that I have set before you life and death, blessings and curses. Now choose life, so that you and your children may live and that you may love the LORD your God, listen to his voice, and hold fast to him. (30:15–20)

The matter could not have been any clearer. We can choose to administer the affairs of our nation's culture, with at least a *respect* for the Word of God and His benevolent hand of blessing, or we can reject Him. The choice is ours. And so are the consequences.

I'M EXPECTING [ISIS IN AMERICA] TO TRY TO PUT IN PLACE—THE OPERATIVES, THE MATERIAL OR WHATEVER ELSE THAT THEY NEED TO DO OR TO INCITE PEOPLE TO CARRY OUT THESE ATTACKS [ON THE UNITED STATES] . . . I BELIEVE THAT THEIR ATTEMPTS ARE INEVITABLE. —CIA DIRECTOR JOHN BRENNAN[15]

No one enjoys hearing words of warning such as those outlined in this chapter. Neither are they pleasant to preach, and they certainly are not enjoyable for me to write on this page. The people of ancient Israel did not like hearing the words either.

However, the Word of God is clear, and so are the pages of history. Israel stands as a testimony to how God will deal with the nations of the world—especially those nations that He has blessed, and those that claim "In God We Trust." Some nations even stamp those very words on their money and their national seals, and declare the phrase to be the national "motto." Well—at least *one* nation does.

And what does Israel's history teach us about how God patiently dealt with His people—before He brought His terrible discipline against them for their hardheartedness?

The LORD, the God of their ancestors, sent word to them through his messengers again and again, because he had pity on his people and on his dwelling place. But they mocked God's messengers, despised his words and scoffed at his prophets until the wrath of the LORD was aroused against his people and there was no remedy. (2 Chron. 36:15–16)

Prophecy watchers around the world, and especially in the United States, have added to their list of modern fulfillments of ancient prophecies the possibility that America is at least on the edge (if not already stepped over the line) of a particular judgment from the Lord—the judgment of broken borders. This is a divine judgment that is well documented, and yet it appears it is being missed by the majority of America's pastors and the churchgoing population. It is as though they have lost their "eyes to see" and their "ears to hear." (See Ezekiel 12:2.) And when, by the mercy of God, a messenger does come along to warn the people, many mock the messenger.

This is what the LORD Almighty says: "Do not listen to what the prophets are prophesying to you; they fill you with false hopes. They speak visions from their own minds, not from the mouth of the LORD. They keep saying to those who despise me, "The LORD says: You will have peace." And to all who follow the stubbornness of their hearts they say, 'No harm will come to you. 'But which of them has stood in the council of the LORD to see or to hear his word? Who has listened and heard his word?" (Jeremiah 23:16–18).

26

THE DEMONIC DELUGE

Human beings are under the control of a strange force that bends them in absurd ways, forcing them to play a role in a bizarre game of deception.
—JACQUES VALLEE, MESSENGERS OF DECEPTION

"THERE ARE TWO EQUAL and opposite errors into which our race can fall [concerning demons]. One is to disbelieve in their existence. The other is to believe, and to feel an excessive and unhealthy interest in them. They themselves are equally pleased by both errors and hail a materialist or a magician with the same delight." C. S. Lewis, the celebrated Christian apologist, penned those words in his renowned spiritual allegory *The Screwtape Letters.*[1]

Whether one "believes" in demonic reality or not is of little consequence. Evil abounds in our midst. That much is undeniable. The Bible leaves little room for doubt; an outpouring of demonic deception and a growing worldwide fascination with the diabolical realm of darkness will be a definitive marker of the last-days generations.

Consider how the demonic realm is presently manipulating

the exponential technology innovation. The techno-media are often used to propagate graphic sexual perversion, demon possession, witchcraft, vampirism, cannibalism, zombie themes, gratuitous and graphic violence, sorcery, sexual violence, murder, racial hatred, rape, mayhem, pornography, drug abuse, and other equally morbid matters of a dark spiritual nature.

Undeniably, there is a growing global lust for virtual experiences capable of immersing one into the abyss of the "dark side." From sex robots to 3-D immersive technology used to emulate rape and murder, we are witnessing the unprecedented flooding of the continents with the demonic deluge of the last days. There appears to be no end to the pit of darkness awaiting the world just around the corner.

> THE LORD SAW HOW GREAT THE WICKEDNESS OF THE HUMAN RACE HAD BECOME ON THE EARTH, AND THAT EVERY INCLINATION OF THE THOUGHTS OF THE HUMAN HEART WAS ONLY EVIL ALL THE TIME. —GENESIS 6:5

While the perverse realm of darkness has always been available in one form or another, there has never before been a truly effective means to proliferate its vile influence throughout the globe, and especially to implant it directly into the hearts of our children—until now.

Observe a few examples of what the Word of God declares about the demonic outpouring and the proliferation of evil specifically marking the last days:

The Spirit clearly says that in later times [the last days] some will abandon the faith and follow deceiving spirits and things taught by demons. (1 Tim.4:1)

Because [the world] did not receive the love of the truth so as to be saved. . . . God will send upon them a deluding influence so that they will believe what is false. (2 Thess. 2:8–11 NASB)

Above all, you must understand that in the last days scoffers will come, scoffing and following their own evil desires. (2 Peter 3:3)

But mark this: There will be terrible times in the last days. People will be lovers of themselves, lovers of money, boastful, proud, abusive, disobedient to their parents, ungrateful, unholy, without love, unforgiving, slanderous, without self-control, brutal, not lovers of the good, treacherous, rash, conceited, lovers of pleasure rather than lovers of God—having a form of godliness but denying its power. Have nothing to do with such people. (2 Tim. 3:1–5)

Therefore God gave them over in the sinful desires of their hearts to sexual impurity for the degrading of their bodies with one another. They exchanged the truth about God for a lie, and worshiped and served created things [demons are among those created beings] rather than the Creator—who is forever praised. Because of this, God gave them over to shameful lusts. Even their women exchanged natural sexual relations for unnatural ones. In the same way the men also abandoned natural relations with women and were inflamed with lust for one another. Men committed shameful acts with other men, and received in themselves the due penalty for their error. Furthermore, just as they did not think it worthwhile to retain the knowledge of God, so God gave them over to a depraved mind, so that they do what ought not to be done. They have become filled with every kind of wickedness, evil, greed and depravity. (Rom. 1:24–29)

Notice the number of references to the demonic influence of the last days in the book of Revelation, which deals with the end-times:

The rest of mankind that were not killed by these plagues still did not repent of the work of their hands; they did not stop worshiping demons, and idols of gold, silver, bronze, stone and wood—idols that cannot see or hear or walk. Nor did they repent of their murders, their magic arts, their sexual immorality or their thefts. (Rev. 9:20–21)

Then another sign appeared in heaven: an enormous red dragon [Satan] with seven heads and ten horns and seven crowns on its heads. Its tail swept a third of the stars [demonic realm of Satan] out of the sky and flung them to the earth [in the last days]. (Rev. 12:3–4)

Then the dragon [Satan] was enraged at the woman and went off to make war against the rest of her offspring—those who obey God's commandments and hold to the testimony of Jesus. (Rev. 12:17)

And I saw coming out of the mouth of the dragon and out of the mouth of the beast and out of the mouth of the false prophet, three unclean spirits like frogs; for they are spirits of demons, performing signs, which go out to the kings of the whole world, to gather them together for the war of the great day of God, the Almighty. (Rev. 16:13–14 NASB)

With a mighty voice [the angel] shouted: "Fallen! Fallen is Babylon the Great! She has become a dwelling for demons and a haunt for every [evil] spirit, a haunt for every unclean bird, a haunt for every unclean and detestable animal. For all the nations have drunk the maddening wine of her adulteries. (Rev. 18:2–3)

Consider the popular programs and websites specifically dedicated to paranormal manifestations, UFO activity, alien abduction, Nephilim research, kabbalistic prophetic secrets, life-after-death stories, satanic worship rituals, demonic possession, séances, spirit channeling, vampires, zombies, haunted properties, and the like. The demonically seductive messages are blasted around the world by satellite transmission at the speed of light. Even in remote, Third World countries, little children are able to watch or listen to the programming with handheld digital devices—twenty-four hours a day, seven days a week.

Of course, there are legitimate organizations and ministries involved in researching some of those topics. Many seek answers to the spiritual mysteries of our day. However, a large number are not so biblically inclined. They exist for the sole purpose of arousing the world's fascination with the titillating vices of spiritual depravity.

The prophecies are clear: a demonic deluge will sweep the planet in the last days—an unprecedented outpouring of evil like the world has never seen will be a marker of the end-times. And that outpouring will eventually culminate in the appearance upon the world scene of the "abomination of desolation (see

Daniel 11:31; 12:11 NASB; Matthew 24:15 NASB).
The world is being prepared for his arrival.

[THE LAST-DAYS GENERATION] STILL DID NOT REPENT OF THE
WORK OF THEIR HANDS; THEY DID NOT STOP WORSHIPING
DEMONS . . . NOR DID THEY REPENT OF THEIR MURDERS, THEIR
MAGIC ARTS, THEIR SEXUAL IMMORALITY OR THEIR THEFTS.

—REVELATION 9:20–21

27

EMISSARIES OF DECEIT

I've always had a really active imagination. Lots of kids have imaginary friends. Mine just took on a rather demonic form.

—CLAIRE DANES, HOLLYWOOD ACTRESS

A PUBLIC POLICY POLLING survey in 2012 found that 57 percent of Americans believe in demonic possession. This large number shocked the "scientific" community, indicating that those who believe in the power of the demonic do not represent a mere superstitious minority. Rather, judging from the survey results, it would appear those holding such beliefs make up a majority of America's overall faith community.[1]

Today's Roman Catholic Church, comprising more than 1.2 billion of the world's professing Christian population, maintains there is a burgeoning global demonic influence. In 2015, Catholic exorcists in Mexico conducted a widely reported exorcism ritual aimed at purging the entire nation of its demonic grip. By March 2016, Mexico was being seized by a swell of satanic ritual killings. Catholic exorcists claimed there was an unprecedented demand for their services.[2]

Other countries under Catholic control and/or influence insisted that exorcism services be performed over their nations as well. Those nations claimed a marked increase in what they described as demonic activity.[3]

The Bible holds the key to understanding why there appears to be such an onslaught of demonic manifestation and attraction in our day. If the age in which we live is indeed the end-times, then Satan is now in the process of ramping up his activity—and for a very good reason:

> Therefore rejoice, you heavens and you who dwell in them! But woe to the earth and the sea, because the devil has gone down to you [the last-days generation]! He is filled with fury, because he knows that his time is short. (Rev. 12:12)

Knowing his time is short; Satan will do all he can to redeem the time. He is not going down without a hellish fight. He intends to have it all. He is playing for keeps. I fear many Christians are not.

A SHINY NEW MICROPHONE

Admittedly, there are those, even in the Christian faith community, who dismiss reports of demonic-entity manifestations as mere fantasy and sensationalism. However, a number of prophecy experts have pointed out that it is no longer necessary to "haunt" people by appearing before their eyes in some type of ethereal form. For the first time in history, the demonic realm has its own manipulated technological platform of ubiquitous "manifestation." Demons can literally hide in plain view while their manifestations are simply dismissed by the majority of the population as everyday technological fantasy.

The stage has been set. The delusion is in place. The propaganda goes forth, full steam ahead. The frog is slowly being boiled alive, and all the while it thinks it is merely in a warm and luxurious bath. I find it ironic that we often think of that proverbial boiling frog as incredibly stupid.

AND NO WONDER, FOR SATAN HIMSELF MASQUERADES AS AN ANGEL OF LIGHT. —2 CORINTHIANS 11:14

The secular and insanely powerful entertainment industry is infatuated with graphically rendering every manner of imaginable evil. The portrayals are as realistic, grandiose, and vociferous as is technologically possible—even in 3-D. Blood, gore, mayhem, rape, murder, and other forms of abject wickedness are the driving ingredients behind much of the fare offered up as daily "entertainment."

A number of actors, television hosts, and musicians openly speak of their "channeling" of the spirit world in order to receive or enhance their "talent." This is certainly not to suggest that all entertainers or media personalities, or even a majority of them, are possessed by demons. However, many famous personalities with huge platforms do claim it, in one fashion or another. And as such, the demonic realm has a growing pulpit from which to disseminate their influential propaganda—a hellish message that stands in direct opposition to the knowledge of God (see 2 Corinthians 10:1–5).

In a 1999 *US Weekly* interview, the late and globally celebrated Robin Williams said:

> Yeah! Literally, it's like possession—all of a sudden you're in, and because it's in front of a live audience, you just get this energy that just starts going. But there's also that thing—it is possession. In the old days you'd be burned for it. (*In a medieval judge's voice*) "You must now die! Strap him up! Come forward! He is no longer one of us!" But there is something empowering about it. I mean, it is a place where you are totally—it is Dr. Jekyll and Mr. Hyde, where you really can become this other force. Maybe that's why I don't need to play evil characters [in movies], 'cause sometimes onstage you can cross that line and come back.[4]

International megastar Beyoncé admits to being possessed by a spirit she calls Sasha Fierce. In multiple interviews over the years, Beyoncé has mentioned Sasha as though she is talking about herself. In one of those unabashed interviews she admitted:

> It was way better than I expected. And Sasha was in full effect . . . When people . . . meet me and they speak with me, they're expecting Sasha . . . I'm really kind of shy and . . . more reserved, and umm . . . nothing like Saasha . . . I guess I wouldn't be very entertaining on the stage until Sasha comes out . . . She can do things that I cannot do . . . I can try, but then, it just doesn't happen. . . all these things that when I'm just by myself—I can't do. And I remember right before I performed, I raised my hands up [in the video she demonstrates the act as if in a position of worship] and it was kind of the first time I felt something else come into me—and I knew that was going to be my coming-out night.[5]

World-renowned actor Denzel Washington said of one of his movie performances, "Basically what I did was got on my knees and sort of communicated with the spirits—and when I came out—I was in charge. It was a powerful scene. I couldn't have acted that [on my own]."[6]

Television talk show host Oprah Winfrey likewise has admitted to channeling spirits before engaging in a performance: "I ask my body to be the carrier for the spirits of those who have come before me in a way that is most meaningful to the character. Just become the vehicle for that character . . . I tried to empty myself and let the spirit inhabit me."[7]

The hugely successful Hollywood actress Shirley MacLaine wrote this candid testimony in one of her best-selling books: "I had seen so many channels and mediums over the past few years. I decided I would apply the same thing to show business. I simply channeled a character that we created . . . This time I allowed the character to inhabit me . . . I trusted the magic would work."[8]

Endlessly the "testimonies" go on—from music stars, rock bands, Hollywood performers, and talk show hosts to Super Bowl halftime entertainment headliners—there seems to be no end to the famous personalities who seek out the "possession of the spirits" in order to be the best at their craft. Their shameless message is now streamed around the globe, live and in high-definition living color. And many of our children adore these people.

What does the message proclaim to an eagerly awaiting world? "If you also desire wealth, fame, and power, do as your heroes have demonstrated. Call upon us. Let us inhabit you! Untold ecstasy awaits you as well. You have been shown the way. Now . . . *indulge!*"

Only in the last few decades of human existence has the demonic realm had this kind of world stage on which to proclaim its diabolical deception.

THE PORNOGRAPHY PLAGUE

One of the most pervasively destructive of all the emissaries of—and an unintended consequence of modern technology—is the explosion of pornography. And America, the world's largest Christian nation, produces 89 percent of all the pornography on the planet.[9]

Damon Brown, writing for *Computer Games* magazine, explained:

> It seems so obvious: If we invent a machine, the first thing we are going to do—after making a profit—is use it to watch porn. When the projector was invented roughly a century ago, the first movies were not of damsels in distress tied to train tracks or Charlie Chaplin–style slapsticks; they were stilted porn shorts called stag films. VHS became the dominant standard for VCRs largely because Sony wouldn't allow pornographers to use Betamax; the movie industry followed porn's lead. DVDs, the Internet, cell phones. You name it, pornography planted its big flag there first, or at least shortly thereafter.[10]

There it is again—the obvious truth is staring us right in the face. This generation's technological advances have become a platform for the demonic realm unparalleled in history.

Even the U.S. Department of Justice, as far back as 1996, recognized that "never before in the history of telecommunications media in the United States has so much indecent (and obscene) material been so easily accessible by so many minors in so many American homes with so few restrictions."[11]

Sociologist and marriage and family therapist Dr. Jill Manning, speaking at a 2005 U.S. Senate hearing on pornography, underscored the uniqueness of our generation. She observed, "Research reveals many systemic effects of Internet pornography that are undermining an already vulnerable culture of marriage and family. Even more disturbing is the fact that the first Internet generations have not reached full-maturity, so the upper-limits of this impact have yet to be realized."[12]

Manning went on to emphasize, "Since the advent of the Internet, the pornography industry has profited from an unprecedented proximity to the home, work and school environments. Consequently, couples, families, and individuals of all ages are being impacted by pornography in new and often devastating ways."[13]

Internet technology, and its use for the pumping of porn into the minds and psyches of our children, has not yet reached the maturity of a singular generation. The brunt of the coming destruction has not come close to its full realization. I doubt if we are ready for the demonic outpouring that awaits us on the other side of this unmitigated disaster. The statistics bear out the dreadful facts:[14]

- "At a 2003 meeting of the American Academy of Matrimonial Lawyers, two thirds of the 350 divorce lawyers who attended said the Internet played a significant role in the divorces in the past year, with excessive interest in online porn contributing to more than half such cases. Pornography had an almost non-existent role in divorce just seven or eight years ago."

- In 2003, according to a Focus on the Family poll, 47 percent of families said pornography is a problem in their home.
- Two in five abductions of children ages fifteen to seventeen are due to Internet contact.
- In 2004 it was reported that 76 percent of victims in Internet-initiated sexual exploitation cases were between the ages of thirteen and fifteen; 75 percent were girls. "Most cases progressed to sexual encounters"—93 percent of the face-to-face meetings involved illegal sex.
- The U.S. Department of Justice reported in 2001 that children ages ten to seventeen receive unwanted sexual solicitations online.
- In 2001, 51 percent of pastors said cyberporn is a possible temptation; 37 percent say it is a current struggle.
- Over half of evangelical pastors admitted to viewing pornography within the last year.
- In 2005, 57 percent of pastors said that addiction to pornography is the most sexually damaging issue to their congregations.
- 75 percent of pastors said they do not make themselves accountable to anyone for their Internet use.[15]

WHEREIN IN TIME PAST YE WALKED ACCORDING TO THE COURSE OF THIS WORLD, ACCORDING TO THE PRINCE OF THE POWER OF THE AIR, THE SPIRIT THAT NOW WORKETH IN THE CHILDREN OF DISOBEDIENCE. —EPHESIANS 2:2 KJV

Today, the Internet features a plethora of reputable ministries offering support to those caught in the demonic grip of pornography. The director of one such ministry wrote:

From a spiritual standpoint, pornography addiction is a form of idolatry and with idolatry comes demonic oppression and all manner of evil. Pornography addiction is the practice of sexual immorality, (whether it be lusting in the heart or in person), which God's Word says is idolatry. . . . (Ephesians 5:3–5) The kingdom of God is righteousness, joy and peace in the Holy Ghost (Romans 14:17). Idolatry stands in opposition to that and prevents the joy and peace that are available in the Kingdom of God from becoming a part of your life. Instead of experiencing daily righteousness, joy and peace, you will experience the death and oppression that is associated with pornography addiction, which the Bible calls bondage.[16]

Along with the plague of pornography comes the heartbreaking reality of the corresponding sex-slave industry. Millions of women and children (including a growing number of little boys) are being kidnapped or lured into the porn industry. The problem is a global one. And the scourge has now reached epidemic proportions.[17]

Never before has the domain of Satan had the ability to reach the entire planet—every moment of every single day—at once. There can be no doubt; opportunity for Satan's last-days efforts to influence and seduce has mushroomed.

WE'RE THE FIRST!

Only in our generation—how many times have we come to that profoundly prophetic conclusion as we have moved through this study? Surely, you see the pattern by now.

It is not that evil is necessarily any worse than it has ever been; it is just that evil has never before had the means to flourish as it does now. That undeniable ability is undoubtedly a prophetic marker of our times.

Maybe the last-days phenomenon of a technologically aided global outpouring of evil helps explain what is also occurring even in some of America's most "conservative" churches.

Many believe the biblical end-times "days of apostasy" have arrived—and with hardly a whimper from the pews.

28

DID GOD REALLY SAY . . . ?

Now the serpent was more crafty than any of the wild animals the LORD
God had made. He said to the woman, "Did God really say . . . ?"
—GENESIS 3:1

"MOST OF THE PLANET'S inhabitants declare themselves believers; this should lead to dialogue among religions. We should not stop praying for it and collaborating with those who think differently. Many think differently, feel differently, seeking God or *meeting God in different ways.* In this crowd, in this range of religions [Buddhists, Islamists, Orthodox Jews], there is only one certainty that we have for all: *we are all children of God.*"[1]

Those were the words of Pope Francis as he spoke in his first-ever video, produced in January 2016. In that video, the pope claimed all the religions of the world were merely seeking God "in their own way." Critics of the video speech asserted that the pope had just declared each of the world's religions to be valid "in their own way" as a means for providing eternal salvation. To a large swath of the world's population, a statement like that would have sounded "tolerant" and "admirable." However, to those who know what the contextual Word of God actually says on that topic, it would be considered biblical apostasy.

THE VATICAN GETS IT WRONG

The biblical truth of the matter is that there is only one mediator between God and man—Jesus Christ (1 Tim. 2:5). If one denies Jesus as the Son of God, Savior, and Lord—he or she does not have the "Father," or eternal life (1 John 2:22–23; 5:12). There is only one name by which humanity can be saved—the name of Jesus (Acts 4:12). There is only one "way" to eternal life—that way is found only in Jesus Christ (John 14:6).

Furthermore, not all people are "children of God." Only those who have professed Jesus Christ as Lord are His sons and daughters (John 1:12–13)—and joint heirs with Jesus (Rom. 8:17).

And finally, if one does not come through Jesus Christ as Savior and Messiah, that person may indeed be a "creation" of Yahweh, however his or her true "father" is none other than Satan himself (1 John 3:10).

How in the world could Pope Francis have been so mistaken on the basic fundamentals of the Christian faith? How could he be a party to plunging the largest portion of Christianity into beliefs matching end-time apostasy? It was as if the pope had literally uttered those ancient words, *Did God really say . . . ?*

Even though a full 70 percent of all Americans claim to be "Christian," only 36 percent of America believes the Bible to be God's literal word.[2]

Perhaps this explains how the pope could utter such biblical untruth, with barely a protest from the American church.

A TALKING SNAKE?

More than likely it was not a talking snake in the garden of Eden confronting Eve with the sinister challenge—"Did God really say . . . ?" If Eve had encountered such a creature, she probably would have done what most anyone would have done—*scream and run!*

Please understand: this is not a challenge to the authority of God's Word, but rather it is a challenge to our understanding of the original Hebrew language and the bigger picture presented in that chapter.

> THE SPIRIT CLEARLY SAYS THAT IN LATER TIMES SOME WILL
> ABANDON THE FAITH AND FOLLOW DECEIVING SPIRITS AND THINGS
> TAUGHT BY DEMONS. —1 TIMOTHY 4:1

The word translated "serpent" in the Genesis 3 account comes from the Hebrew root word *nachash* (*Strong's* #5172). root word literally means "a diligent observer, one who whispers magically, or one who uses enchantment to manipulate."[3] There it is! That understanding fits the personage of Satan to a tee. No wonder John metaphorically referred to Satan as "that ancient serpent" (Rev. 12:9; 20:2).

When the apostle Paul referenced Satan's appearance to Eve in 2 Corinthians 11:3, he also referred to Satan as a serpent. However, Paul also presented the *serpent* with a human quality (cunning), rather than a quality of a literal reptile.

The Greek word Paul used is *Strong's* #3789, *ophis*. This

biblical word can mean a literal snake, but it also carries with it the connotation of "a sly and cunning person, or an artful malicious person—especially Satan."[4]

The usage of these words is no different from our current use of the English language, in the same context. For example, if a person has lied to us, or deceived us, would we not sometimes refer to that person as a "snake" or a "snake in the grass" or even, "that old snake"? This is the same way the word is used in the Bible when speaking of the person of Satan. Do not be fooled by the children's bedtime-story image of a talking snake. The reality is much more sinister. It is demonic—and it is devastating.

THE *NACHASH* SPIRIT

Sadly, there are strong statistical indicators that the "spirit of *nachash*" is alive and well in America's churches—manifesting itself as "political correctness." *Nachash* is the *spirit of apostasy*, and it has overwhelmed even many of the most "conservative" of the world's evangelical churches and denominations. This *falling away* is also in accordance with end-time prophecy (1 Tim. 4:1; Matt. 24:10, 2 Thess. 2:3 KJV).

In many cases, it is not so much what the churches and their pastors are saying that is the greatest danger—it is what they are *not* saying. Perhaps they too have listened to the cunning, manipulative, and malicious whispering of *nachash*, questioning: "Did God really say . . . ?" Many of America's pulpits have gone silent, just when they need to be crying out the loudest.

The beginning of the apostasy probably gathered its greatest head of steam in the adolescence of America's existence, in the days most infamous for America's full-fledged spirit of cultural rebellion—the '60s and '70s.[5]

> LET NO ONE IN ANY WAY DECEIVE YOU, FOR IT [THE RETURN
> OF JESUS] WILL NOT COME UNLESS THE APOSTASY [FALLING
> AWAY FROM THE TRUTH] COMES FIRST, AND THE MAN OF
> LAWLESSNESS IS REVEALED, THE SON OF DESTRUCTION.
> —2 THESSALONIANS 2:3 NASB

The Vietnam War was fully under way, and violent protests were riddling America's college campuses and public squares. The drug culture bloomed—which opened the door to America's "sexual revolution."

In 1966, *Time* magazine had run its famous cover: "Is God Dead?" In 1970, a Gallup Poll found that 75 percent of Americans believed religion was quickly losing influence—the highest percentage in the history of the poll since it was first conducted in 1957.[6]

By the time William Peter Blatty's novel *The Exorcist* was published in 1971, the secularization process of the American culture was plunging headlong into the mainstream.

In 1973 America's rebellious spirit resolved to legalize the wholesale slaughter of infants in the mother's womb. Ironically, that same year, America also determined to protect baby turtles in their womb (eggs on the beach) by enacting the Federal Endangered Species Act.[7] In the year we "lost our collective minds," we decided that turtle eggs and eagle's nests were more precious than our own human children and the womb of their mother. America's baby-killing holocaust, along with the accompanying apostasy, was in full swing.

At the same time period in American life, the doctrine of

evolution as "fact" had become conventional teaching in public school curricula across the nation. Now pastors, who had grown up in those secularized and "God-less" schools, were grappling in their pulpits with attempts to "reconcile" the Word of God with the "truth of evolution." *Nachash* had finally commandeered many of America's pulpits, whispering, *Did God really say . . . ?* Generations of young Americans, who would later grow up to be the new batch of teachers and societal power brokers, began to fall away from God's Word.

BIBLICAL ILLITERACY AMONG GOD'S PEOPLE
Writing in the December 6, 2003, issue of *World* magazine, Dr. Gene Edward Veith addressed the rising tide of doctrinal illiteracy among those identifying as born-again Christians. Citing a Barna poll demonstrating the stark reality of the "falling away" movement that was already reaching epidemic proportions, he reported the following statistics:

- 26 percent believe all religions are basically equal
- 50 percent believe that good works will get you to heaven
- 35 percent do not believe that Jesus rose from the dead
- 45 percent do not believe that Satan exists
- 33 percent accept same-sex marriage
- 38 percent say it is okay to live together before marriage[8]

By late July 2014, George Barna, of the Barna Group, revealed even more amazing research compiled over a period of two years.[9]

Barna said, in an interview with American Family Radio: "What we're finding is that when we ask [America's "conservative" pastors] about all the key issues of the day, [90 percent of them are] telling us, 'Yes, the Bible speaks to every one of these issues.' Then we ask them: 'Well, are you teaching your people what the Bible says about those issues?'—and the numbers drop . . . to less than 10 percent of pastors who say they will speak to it."

Barna continued, "So the thing that struck me has been that when we talk about the separation of church and state, it's that churches have separated themselves from the activities of the state—and that's to the detriment of the state and its people."

When asked why they did not engage the culture to which they had been called to minister, and why they did not preach the imperative truths of the Bible, the pastors' answers were shocking. They admitted they did not address the matters in question: for fear of losing members, to avoid losing financial support, because the subjects are too controversial, and/or because they were not familiar enough with the details of the issues.

Just one year later, in April 2015, Barna released yet another set of startling statistics. This time the questions concerned what Americans believe about the person of Jesus Christ:

- 44 percent said Jesus was not divine, and merely a man
- 52 percent believe that Jesus was a sinner
- 37 percent do not believe faith in Jesus alone is enough for eternal salvation.[10]

Considering a little over 70 percent of all Americans claim to be "Christians," it soon becomes evident that even out of professing "believers," a striking percentage obviously do not believe Jesus was the divine, sinless, all-sufficient Son of God, and the only way to salvation. Yet, this is exactly what the Bible teaches as foundational truths about the person of Jesus Christ. *Nachash?*

AT THAT TIME MANY WILL TURN AWAY FROM THE FAITH AND WILL

BETRAY AND HATE EACH OTHER. —MATTHEW 24:10

There is sufficient evidence to indicate that at least part of America's slipping away from the core biblical truths is the fault of the institutional educational system. As an example, observe the words of Dr. James D. Tabor, chair of the Department of Religious Studies at the University of North Carolina: "Dead bodies don't rise—not if one is clinically dead—as Jesus surely was . . . so if the tomb was empty the historical conclusion is simple—Jesus' body was moved by someone and likely reburied in another location."[11]

NACHASH'S DEADLY ELIXIR

Think of the recipe for doctrinal disaster currently brewing in our culture. If an increasing number of deluded professors are teaching abject deviation from Scripture, coupled with 90 percent of America's "conservative" preachers who are not confronting society as it continues to turn from the foundational truths of God's Word, is there any wonder America's faith in Jesus Christ, and belief in the Word of God, is in decline?

And if the preachers will not proclaim the truths America so desperately needs in this dark hour, *who will do it*? Will it be the public school system? Will Congress lead the way? Will the Supreme Court raise the banner? Will the entertainment industry take up the charge?

Who will make certain the next generations know that real marriage is between one man and one woman, and that the human race did not evolve from an accidental chemical soup, and that babies in a mother's womb are real people and the literal future of our nation and of the church? Who will teach them that human babies are infinitely more valuable than a turtle's egg? Who will tell them that the supernatural resurrection of the nation of Israel is one of God's most definitive signs of Yahweh's existence, glory, and promise to the world of the soon return of Jesus Christ? How will future generations of parents know what God's Word says so that they are properly equipped to instruct their children, especially if the preachers fail to tell them? Who will tell them if the shepherds do not tell them? Who will lead the way if political correctness is more important in America's churches than is biblical correctness?

Not only is the lion roaring—but *Nachash* is hissing and spitting. God's people are being destroyed right before our eyes. How about it? Do you see anything prophetic in this mix?

"MY PEOPLE ARE DESTROYED FROM LACK OF KNOWLEDGE. "BECAUSE YOU HAVE REJECTED KNOWLEDGE, I ALSO REJECT YOU AS MY PRIESTS; BECAUSE YOU HAVE IGNORED THE LAW OF YOUR GOD, I ALSO WILL IGNORE YOUR CHILDREN." —HOSEA 4:6

29

DENIZENS OF DARKNESS

The Light shines in the darkness, and the darkness did not comprehend it.
—JOHN 1:5 (NASB)

THE UNITED STATES OF America is still the world's largest Christian nation. Nearly 250 million Americans claim to be Christians. Some nations have higher percentages of professing Christians, but the raw numbers are not as high as America's. Protestant denominations account for 51.3 percent of America's Christians, while Roman Catholicism by itself, at 23.9 percent, is the largest individual denomination.[1]

However, not only is America's Christian community in serious trouble regarding foundational doctrine beliefs, but it is also suffering from ever-declining membership. A little more than 70 percent of polled American adults identified themselves as Christian in 2014.[2]

As recently as 1990, polling data indicated nearly 90 percent of Americans claimed to be Christian. So, according to the most reliable information available, in fewer than twenty-five years, the number of people in the United States claiming to be Christians went from 90 percent to 70 percent.[3]

The light of the gospel is growing dimmer in America. What happens in the rest of the world if the light of its largest and most powerful Christian nation is eventually all but gone?

THE ISSUES

In September 2015, the Barna Group published the results of a study determining what topics America's conservative congregations most wanted to hear addressed from their pulpits. That study lists twenty-two areas polling high enough to be analyzed.

The participants were then asked to rate their desire to hear preaching on those twenty-two topics from between "extremely important" and "very important." However, when asked how often they actually heard preaching on those topics rated among their highest priorities, there was a wide margin of difference.[4]

For example, congregants of conservative evangelical churches said they deeply desired biblical instruction on: abortion (91 percent), same-sex marriage (86 percent), and the importance of Israel in its biblical role in the world (82 percent).

When asked how many of those respondents actually heard their pastors address those issues, they said: abortion, 50 percent; same-sex marriage, 46 percent; and Israel's role in biblical matters, 24 percent.

What do we say when the world's largest Christian nation has killed almost sixty million of its unborn on the altar of convenience since the rebellion year of 1973? At the rate of over 1.2 million abortions a year, that number is enough to exterminate the attendees at America's largest football stadium (Michigan Stadium at Ann Arbor, Michigan—capacity 107,000), almost ten times over—every single year—year in and year out. Can you imagine if a terrorist's bomb went off in that stadium, ten times a year, and killed over 100,000 people each time—and virtually no one mentioned it from a pulpit in America?[5]

> "IT WAS THE SAME IN THE DAYS OF LOT. PEOPLE WERE EATING AND DRINKING, BUYING AND SELLING, PLANTING AND BUILDING. BUT THE DAY LOT LEFT SODOM, FIRE AND SULFUR RAINED DOWN FROM HEAVEN AND DESTROYED THEM ALL. IT WILL BE JUST LIKE THIS ON THE DAY THE SON OF MAN IS REVEALED." —LUKE 17:28-30

THE CULTURE OF DEATH—DEADLY CORRELATIONS

While not wishing to diminish the heartbreak of suicide, and recognizing it is a matter of supreme complexity, deeply impacting many lives and relationships, there is still a disturbing correlation we must address.

Consider the connections. A tidal wave of pornography is infecting our marriages, homes, families, and churches. The number of our nation's "professing Christian" is plummeting, and our biblical literacy rates appear to be taking a real bruising as the overall Christian world sinks deeper into apostasy. Substance addiction rates continue to increase. And at the same time we see these evidences of the prophesied demonic outpouring of the last days sweeping the globe, we also see marked increases in suicide rates as well.

Global suicide has increased 60 percent in the past forty-five years. And on average, one person dies by suicide every forty seconds somewhere in the world.[6]

The *New York Times* reported in 2013 that from 1999 to 2010, the suicide rate in the United States alone, among those ages thirty-five to sixty-four, rose by nearly 30 percent.[7]

Nine of the top ten causes of death in the United States remained the same from 2011 to 2012. Death by suicide was the only one that rose. Now, for the first time, more people in America die of suicide than in car accidents. "This shows that Americans are getting more efficient at managing health conditions, but maybe 'we're not able to manage mental health as well, resulting in devastating results,' Solveig Cunningham, an Emory University researcher, told the AP, referencing the suicide rate."[8]

By 2014, the suicide rate in the U.S. was reported at its highest levels in a quarter of a century, according to the Center for Disease Control and Prevention.[9]

This statistic correlated with another sobering truth; at the same time suicide rates were at a historic high, so was America's number of anxiety drug overdoses. In February 2016, *Time* and NBC News reported that these specific types of overdoses had quadrupled over the past four decades.[10]

Certainly not all mental illnesses and overdose issues are the result of demonic attack or influence. However legitimate experts who deal in the biblical deliverance ministries of demonic oppression testify that certain suicidal thoughts and actions are directly connected to some level of demonic bondage.[11]

Added to this ever-growing mix of *Nachash* lies, we now know that addiction to drugs and alcohol is identified as America's most neglected disease. Overdose deaths from opioids (narcotic pills such as OxyContin, Percodan, and methadone, as well as heroin) have become the fastest growing drug problem throughout the United States.[12]

THE GLOBAL SPIRITUAL SHIFT

A professional paper written by a PhD candidate at the University of Sydney, Australia, examines the global spiritual paradigm shift, especially as it relates to the existence of Internet technology. Its author wrote:

> Scholars observing the paradigm shifts of postmodernity have been quick to note that although the social influence of institutionalized religion may be waning, religiosity has not disappeared: the sacred has simply relocated.
>
> The ensuing milieu "popular occulture" [has become] a melting pot of Paganism, Esotericism, Jungian psychology, folk medicine, modern superstitions, and paranormal theories.
>
> Post-modern spirituality has turned to the self as the ultimate arbiter of truth. The Internet has always been a spawning ground for alternative and bricolage spiritualities that incorporate themes from fiction, film, music, television, and art.[13]

Do you see a pattern in all we have laid out in the last several chapters? How do *you* estimate that the pattern ties into everything else we have learned along the way?

Many prophecy scholars see the connections as strikingly spiritual, and can only be interpreted to indicate that we are living in challenging and prophetic times.

30

THE SHEMITAH SHAKING

The [United States] had been brought into existence to be a vessel of God's purposes [and] had now transformed into its very opposite—a civilization turned in upon itself, at war against its own foundations, and at war with God.

—JONATHAN CAHN, *THE MYSTERY OF THE SHEMITAH*

LIKE A SARDONIC SALUTATION to the 2016 New Year, a series of enormous financial collapses struck the Chinese stock markets as well as other major market centers of the world. The first week of 2016 amounted to the worst opening in global stock market history.[1]

By the end of the first day of stock market trading, CNBC posted its headlines: "Dow closes down triple digits, posts worst opening day in 8 years."[2]

And to make matters just a bit too eerie for some folks, that unwelcome news came precisely at the end of a widely publicized *Shemitah* year, a very unique year coinciding with the Hebrew calendar (September 2014 through September 2015).

That year had been predicted, some months earlier, to be a harbinger of devastating prophetic judgments—not only during that specific year, but also perhaps for some time to come. Prophecy watchers held their breath.

WHAT IS A SHEMITAH YEAR?[3]

As soon as the ancient Jews settled in the Holy Land after coming out of Egypt, they began to count and observe seven-year sequences. Each seven-year cycle concluded with a sabbatical year (a year of rest), known as *Shemitah*, a Hebrew word meaning, "to release."

In the Shemitah year, among other things, the land was not worked; instead it was "released" and allowed to "rest." Each "year" in that cycle of "sevens" started with Rosh Hashanah (the Feast of Trumpets), occurring in the autumn month of Tishri. The month of Tishri usually occurs in September–October on the Gregorian calendar.

When the original twelve tribes lived in Israel, the year that followed seven of those complete Shemitah cycles, the fiftieth year (7 x 7 +1 = 50), was observed as the *Jubilee* year, or in Hebrew, *Yovel.*

In the year of Yovel, not only was the land not worked, as in the Shemitah year, but also in that Jubilee year all slaves were freed. Another feature of the ancient Yovel was that all land and houses sold during the past fifty years were returned to their original owners. While Shemitah is still observed today among the Orthodox Jews, the year of Jubilee is not, for a variety of biblical and legal reasons.

During the Shemitah year, in the levitical years of Israel's history, three prominent features of the *year of release* were observed.

1. The Shemitah year waived all outstanding debts between debtors and creditors (Deut. 15:1–2).

2. During that year, all residents of Israel were required to cease from working, planting, and harvesting their fields. They also relinquished personal ownership of their fields. Whatever fruit of the land grew entirely on its own was considered property of the community—it was free for anyone to consume (Lev. 25:3–6)

3. The yearlong abstaining from cultivation of the fields also afforded the people the opportunity to focus as a community upon the things of God. They were encouraged to use the year as a time of honing their spiritual awareness (Lev. 25:20–22)

THE PROPHETIC CONNECTION

Messianic rabbi Jonathan Cahn, *New York Times* best-selling author of *The Harbinger*, is probably the best-known personality alerting the prophecy world to the 2014–2015 Shemitah year event. His blockbuster book *The Mystery of the Shemitah* became the global benchmark for shedding light on the matter.[4]

The Shemitah occurs on Elul 29, every seven years on the Hebrew calendar. The Hebrew month of Elul corresponds to August–September on the Gregorian calendar. In 2015 the Shemitah fell on September 13. At the end of this particular Shemitah cycle came a Jubilee year, making this a so-called super Shemitah.

In September 2014, Cahn released his book about the upcoming Shemitah year. In that book he claimed that the five great economic crashes of the last forty years—1973, 1980, 1987, 2001, and 2008—had each occurred in Shemitah cycles.

Of course, we also recognize several of those dates as carrying other ominous messages. The year 1973 was the year of *Roe v. Wade*, launching America's reprehensible holocaust of the unborn. September 2001 brought the worst mainland terrorist attack in global history. Cahn's summation of the book's message was, "America is progressing towards God's judgment."[5]

Rabbi Cahn also explained that though the Hebrew word *shemitah* can mean a "release," it can also mean "to fall, to collapse, or to shake." In other words, Cahn postulated, the year of the Shemitah can also bring God's judgment.

SHEMITAH CORRELATIONS

In *The Mystery of the Shemitah*, Cahn claims that 100 percent of the worst U.S. economic calamities since World War II were each aligned with the shemitah. In fact, as noted in an article titled "Holy Shemitah!" by WND, "all of the great economic crashes in U.S. history, including the Great Depression, line up with Shemitah years."[6]

As Elul 29, 2015, approached, Cahn wrote, "In the past, [the Shemitah has] ushered in the worst collapses in Wall Street history. What will it bring this time? Again, as before, the phenomenon does not have to manifest at the next convergence."[7]

Cahn explained, "The phenomenon may manifest in one cycle and not in another and then again in the next. And the focus of the message is not date-setting but the call of God to repentance and return. At the same time, something of significance could take place, and it is wise to note the times."[8]

"For as long as I've spoken of the Shemitah and the future," Cahn wrote, "I've issued that warning and caution: God is sovereign, and nothing had to happen on any date, month, season, Shemitah, or year."[9]

Nevertheless, the naysayers railed against the Shemitah observations as the portentous date of September 13, 2015, approached. Some scholars protested that Hebrew calendar dates were of uncertain determination, and they insisted that even various orthodox sects used differing calculations for determining feast days and various other holidays. Others noted that the scriptural commands concerning the Hebrew calendar cycles, and the blessings and curses that may go with them, were given to ancient Israel. Therefore the Shemitah cycle was not for America or any other nation, nor was it even for *modern* Israel.

Regardless, Cahn's observations, and those of others who were following the phenomenon from a prophetic point of view, were aimed at pointing to the possibility that ominous warnings might be given to the world on or near that date. Many prophecy watchers believed this particular Shemitah cycle could very well hold manifold prophetic significance.

Accordingly, a number of Bible scholars wondered, "If in the past God might have used the Shemitah cycle to bring about obvious calamities in order to get the world's attention, why should we not carefully observe this Shemitah cycle as well?"

And so, they waited—and they watched. What eventually unfolded was rather overwhelming.

"ELUL 29, THE SO-CALLED SHEMITAH 'WIPEOUT DAY,' CAME AND WENT AND NOTHING HAPPENED. ISN'T IT TIME THIS FALSE PROPHECY ITSELF GOT WIPED OUT? —DR. JOEL MCDURMON[10]

WHATEVER HAPPENED TO THE SHEMITAH?

The exact date of Elul 29, 2015, passed in a fairly uneventful way, further fueling the fires of the naysayers. Some even said, "See . . . we told you! Nothing happened!"

However, a more realistic evaluation shows that the entire Shemitah year of 2014–2015 (as well as the months immediately following September 13, 2015) certainly was not so prophetically quiet. In fact, that time period has proven to be monumentally prophetic, even in unprecedented ways. Many believed this fact gave a strong measure of credence to the predictions of significant prophetic occurrences coming to pass in yet another Shemitah cycle.

With the approach of Elul 2015, every major global market was in collapse. The Dow Jones Industrial and the S&P 500 had been in a steep decline since May. The Russell 2000 Index began collapsing in June, as did China's Shanghai Composite Index. Finally, in late July, the NASDAQ also began its downward spiral.[11]

At the opening of Shemitah, the news erupted around the world that the United States was no longer the strongest economic power on earth. The title had passed to China.[12]

But as Rabbi Cahn later pointed out, "In the summer of 2015, China's stock market, the Shanghai Exchange, began to collapse as well. By the end of the summer, and of the Shemitah, China's financial realm had been decimated. The Shemitah had wiped away a colossal 43 percent."[13]

That same report indicated that the 2015 Shemitah "wiped out"

- an estimated 16 percent of the British markets,
- 18 percent of the French markets,
- one-fourth of the German markets,
- 4,000 points from the Indian markets,
- 12,000 points from the Brazilian market,
- $2 trillion of the U.S. markets,
- a colossal $11 trillion from the world's financial realm.

Here is how various global mainstream media sources reported the gloomy economic situation:

- NEW YORK TIMES: "Markets suffer their worst start to the year since Great Depression"[14]
- CNBC: "Dow closes down triple digits, posts worst opening day in 8 years"[15]
- FORTUNE: "Investors Have Lost 1.78 Trillion [in investments] so far this Year"[16]
- LA TIMES: "Some countries are using negative interest rates to fight slowdowns: Is the U.S. next?"[17]

Those major headlines, and many others like them, certainly did not appear to be the "See! Nothing happened" scenario being proclaimed by the Shemitah detractors. And that was only the economic news. Many more prophetic things occurred as well.

SHEMITAH BY THE CALENDAR

MARCH 2015
Israel's prime minister, Benjamin Netanyahu, addressed a joint session of Congress on the day before the Jewish celebration

of Purim. President Obama publicly repudiated Netanyahu's presence in Congress and the premise of the prime minister's speech. He contemptuously assured Netanyahu that the United States will continue with the brokering of the deal and that an agreement *will* be reached and enacted.[18]

APRIL 2015

On April 2, Obama declared that a provisional deal had in fact been reached with Iran just one day earlier—on April 1. That date happened to correspond with the infamous Jewish calendar date of Nisan 13, the very date on which the book of Esther declares that the king of ancient Persia approved a "pact" to begin its campaign to destroy every Jew living within its domain (Esth. 3:11–12).[19]

MAY 2015

Pope Francis called for Palestinian statehood and continued to use his pulpit to stoke the fears of man-made "climate change" and "global warming."[20]

JUNE 2015

The Supreme Court of the United States ruled in the *Obergefell v. Hodges* decision. Most of America immediately interpreted the decision to be the new "law of the land" allowing gay marriage in all fifty states.

This ruling was made despite the Supreme Court's previous ruling, exactly two years earlier, in the *U.S. v. Windsor* case. In this case (regarding DOMA), the court stated in the majority opinion, "Regulation of domestic relations [marriage] is an area that has long been regarded as a virtually exclusive province of the States . . . Federal intrusion on state power is a violation of the Constitution because it disrupts the federal balance."[21]

By their own words the Supreme Court "violated the Constitution" with the *Obergefell* ruling, and rendered a pro-gay-marriage decision. This action plunged America, and the world, headlong into the Sodom and Gomorrah spirit, perhaps one of the biggest of all the Shemitah "judgments."

The United States, under the Obama administration, then engaged in the process of aggressively exporting the Sodom and Gomorrah spirit to other nations—even threatening to withhold desperately needed aid to nations that refuse to submit to the abomination of "gay marriage."[22]

Jesus defined that spirit as a definitive marker of the very last days (Luke 17:28).

JULY 2015

Pope Francis called for a "new world order" and for "the goods of the Earth to be shared by everyone."[23]

Planned Parenthood was caught admitting in a "video sting" that they were selling aborted baby body parts for profit. The first of many videos was released during this month. The scandal vibrated around the world as a number of similar videos were released over the next months.[24]

SEPTEMBER 2015 (THE MONTH OF PRIMARY FOCUS)

For the first time in American history, a federal judge jailed an elected state official over "gay rights." Kentucky county clerk Kim Davis refused to recognize gay marriage by signing off on state-issued marriage certificates.[25]

President Barack Obama met with Pope Francis at the

White House on the pope's first official visit to the United States. By now, both Obama and the pope had been heavily pushing the "man-made global warming" agenda around the world.[26]

Pope Francis addressed a joint session of the U.S. Congress— the first time in history a pope has done so. In that speech, the most recognized leader of the largest denomination of the Christian faith never mentioned the name of Jesus. Nor did he use the words *Bible, Christian, terrorists, ISIS, abortion, Muslim, jihad, Middle East, the selling of aborted baby body parts, the genocide against Christians in the Middle East,* and many other words related to hugely important issues of the day. Instead he focused his message primarily on "climate change," U.S. borders, and "world peace."[27]

[THE UN] WOULD VOTE TO DECLARE THAT THE EARTH IS FLAT, IF THE PALESTINIANS PROPOSED IT. —RON PROSOR, ISRAELI AMBASSADOR TO THE UN[28]

The "Palestinian Flag" was flown over the UN headquarters for the first time. This act was a direct affront to Israel and violated the United Nations' own rules. The "state of Palestine" is neither a sovereign state nor a UN member-state. Palestinian envoy Riad Mansour welcomed the "historic vote," which he called "yet another significant step in affirming the international consensus in favor of Palestinian independence. The Palestinian people are in despair as they continue to suffer under Israel's nearly half-century foreign occupation."[29]

Pope Francis addresses the United Nations' largest gathering of world leaders. What was the crux of his message? You guessed it—climate change, and a new world order.[30]

On September 25, Russia announced an accord it had reached with Iran, Syria, and Iraq. The accord regards the war on ISIS in the Middle East.[31]

OCTOBER 2015

Prime Minister Netanyahu addressed a sparsely attended session of the United Nations General Assembly. In that address, he once again pleaded against negotiating with Iran concerning their possession of nuclear weapons. He warned, "The days when the Jewish people remained silent in the face of genocidal enemies are over."[32]

Russia showed up in Syria and planted its military might in the Middle East amid the Syrian civil war and ongoing ISIS battle.[33]

Vladimir Putin ramped up talks of a looming World War III.[34]

A few weeks after Netanyahu's UN plea, President Obama officially put the Iran nuclear deal into effect.[35]

NOVEMBER 2015

China announced it would send troops to Syria to bolster Russia's efforts to prop up Syrian president Bashar Assad.[36]

DECEMBER 2015

China established its first naval base in Northern Africa. From that base it planned to supply troops to assist Russia in Syria.[37]

Pope Francis again called for a "one world order," declaring,

"Christians and Muslims are brothers and sisters. Those who claim to believe in God must also be men and women of peace."[38]

Saudi Arabia formed an "anti-terrorism" coalition of thirty-five Muslim nations. They began military exercises, backed by the United States.[39]

JANUARY 2016

Pope Francis called all people "Children of God," and declared that all the world's faith systems were simply seeking "their own ways to God." He was immediately denounced by evangelical leaders, who stated the pope spoke completely outside the truth of God's Word on both of these matters (John 1:12–13; Acts 4:12 John; 14:6). Some even called the pope's remarks "apostasy."[40]

FEBRUARY 2016

Vladimir Putin again affirms the distinct possibility of a soon coming World War III.[41]

Supreme Court Justice Antonin Scalia died on February 13. Many believe Judge Scalia's death put the Constitution, and basic constitutional rights, in a precarious position, since Scalia was known for being a strict constitutionalist and unapologetically a man of deep faith and a conservative. The Supreme Court was now ideologically split.[42]

The global markets continue their declines, causing many to speak of deepening recession, or even an out-and-out depression. Near the end of February, MarketWatch.com ran this headline article, "Chilling ways the global economy echoes 1930s Great Depression era."[43]

MARCH 2016

By March, the *Times* UK reported that the world's financial markets had entered a state of alarming instability. The headlines declared, "Global fears as markets lose faith in central banks." The article emphasized that the Bank for International Settlements, known as the central bank for the world's central banks, had affirmed in its last quarterly report, "The uneasy calm in financial markets last year has given way to turbulence."[44]

SURELY THE SOVEREIGN LORD DOES NOTHING WITHOUT REVEALING

HIS PLAN TO HIS SERVANTS THE PROPHETS. —AMOS 3:7

AN UNFOLDING STORY

A number of prophecy watchers are still not anxious to acknowledge that the Shemitah year of September 2014–September 2015, and the months that followed it, was a definitive declaration from the throne of heaven. Whether one chooses to call it the Shemitah effect or not, the rapid convergence of astounding prophetic relationships continued to march forward. Could it be we were being warned—from the throne of Yahweh?

Perhaps so, but sadly, most of humanity merely continued to "eat, and drink, and to be given in marriage" (see Matthew 24:38; Luke 17:27, cf. Genesis 6–7). At the same time Yahweh may very well be in the process of constructing an "ark" of warning in the world's backyard.

PART IV

EQUIPPING THE SAINTS "FOR SUCH A TIME AS THIS"

For if you remain silent at this time, relief and deliverance for [God's People] will arise from another place, but you and your family will perish. And who knows but that you have come to your royal position for such a time as this?

—ESTHER 4:14

31

BALANCE

The Christian ideal has not been tried and found wanting. It has been found difficult; and left untried.
— G. K. CHESTERTON, *WHAT'S WRONG WITH THE WORLD?*

THE CONVERSATION BEGAN IN a casual manner.

The young woman, identified by her name tag as Ms. Thompson, had just finished recording the man's personal medical history and was in the process of taking his blood pressure. As she cinched up the cuff and began pumping up the pressure ball, she asked a question:

"What in the world is wrong with us?"

"What do you mean?" the patient asked. "What's wrong with who?"

The cuff hissed as Ms. Thompson released most of its pressure. It was obvious the matter was heavy on her heart.

"I'm sorry. I *meant* the world!" she sighed. "It's so messed up. It's not just our country. It's everywhere. There's so much evil going on! It's on the news; it's in conversations with people at work, and even at church. I feel as though we're right at the verge of World War III or something!" She paused, and sighed again.

"*Phfff.* Maybe I just need to quit watching the news so much," she reflected, laughing at her own comment.

The man's expression betrayed a hint of sympathy.

"Look what's happening in the Middle East!" she continued. "They're killing all those Christians—even the women and children! Burning them alive and cutting off their heads! It's horrible!

"And look how we're treating Israel! And the rest of the world is turning their back on Israel too! Sometimes I just can't believe what I'm seeing!"

But she still wasn't finished.

"But it's not just that—I think we might even be in the end-times. And I'm not the only one that thinks that way. People everywhere are talking about it."

After she had vented her sentiments, she looked at the man and apologized, "Please forgive me. I shouldn't have even gone there. When you said, 'God bless you' when we first met, I just assumed—"

"Oh no—not a problem," the man interjected. "Actually, we're probably in pretty close agreement."

"Thanks," she replied and slowly exhaled. "I'm so glad you don't think I'm crazy or something."

"Actually, I do think it's a very real possibility that we might be living in the last days," her patient responded, "but let me explain, because I believe there's a balance to the matter."

He now had her attention.

"First let me say this: What is wrong with us, Ms. Thompson, is that we live in a fallen world. The existence of abject evil has been a reality since the days of the garden of Eden. But the Bible tells us that those days of evil will eventually come to an end—with the return of Jesus Christ. The Bible calls that time the *last days* or *the Day of the Lord.* And that same Bible tells us about the prophetic times that we're living in right now.

"Jesus told us we couldn't know the day or the hour," the patient continued, "so I don't worry about trying to pinpoint the day of His return, nor do I live my life in a state of constant anxiousness either. Life can be tough enough without living every day as though the sky is falling.

"But here's the real kicker," he went on, "times have *always* been tough, even downright scary, for almost every generation that has ever lived. Think of the butchery, wars, brutality, conquering, disease, starvation, murder, pestilence, rape, torture, and persecution throughout the ages.

"But," he interjected, "and *this* is really important . . . there is something very different about *our* generation. It's something that makes us especially responsible to pay attention and to 'discern the season.' And, it's overlooked by most of the naysayers."

"What's that?" she asked, practically pleading for the answer.

"You mentioned it earlier," he said, smiling.

Ms. Thompson began to think back through her previous comments.

"You mentioned the nation of Israel," he explained.

Her eyes brightened.

"The fact that Israel is back in the land," he continued, "is the fulfillment of a twenty-five-hundred-year-old prophecy, found only in the Bible, and fulfilled only in our generation. Many believe God's last-days prophetic timetable started with the return of Israel—and we're living on the other side of that clock being wound up and let loose!"

"Yes!" She nodded. "I never thought of that before."

The man went on. "So, I tell believers to simply get on with life, enjoy the time the Lord has given you; we're not guaranteed another day. The Lord may tarry several hundred more years; we just don't know. But we have to be ready, regardless. However, at the same time, we shouldn't be spiritually blind about what's going on in the world around us, either."

He continued with added perspective, "But, if we're intelligently aware of the prophetic times we're living in, we can properly prepare our families, ourselves, and even our church families for the possibility of tough days ahead. We've been so blessed in America. We haven't seen real persecution here—not like the kind of misery our brothers and sisters around the world have been suffering for decades.

"Plus, I think it would do us well to understand the urgency of reaching people for the Lord, while there is still time. The real problem is getting people to wake up and to understand the times!"

"I believe you're right," Ms. Thompson responded. "It's as though most people don't even see it; they just amble on through life thinking everything is normal because most of the elements of their daily lives are still in place."

"Exactly! Which is why I also encourage Christians to *stay engaged.* Jesus instructed us to be the 'salt' and the 'light' [Matt. 5:13–16]. When the darkness grows darker, we've got to turn the lights up brighter. Now is certainly not the time for God's people to grow more silent, more complacent, and more timid." He smiled at the young woman, her face indicating she now had an entirely new perspective on the matter.

Ms. Thompson cocked her head with a knowing look, as though she had finally discovered the answer to a mystery she had been long pondering. "Are you some kind of preacher or something?" she asked.

The man laughed. "How'd you know?"

ARTICULATING THE ANSWER

As you might have guessed, I am that man. The situation represented here actually occurred. The woman's real name is not "Ms. Thompson," but the rest of the account is accurate.

Conversations very similar to the one I had with Ms. Thompson are taking place around the planet every day. With the advent of worldwide and instantaneous communication technologies, these types of exchange are, more than ever before, easier to engage. As a result, people all over the world are anxious, perhaps unusually so, and they are looking for answers. They feel in the core of their beings that something is not quite right with the world. But most people seem unable to put their finger on it, or at least, they are not able to articulate what they believe they might be seeing. Our responsibility is to communicate that answer in an accurate and biblical way. And most important, we must communicate the truth with compassion.

If I do not know the person's relationship with the Lord, I usually begin with a few probing questions: "Are you born-again? Are you absolutely certain you will spend eternity with your Creator when you pass from this life? Are you spiritually prepared for the coming days of God's prophetic outpouring?"

In being prepared to help people answer these questions, we are greatly accountable. The scripture clearly instructs us in that responsibility:

But in your hearts revere Christ as Lord. Always be prepared to
give an answer to everyone who asks you to give the reason for
the hope that you have. But do this with gentleness and respect.
(1 Peter 3:15)

The first step of our personal preparedness is to make certain
that our hearts are sincerely set apart unto the Lord. We must
be confident that we are living our lives as consistently as possible from a biblical worldview, giving answers to life's toughest
questions with God's Word as our foundational filter of truth.

Second, to "always be prepared to give an answer" implies
that we must give the matter serious thought and prayer. Lay
out a plan for leading someone to salvation in Jesus Christ.
Memorize important passages of scripture that will help you do
so. Become regularly involved in Bible study—both personal
and corporate study.

And where the passage declares, "to everyone who asks" it
also implies that as you live from a biblical worldview, people
will notice! As you go through your daily routines, some of
those around you will begin to seek biblical advice from you. Be
prepared! There will be plenty of Ms. Thompson opportunities
coming your way.

The third element of 1 Peter 3:15 is vital. We are told, "Do
this with gentleness and respect." The opposite of those attitudes
would be to respond with gruffness, and in a condescending
manner. There's that "balance" again! We must be prepared,
and we must speak the truth. However, we must temper that
truth with compassion and understanding.

SEARCHING FOR ANSWERS

These are seriously spiritual and prophetic times. People are frightened. They are concerned. They know something is wrong; they just don't know what. They are searching for answers. We must not give the impression that their questions are somehow an inconvenience to us. It could very well be that the Lord Himself has actually placed them in our paths so they might be given biblical answers, with kindness and deference. Can the Lord trust *you* in this matter?

Do not be surprised if, after asking those first probing questions, people's responses indicate that they are not certain of their salvation. It happens to me all the time. I have discovered that many people are sensitive to the things of God, especially because of the portentous days in which we now find ourselves, but they do not know what it means to be biblically born again.

Jesus told us our priorities, especially in those times when people are responsive to the gospel message: "[Jesus] told them, 'The harvest is plentiful, but the workers are few. Ask the Lord of the harvest, therefore, to send out workers into his harvest field'" (Luke 10:2).

There are many ways to take people through the gospel plan of salvation, and there is an abundance of good material to assist you in formulating your own biblical plan. The key is—*have a plan!* Be prepared! These days are much too important to squander the opportunities we are given to lead someone to eternal salvation in Jesus Christ.

YOU WILL BE SAVED

One way I have discovered to be particularly effective is in the memorization of one simple, clear-cut, biblical explanation of how to be saved. Armed with this "gospel in a nutshell" verse, you can speak the truth very quickly, or expand upon it for hours, if you have the time to do so.

If you will memorize the following verse and familiarize yourself with its deeper biblical truths, you will not even need a Bible in your hand to share salvation's plan. I use this verse several times a week in witnessing opportunities: "If you declare with your mouth, 'Jesus is Lord,' and believe in your heart that God raised him from the dead, you will be saved" (Rom. 10:9).

And that is the crux of the salvation experience. We must be able to declare unashamedly that Jesus is "God with us." We must proclaim from our very being that Jesus alone is our Savior and our only hope. *Lord* means "savior," "boss," "master," or "ultimate authority." In effect, when we proclaim, "Jesus is Lord," we are declaring that Jesus is God in the flesh, and our only Savior and master.

To "believe in your heart" means moving beyond a simple head knowledge of Christ's resurrection—and moving into the mode of surrendering your life goals and passions to that truth. Remember: even Satan "believes" Jesus rose from the dead. Satan was there! And, he knew the resurrection of Jesus was his ultimate undoing. But Satan surely is not "saved" simply because he "believes." The difference is this; Satan will not bow his knee and surrender his life to promoting the things of God. But a born-again believer *will* do that—at any cost!

However, if we are going to fully prepare ourselves to be the balanced and faithful witnesses we have been called to be, we must first make certain we have the proper perspective. We can never truly help others understand where we are as a historical generation unless we first have that perspective in a contextual biblical focus.

The next chapter will help with that.

32

PERSPECTIVE

Look again at that dot. That's here. That's home. That's us. On it everyone you love, everyone you know, everyone you ever heard of, every human being who ever was, lived out their lives . . . the pale blue dot, the only home we've ever known.
—CARL SAGAN, *PALE BLUE DOT: A VISION OF THE HUMAN FUTURE IN SPACE*

PERSPECTIVE CAN BE AN unforgiving taskmaster.

If you do not possess the proper point of view of a situation, the misinterpretation of what lies before you can sometimes exact a dear price.

Long before the Wright brothers positioned their flimsy flying-machine apparatus atop that hill at Kitty Hawk, human beings had discovered the deadly potentials of the problems associated with vertigo, spatial-distance calculations, time relativity, and other matters of perception.

Even ministers, psychologists, and counselors know the dangers of "losing perspective" as one sojourns through this brief but often vexing life. Most of the counseling sessions I have conducted as a pastor involve helping people regain their biblical viewpoint of life. It certainly is easy to lose sight of reality along the way.

Today's modern pilots go through extensive training; learning to rely on their precision-tuned flight instruments. They discover in that training that their own physical sensations and intuitions can sometimes be incorrect—deadly incorrect. So, they are taught how to read their instruments accurately, and to trust them—lest they find themselves flying upside down, or even *nose down*, headed for the quickly ascending earth! Staying in tune with the "proper perspective" is a matter of life and death for a pilot.

Perspective—how you define it and the way you respond to it—always matters.

PERSPECTIVE ASSESSMENT

In earlier chapters you have been inundated with facts, statistics, headlines, and a historical journaling of prophetic connections. With all this information you may have forgotten some of the more important points that we have covered.

If we are going to be effective ministers in our prophetic times, we must endeavor to keep the proper point of view. We have to be absolutely convinced we are reading our "flight instruments" correctly. Am I flying upside down, or am I straight and level? Am I simply passing through a small cloud, or have I entered a massive fog bank? Am I going crazy, or am I really seeing what I think I am seeing?

Take a moment and reconsider what you have learned from the preceding chapters. We have seen the prophetic rebirth of

Israel, the burgeoning advancement of technology, the intensified efforts towards eradication of Christianity in the Middle East, and now the presence of Russia and China in Syria are causing global concerns of the very real potential of World War III right before our eyes.

How's your perspective now? What are your "flight instruments" telling you? Do you trust them? In what direction do *you* think the world is heading? Your answers to these questions determine your prophetic perspective.

You are living in the midst of these astounding prophecies. You are *not* "flying upside down." You can trust your "flight controls and navigational instruments." The Word of God is coming to life, in our generation. A firm grip on that truth is essential for a realistic and healthy outlook on life, as well as for developing a biblical plan of action.

Please remember what we discovered many chapters back: prophetic unfolding most often occurs in many small steps rather than one huge, instantaneous event. And even if we think we see that one giant occurrence—in reality the whole affair has usually been the end result of a slowly unfolding story.

We have been watching that process occurring throughout most of our lives. From the Persian Gulf War to 9/11, from Iraq and Afghanistan to Arab Spring—then from the birth of ISIS to Russia and China in the Middle East forming alliances with Iran, and the extermination of Christianity in the Middle East to the worldwide talk among the global elite of a coming World War III. Beginning with Saddam Hussein, right up through where we are today, for the most part, the world merely went back to their routine after the initial shock of the events wore off. All the while, prophetic elements were building right before our eyes—and going largely unnoticed. Many had lost their biblical perspective.

A CALL TO PREPARE

If you are a pastor or Bible teacher, and previously you were hesitant to "deal with prophecy," hesitate no longer. You now have a resource in your hand that can assist you in helping others make sense of what is happening prophetically around the globe. Please believe me: they *are* asking the questions, whether you are talking about them or not!

On the other hand, if you find that you are a member in the congregation of one of those "prophecy-poor" American churches that George Barna's research group and the Pew polls have described, now you also have a tool with which to inject the truth into your church. With a humble and courteous spirit, get this book into the hands of your preachers, pastors, teachers, fellow church members, and Bible study leaders.

This book might also serve as a powerful witnessing tool. I pray you will use it creatively. People are wondering, *What in the world is going on? What is wrong with us?* Now you can show them, backed up with plenty of balanced and reliable documentation, and perhaps lead them to the light of truth in Jesus Christ.

In 2015, I authored a book titled *Be Thou Prepared: Equipping the Church for Persecution and Times of Trouble.* The purpose of that book was to answer the dozens of questions modern believers consistently ask concerning the topic of preparedness.

Many Christians, for fear of looking like a "crazy prepper," reach a point of paralysis by analysis and react by making little or no preparation for the potentiality of tough times ahead.

To alleviate anxiety regarding their unpreparedness, they often resort to the virtuous-sounding excuse "I'm just gonna live by faith! I don't need to prepare. The Lord will provide."[1]

Of course we should live by faith! We are not guaranteed another moment of life. Ultimately each breath and heartbeat is in the hands of the Lord. But to say, "I'm not going to prepare; I'm not going be attentive to protecting my family, church, and the innocent," is an unbiblical position entirely.

Certainly we should reasonably prepare! Our daily life is filled with activities of "emergency preparation." This is why we wear safety belts, lock our doors at night, install alarm systems, have fire extinguishers, and purchase all manner of insurance policies. It is also why we teach our children how to dial 911 and why we carry a spare tire and other emergency supplies in the trunk of our vehicles. We live our lives in a constant state of preparedness. How foolish it would be to leave your family and church in a preparedness void in these portentous days.

FACING THE FACTS

Today's church has to face the cold, hard facts of the new world in which we live. Many experts believe religious persecution is only going to increase as we move forward. Is this not also what Jesus made clear on several occasions when He spoke of the signs of the last days? The statistics bear out the plain truth of the matter. The scourge is already upon us.

In February 2016, First Liberty Institute published a report titled *Undeniable: The Survey of Hostility to Religion in America.* That document unveils a list of 1,285 reported cases of hostile activities aimed at America's religious community; much of the aggression aimed squarely at Christians. And the reported instances were recorded only from the start of 2016! In fact, the report indicated attacks on Christians had doubled in the last three years prior to the research being published.[2]

The report revealed, "These cases . . . show a clear expansion during this past year. Quantitatively and qualitatively, the hostility is undeniable. And it is dangerous."[3]

Kelly Shackelford, the chief counsel for First Liberty, reported, "hostility to religion in America is rising like floodwaters . . . This flood is engulfing ordinary citizens who simply try to live normal lives according to their faith and conscience. It is eroding the bedrock on which stand vital American institutions such as government, education, the military, business, houses of worship, and charity. It has the potential to wash away the ground that supports our other rights, including freedom of speech, press, assembly, and government by consent of the people."

Shackelford continued, "The attacks . . . are sweeping away small businesses, careers and ministries. Behind the legalities are tears, anguish and the denial of basic human tolerance, compassion, and common decency."[4]

It is now time for America's churches, and the entire Christian community, to get a *perception realignment*. We are living in critical prophetic days. To deny this truth is to deny the readings of our "flight instruments." The church and individual Christians have a biblical responsibility to prepare, both spiritually and logistically. We need the proper perspective!

There is no need to be anxious; there is no need to panic. We simply must biblically and rationally adjust to the prophetic times in which we are living. Those who refuse to see what is right before them are not only taking a dangerous approach concerning life's realities, they are also robbing themselves of many exciting opportunities to advance the kingdom of Jesus Christ—before His soon return.

The fields truly are "white unto harvest" (John 4:35 YLT)!

"YOU ARE THE SALT OF THE EARTH. BUT IF THE SALT LOSES ITS SALTINESS, HOW CAN IT BE MADE SALTY AGAIN? IT IS NO LONGER GOOD FOR ANYTHING, EXCEPT TO BE THROWN OUT AND TRAMPLED UNDERFOOT. YOU ARE THE LIGHT OF THE WORLD. A TOWN BUILT ON A HILL CANNOT BE HIDDEN. NEITHER DO PEOPLE LIGHT A LAMP AND PUT IT UNDER A BOWL. INSTEAD THEY PUT IT ON ITS STAND, AND IT GIVES LIGHT TO EVERYONE IN THE HOUSE." —MATTHEW 5:13-15

33

THE INGATHERING

They will follow the Lord*; he will roar like a lion.*   —HOSEA 11:10

THE INTERNET WENT ACTIVE with its premier website on Christmas Day 1990.[1]

Sir Tim Berners-Lee, inventor of the World Wide Web, and Belgian computer scientist Robert Cailliau communicated between a web browser and a web server for the first time on that eternally significant date. It happened during the world's celebration of the gospel message having been born—in the flesh—in the person of Jesus Christ. Think of the prophetic correlation of those events!

Jesus' forecast, found in Matthew 24:14, would begin its literal fulfillment, "And this gospel of the kingdom will be preached in the whole world as a testimony to all nations, and then the end will come." However, the actualization of that truth would not take place until a full two thousand years after Jesus uttered those words—*and only in our generation*! Ours is the first generation to possess the technology to proclaim the kingdom truths and the gospel message to every single nation. And that technology was literally born on the same day we were celebrating Messiah's birth. I am overwhelmed just typing these words.

And boy, has the world changed since the day the Internet went live! The entire globe is now "connected," for better or for worse, until death do we part. As we have previously documented, the proliferation of evil and the influence of the demonic realm has never had a larger pulpit. On the other hand, neither has the kingdom of God, and neither have individual Christians!

"Regular" Christians, who previously had to depend on the work of missionaries, evangelists, major ministry organizations, and authors to do the work of God on a global scale (see John 9:4), can now log on to the social media network and reach the world for Christ from their cell phones, in seconds. And they can do this remarkable work twenty-four hours a day, seven days a week. Amazing! Unprecedented! It's the stuff of end-time prophecy.

We have already examined the remarkable ingathering of Jews in the last days, even in the land of Israel itself. But fewer realize the vast ingathering of other biblical people groups taking place every day, around the world.

AND THIS GOSPEL OF THE KINGDOM WILL BE PREACHED IN THE WHOLE WORLD AS A TESTIMONY TO ALL NATIONS, AND THEN THE END WILL COME. —JESUS (MATTHEW 24:14)

MUSLIMS COMING TO CHRIST

While we see Christianity on the steady decline in America, we see it on the rise in other nations. In June 2015, *Christianity Today* published an article proclaiming, "We are living in the midst of the greatest turning of Muslims to Christ in history."[2] The piece was an exposé of missionary David Garrison's book, *A Wind in the House of Islam.*[3]

Garrison's work records the amazing last-days trend that he says demonstrates "we are living in the midst of the greatest turning of Muslims to Christ in history." Garrison's report is the product of two and a half years of research and involved traveling more than 250,000 miles to conduct interviews with more than 1,000 people throughout the Muslim world.

In Garrison's research, a "movement" of believers is defined as a group of more than 1,000 baptized believers or 100 church starts within a Muslim community. In total, he discovered sixty-nine movements that had started in the first twelve years of the twenty-first century. There had been virtually no voluntary movements of converts to Christianity among Muslims in the first twelve centuries of Islam.[4]

Even Al Jazeera, the Middle East's leading news network, disclosed the startling statistics. In each hour of every day, 667 Muslims convert to Christianity. Every single day, 16,000 Muslims come to Jesus Christ as Savior. Every year, 6 million Muslims convert to Christianity in Africa alone. Additionally, millions more have come to Jesus Christ in the combined outpouring in Egypt, India, Morocco, Somalia, Indonesia, Thailand, Malaysia, Singapore, Pakistan, Bangladesh, Saudi Arabia, UAE, and the Maldives.[5]

How is the church in America going to respond to the fact that the Lord is now allowing the influx of Muslims in unprecedented numbers to our own shores, and into our own communities? Will we redeem the opportunities—or retreat in disobedience like Jonah? Jesus' command is clear, "Go ye into all the world and . . . make disciples" (Mark 16:15 KJV; Matt. 28:19). *All the world* includes our own neighborhoods and towns.

We must learn to engage. Every time we engage anyone with the gospel truth of Jesus Christ, we are advancing the kingdom of God—regardless of his or her immediate response to the message. And is this not what we have been raised up to do? Is this not our supreme purpose in life?

One may protest, "But I don't want to witness to Muslims. They have been our enemies for so long!" That was the protest of Jonah, and we all know what happened to him. And don't forget: Jonah was sent to the people of Nineveh. That city was one of the capitals of the ancient Assyrian Empire. The Assyrians were the terrorists of Jonah's day—and now that area is the heart of Middle Eastern Islam.

The people of Nineveh repented in Jonah's day and turned to God. Many of the people of today's "Nineveh" are turning to God through Jesus Christ in our day. Coincidence? Don't be a Jonah. Don't become "fish food"!

CHINA COMING TO CHRIST

There is also an unprecedented revival and ingathering of Christians in China. My good friend and global outreach ministry partner Messianic rabbi Zev Porat lives in Israel. However, his wife, Lian, is from China. Zev and Lian often minister in China, making several trips there each year. Zev's wife speaks Mandarin Chinese, the official language of China and Taiwan. Rabbi Porat testifies of the great revival currently erupting in

China, and especially in the underground church.

Here is yet another definitive prophetic marker of our day. Isaiah spoke of it in one of his striking end-time prophecies. Rabbi Porat was one of the first to remind me of this biblical fact:

> See, they will come from afar—some from the north, some from the west, some from the region of Aswan. (Isa. 49:12)

In the NIV for this verse, the footnote to the word Aswan shows that Sinim is the Masoretic Text translation of the Hebrew word used here. And according to a footnote on the Amplified Bible's rendering of this verse, Sinim is "traditionally interpreted as China."

The *International Standard Bible Encyclopedia* has this to say about Sinim in Isaiah's prophecy:

> The name occurs in Isaiah's prophecy of the return of the people from distant lands: "Lo, these shall come from far; and, lo, these from the north and from the west; and these from the land of Sinim" (Isa 49:12). The land is clearly far off, and it must be sought either in the South or in the East. Septuagint points to an eastern country. *Many scholars have favored identification with China*, the classical Sinae. It seems improbable that Jews had already found their way to China; but from very early times trade relations were established with the Far East by way of Arabia and the Persian Gulf.[6]

The American Tract Bible Society identifies Sinim as

> a people very remote from the Holy Land, towards the east or south; generally believed to mean the Chinese, who have been

known to Western Asia from early times, and are called by the Arabs Sin, and by the Syrians Tsini.[7]

China is on track to have the world's largest population of Christians by 2030. The Council on Foreign Relations reports, "The number of Christians in the early 1980s was estimated at about six million . . . In 2010 the Pew Research Center calculated a total of sixty-seven million . . . Christians in China, approximately five percent of the country's population. Other independent estimates suggest somewhere between 100 and 130 million. Purdue's [Fenggang] Yang projects that if 'modest' growth rates are sustained, China could have as many as 160 million Christians by 2025 and 247 million by 2032."[8]

Just as Isaiah predicted, they are coming to the Lord in the last days, even in the land of China [Sinim]. This revival is not happening with ease. It is coming at great cost to the Chinese Christian community. The Chinese government is a prolific antagonist of the Christian faith and sees Christianity as a direct threat to its communist intentions. Nevertheless, the last-days ingathering of the Chinese people continues. For it is written.

There can be no doubt that in the midst of the simultaneous *falling away* in America and Europe, there is also a great *ingathering* in other parts of the world. In Asia, Africa, and Latin America, the numbers of those coming to Jesus Christ continue to soar, with more coming to faith in the last twenty-five years than at any time in world history.[9]

There can also be no doubt that Satan and his domain will use every opportunity to thwart and stall the advancing of the kingdom work of Jesus Christ. Therefore, we must be especially alert.

I AM SENDING YOU OUT LIKE SHEEP AMONG WOLVES. THEREFORE
BE AS SHREWD AS SNAKES AND AS INNOCENT AS DOVES. —JESUS
(MATTHEW 10:16)

Redeem the time. That is why we are here.

34

ENGAGE AND ADVANCE

The best form of defense is attack.
—ATTRIBUTED TO KARL VON CLAUSEWITZ, PRUSSIAN GENERAL AND
MILITARY THEORIST

THIS IS WAR! ENGAGE the enemy! Advance the troops! We have ground to take! Let's go!

You might imagine hearing those words coming from the command of a military leader as the officer's troops prepare to enter the heat of battle. These two key words sum up practically the entire goal of the church's battle—*engage* and *advance*.

We know the days in which we live are abjectly evil. We also know we are involved in spiritual warfare fought at a technological and demonic level the world has never before experienced. And if the technology forecasts are correct, that war will only become tougher in the coming years.

But our battle is not simply against the exponentially advancing "technology"; rather, it is against the wicked powers that will most assuredly seek to manipulate technology to further enslave the planet. The powers are spiritual. They are demonic. And they are playing for keeps. And it was all foretold from the beginning.

> THE WORLD IS A DANGEROUS PLACE TO LIVE, NOT BECAUSE OF THE PEOPLE WHO ARE EVIL, BUT BECAUSE OF THE PEOPLE WHO DON'T DO ANYTHING ABOUT IT. —ALBERT EINSTEIN[1]

JUST LIKE THIS

There is a defining characteristic of the days just before the return of Jesus that we simply cannot ignore. The definition of those days comes from the mouth of Jesus Himself, and there can be little room for misinterpretation of His words. Observe how Jesus described the time—perhaps *our* time:

> Just as it was in the days of Noah, so also will it be in the days of the Son of Man. People were eating, drinking, marrying and being given in marriage up to the day Noah entered the ark. Then the flood came and destroyed them all. It was the same in the days of Lot. People were eating and drinking, buying and selling, planting and building. But the day Lot left Sodom, fire and sulfur rained down from heaven and destroyed them all. It will be just like this on the day the Son of Man is revealed. (Luke 17:26–30)

Jesus said it would be "just like this" in the days just before His return. So—how *were* those days? According to Jesus, there was a general apathy among Earth's population toward the things of God—and there will be again. Civilization will be filled with unbelief, ignoring the prophetic signs all around them.

In both days there was also a spirit of mocking God, as well as mocking His messengers. In Noah's day, he and his family were the witnesses. And their witness was accompanied by 120 years of preaching that the judgment of God would indeed fall upon the world—assured by the presence of an aircraft carrier–sized ship in Noah's backyard! But the hearts of the population in general were still only intent upon wickedness. They mocked and scoffed and went on with their lives as though the world would last forever. But "the flood came and destroyed them all."

"WHILE THE UNITED STATES IS FOCUSED ON ITS OWN POLITICS, THE WORLD IS UNRAVELING. THE DANGER SIGNALS ARE EVERYWHERE."

—FRANKLIN GRAHAM[2]

In Lot's day it was the constant testimony of "righteous Lot" and his family that stood as God's witness of His word in their time (see 2 Peter 5:6–8 HCSB). The wickedness and perversion of the Sodom and Gomorrah societies were under judgment. Two angels even showed up at Lot's house, in full view of the townspeople. But the people's hearts were only filled with evil intent—even in the face of God's divine messengers. They mocked God's grace, and they mocked His warning. And so the fires of heaven fell and destroyed them all.

In both of these troublesome situations, God's witnesses

lived in and through the midst of the most terrible times those civilizations had ever seen. Yet, God preserved them in the heart of those dreadful days and used them as witnesses of His glory and His coming judgment.

Jesus said, "It will be just like this," before He returns. I really do not see how He could have been any clearer.

The signs are all around us. From the return of Israel to the presence of Russia and China in the Middle East—to the meteoric rise of prophetic end-time technologies . . . how can people miss the signals? But they do. They are content to eat, drink, marry, and be given in marriage—right up until judgment falls.

However, that is why we are here! We are the Noahs of our generation. We are the Lots. We are the witnesses of the kingdom of God, prophesying to a last-days world—and especially to *America*!

Award-winning journalist and author Cheryl Chumley, in her latest title, *The Devil in DC: Winning Back the Country from the Beast in Washington* wrote:

> Let's not cede the battle just yet. Our country may be only of earthly substance, rather than heavenly, and we may all be here just biding our time until the Second Coming. But until then, we need something to do, and why not make it something for the greater good—for the glory of God? It seems only proper for those who see the evil to fight it, and for those who discern the wicked to teach others to be aware and act.[3]

ENGAGE AND ADVANCE!

I agree with Ms. Chumley. We are here for the greater good. We have been placed here to fulfill God's purpose. Therefore, let us engage! Let us be the faithful witnesses of our "day." Let us not grow weary of doing good. We must determine to be the salt and light Jesus has called us to be. And let us get on with the work of advancing the kingdom of Jesus Christ.

THEN ONE OF THE ELDERS SAID TO ME, "DO NOT WEEP! SEE, THE LION OF THE TRIBE OF JUDAH, THE ROOT OF DAVID, HAS TRIUMPHED. HE IS ABLE TO OPEN THE SCROLL AND ITS SEVEN SEALS." —REVELATION 5:5

We can live these days cowering in anxiousness, or we can live these days enjoying life, thanking Yahweh that He has entrusted us with His kingdom work. God has promised He can preserve us in the midst of our day as well. We have been given that assurance in no uncertain terms. Let us take Him at His promise, and put our shoulder to the plow!

If [God] did not spare the ancient world when he brought the flood on its ungodly people, but protected Noah, a preacher of righteousness, and seven others; if he condemned the cities of Sodom and Gomorrah by burning them to ashes, and made them an example of what is going to happen to the ungodly; and if he rescued Lot, a righteous man, who was distressed by the depraved conduct of the lawless (for that righteous man, living among them day after day, was tormented in his righteous soul by the lawless deeds he saw and heard)—if this is so, then the Lord knows how to rescue the godly from trials and to hold the unrighteous for punishment on the day of judgment. (2 Peter 2:5–9)

We *do* know we are living in very prophetic times. However, we do not know, nor can we know, the hour of Christ's return. It may yet be another hundred years, maybe even two hundred. But according to the prophetic signs most biblical prophecy watchers see, the Lord's return *could* be today! It does not matter. The point is we are not assured of another beat of our heart. Our responsibility is to be a faithful witness with whatever time the Lord has given us.

WE END WHERE WE BEGAN

In its early pages, this book started with an account of Israel's prime minister Benjamin Netanyahu addressing the United States Congress. In that congressional speech he invoked the lesson of the book of Esther and the Feast of Purim.

One thing Netanyahu did not address in that admonition was Esther's hesitancy to be obedient to her moral duty. She almost buckled under the weight of the matter. She felt the fear of possible death, if she were to literally *engage and advance*, as her cousin Mordecai had asked her to.

She sent back word through her messenger that she would not do what Mordecai asked. Esther insisted it was too dangerous, to which her cousin (who had raised Esther as his own daughter) replied, "If you remain silent at this time, relief and deliverance for the Jews will arise from another place, but you and your father's family will perish. And who knows but that you have come to your royal position for such a time as this?" (Esther 4:14)

There it is! There is our calling, exactly. If we cling to our life—we just might lose it. However, on the other hand, if we are willing to "lose" our life in the kingdom work and the advancement of the cause of Jesus Christ, we will gain it, and perhaps the souls of many others along the way.

In these prophetic times, I am convinced that you and I have been raised up . . . *for such a time as this*!

The Lion has roared.
Will you heed His call?

Even so, come Lord Jesus!
May Yahweh bless you and keep you as we walk this journey of faith together . . . In the name of His Son, Yeshua HaMashiach—amen.

NOTES

INTRODUCTION

1. James Jay Carafano, "Russia May Be Leaving Syria but Putin Will Have Assad's Back for a Long, Long Time," Fox News, March 14, 2016, http://www.foxnews.com/opinion/2016/03/14/russia-may-be-leaving-syria-but-putin-will-have-assads-back-for-long-long-time.html?intcmp=hpbt1.

CHAPTER 1: IS THE SKY FALLING?

1. Jon Austin, "Yellowstone about to Blow? Scientists Warning over SUPER-VOLCANO That Could Kill MILLIONS," *Express* (UK), March 31, 2016, http://www.express.co.uk/news/science/632054/Yellowstone-about-to-blow-1-in-10-chance-super-volcano-will-kill-millions.
2. Ibid.
3. Ibid.
4. Scientist Warning: Scientists Warn of Yellowstone Super Volcano—Shepard Smith Reporting," Youtube video, 4:35, from the January 8, 2016, Fox News broadcast, posted by "Mass Tea Party—Wake Up America!" January 8, 2016, https://www.youtube.com/watch?v=QdgEmkYBWBY5.
5. Austin, "Yellowstone about to Blow?"
6. Ibid.
7. Michael Martinez, Stephanie Elam, and Rosalina Nieves, "The Quake-Maker You've Never Heard Of: Cascadia," *CNN*, February 13, 2016, http://www.cnn.com/2016/02/11/us/cascadia-subduction-zone-earthquakes.

CHAPTER 2: EVERYBODY'S TALKING ABOUT IT!

1. Pew Research Center, "Jesus Christ's Return to Earth," July 14, 2010, http://www. pewresearch.org/daily-number/jesus-christs-return-to-earth/; Dominique Mosbergen, "How Many U.S. Christians Believe Christ's 'Second Coming' Will Happen Soon? More Than You May Think (SURVEY)," *Huffpost Religion*, April 1, 2013, http://www. huffingtonpost.com/2013/04/01/christ-second-coming-survey_n_2993218.html.

2. David A. Patten, "Rev. Billy Graham Prepares 'Perhaps . . . My Last Message,'" NewsMax, http://www.newsmax.com/Newsfront/Graham-evangelist-final-message/2013/10/05/id/529474.

3. Nicola Menzie, "Billy Graham Turns 95: Milestones in Influential Evangelist's Ministry and Preaching Career," *CP*, November 7, 2013, http://www.christianpost.com/news/ billy-graham-turns-95-milestones-in-influential-evangelists-ministry-and-preaching-career-photos-videos-108163.

4. Patten, "Rev. Billy Graham Prepares 'Perhaps . . . My Last Message,'" emphasis added.

5. Franklin Graham's Facebook page, posted March 17, 2015, https://www.facebook.com/ FranklinGraham/posts/886848164704699.

6. Jeremy Burns, "Billy Graham's Daughter: We're Coming Close to the End of Human History as We Know It," Charisma News, May 29, 2015, http://www.charismanews. com/culture/49887-billy-graham-s-daughter-we-re-coming-close-to-the-end-of-human-history-as-we-know-it.

7. Bill Chappell, "World's Muslim Population Will Surpass Christians This Century, Pew Says," *The Two-Way* (blog), April 2, 2015, http://www.npr.org/sections/ thetwo-way/2015/04/02/397042004/muslim-population-will-surpass-christians-this-century-pew-says.

8. Thomas D. Williams, "After Paris, Pope Francis Tells Christians to Be Ready for the End of the World," Breitbart, November 15, 2015, http://www.breitbart.com/big-government/2015/11/15/paris-pope-francis-tells-christians-ready-end-world.

9. Adam Edelman, "President Obama's Iran Nuclear Deal Is Proof That We Are Living in Bible's 'End of Days,' Former Rep. Michele Bachmann Claims," *New York Daily News*, August 10, 2015, http://www.nydailynews.com/news/politics/iran-nuke-deal-proff-biblical-times-bachmann-article-1.2320818.

10. Gideon Rachman, "Battered, Bruised and Jumpy—the Whole World Is On Edge," *Financial Times*, December 28, 2015, http://www.ft.com/intl/cms/s/0/c523a45a-a973-11e5-955c-1e1d6de94879.html#axzz3vqA3TwRb.

11. Robin Wigglesworth, "China Plunge Spreads to Global Markets," *Financial Times*, January 5, 2016, http://www.ft.com/cms/s/0/ea7434e6-b2af-11e5-aad2-3e9865bc6644. html.

12. Evelyn Cheng, "Dow Closes Down Triple Digits, Posts Worst Opening Day in 8 Years," CNBC, January 4, 2016, http://www.cnbc.com/2016/01/04/us-markets.html.

13. Marcus Leroux, "Markets Suffer Their Worst Start to the Year since Great Depression," *Times* (UK), January 17, 2016, http://www.thetimes.co.uk/tto/public/assetfinance/article4667135.ece.

14. Patrick Hosking and Philip Aldrick, "Global Fears as Markets Lose Faith in Central Banks," *Times* (UK), March 7, 2016, http://www.thetimes.co.uk/tto/business/economics/article4707169.ece.

15. Jason Taylor, "ISIS Plotting 'to Slaughter THOUSANDS' in 2016 in Bid to Spark Huge FINAL BATTLE with West," *Express* (UK), January 1, 2016, http://www.express.co.uk/news/world/630316/ISIS-secret-plot-world-masterplan-2016-final-battle.

16. Anne Speckhard, "End Times Brewing: An Apocalyptic View on al-Baghdadi's Declaration of a Caliphate in Iraq and the Flow of Foreign Fighters Coming from the West," *Huffington Post*, June 30, 2014, http://www.huffingtonpost.co.uk/anne-speckhard/isis-iraq_b_5541693.html.

17. Amir Taheri, "Obama and Ahmadinejad," *Forbes*, October 26, 2008, http://www.forbes.com/2008/10/26/obama-iran-ahmadinejad-oped-cx_at_1026taheri.html.

18. Pew Research Center, "Mapping the Global Muslim Population," October 7, 2009, Pew Forum, http://www.pewforum.org/2009/10/07/mapping-the-global-muslim-population.

19. "End-Times Prophecy Invoked at Gop Debate: Former Senator Warns against Trap of Islamic State," WND, December 15, 2015, http://www.wnd.com/2015/12/end-times-prophecy-invoked-at-gop-debate.

20. Joel C. Rosenberg, "Islamic Extremists Are Trying to Hasten the Coming of the Mahdi," *National Review*, September 11, 2015, http://www.nationalreview.com/article/423852/islamic-extremists-are-trying-hasten-coming-mahdi-joel-c-rosenberg.

CHAPTER 3: WHEN THE LION ROARS

1. Ewen MacAskill and Chris McGreal, "Israel Should Be Wiped Off Map, Says Iran's President," *Guardian* (UK), October 26, 2005, http://www.theguardian.com/world/2005/oct/27/israel.iran.

2. JPost.com staff, "'Iran would definitely use nuclear weapon on Israel,'" *Jerusalem Post*, January 25, 2013, http://www.jpost.com/Iranian-Threat/News/Iran-would-definitely-use-nuclear-weapon-on-Israel.

3. *Washington Post* staff, "The Complete Transcript of Netanyahu's Address to Congress," *Washington Post*, Marxh 3, 2015, https://www.washingtonpost.com/news/post-politics/wp/2015/03/03/full-text-netanyahus-address-to-congress.

4. Ibid.

5. Jack Minor, "Obama's Iran Deal Falls on Ominous Bible Date," WND, April 6, 2015, http://www.wnd.com/2015/04/obamas-iran-deal-announced-on-ominous-bible-date.

6. Herb Keinon, "Analysis: Netanyahu's Speech to Congress Is Purim on the Potomac," *Jerusalem Post*, March 2, 2015, http://www.jpost.com/Israel-News/Politics-And-Diplomacy/Analysis-Netanyahus-speech-to-Congress-is-Purim-on-the-Potomac-392724.

7. The quotes that follow are from "Full Transcript: Prime Minister Netanyahu's Speech at the United Nations General Assembly, 2015 (Video)," *Algemeiner*, October 1, 2015, http://www.algemeiner.com/2015/10/01/full-transcript-prime-minister-netanyahus-speech-at-the-united-nations-general-assembly-2015-video/#.

8. *Times of Israel* staff, "Full text of Netanyahu's 2013 speech to the UN General Assembly," *Times of Israel*, October 1, 2013, http://www.timesofisrael.com/full-text-netanyahus-2013-speech-to-the-un-general-assembly/.

9. Erick Stakelbeck, "Russia-Iran 'Nightmare' Alliance: Why You Should Be Concerned," CBN News, November 5, 2015, http://www1.cbn.com/cbnnews/world/2015/November/Russia-Iran-Nightmare-Alliance-Why-You-Should-Be-Concerned.

10. Colleen Mccain Nelson, "Obama Says Syrian Leader Bashar al-Assad Must Go: U.S. President Says Syrian Civil War Won't End with Assad in Power," *Wall Street Journal*, November 19, 2015, http://www.wsj.com/articles/obama-says-syrian-leader-bashar-al-assad-must-go-1447925671.

11. John Gambrell, "Iran Fires 2 Missiles Marked with 'Israel Must Be Wiped Out,'" Yahoo! Finance, March 9, 2016, http://finance.yahoo.com/news/iran-fires-2-missiles-marked-israel-must-wiped-071612751.html.

CHAPTER 4: OH, AND BY THE WAY . . .

1. Billy Hallowell, "'Left Behind' Producer Reveals Potential End-Times Prophecy Moment He Noticed During GOP Debate," TheBlaze, December 17, 2015, http://www.theblaze.com/stories/2015/12/17/end-times-filmmaker-reveals-potential-bible-prophecy-moment-during-gop-debate-that-could-have-stirred-things-up-had-candidates-done-this-simple-thing.

2. WND, "America Enters World War Three," *Whistleblower* magazine, December 13, 2015, http://www.wnd.com/2015/12/america-enters-world-war-three.

3. Breitbart TV, "Hagel: 'I Think We Are Seeing a New World Order,'" Breitbart, October 29, 2014, http://www.breitbart.com/video/2014/10/29/hagel-i-think-we-are-seeing-a-new-world-order.

4. U.S. Dept. of Defense, "Remarks by Secretary Hagel at a Town Hall with Recruit Training Command School Student Instructors at Naval Station Great Lakes, North Chicago, Illinois," news transcript, May 6, 2014, http://archive.defense.gov/transcripts/transcript.aspx?transcriptid=5426.

5. Adm. James A. Lyons, "LYONS: The Islamic Cloud over Brennan and Hagel: National Security May Not Be a First Priority," *Washington Times*, February 19, 2013, http://www.washingtontimes.com/news/2013/feb/19/the-islamic-cloud-over-brennan-and-hagel.

6. Jack Moore, "Vladimir Putin Says 'Islamization' of Turkey Is Bigger Problem Than Downing of Russian Jet," *Newsweek*, November 25, 2015, http://www.newsweek.com/vladimir-putin-says-islamization-turkey-bigger-problem-downing-russian-jet-398183.

7.   Jessilyn Justice, "Pope Francis Calls for a New World Order—Again," Charisma News, July 8, 2015, http://www.charismanews.com/world/50444-pope-francis-calls-for-new-world-order-again.

8.   Eli Rosenberg, "Pope Francis Acknowledges 'State of Palestine' as He Prays in Bethlehem," *New York Daily News*, May 25, 2014, http://www.nydailynews.com/news/world/israeli-palestinian-leaders-accept-pope-invite-article-1.1804924.

9.   Dave Hunt, "The Current End-Time Apostasy of the Church—Part I" (presentation), Berean Call, December 2005, https://www.thebereancall.org/content/september-2011-classic.

10.   Susan Berry, "America's Openly Gay Ambassadors Boast: ObamaTrade 'Will Export' LGBT Agenda," Breitbart, June 15, 2015, http://www.breitbart.com/big-government/2015/06/15/americas-openly-gay-ambassadors-boast-obamatrade-will-export-lgbt-agenda. This global spread of LGBT "values" is nothing less than a spread of the spirit of Sodom and Gomorrah.

11.   "George Will: 'Global Warming Is Socialism by the Back Door,'" Real Clear Politics Video, April 28, 2014, http://www.realclearpolitics.com/video/2014/04/28/george_will_global_warming_is_socialism_by_the_back_door.html; Larry Bell, "Pope's Faulty Climate Message Based on Global Socialism," NewsMax, September 28, 2015, http://www.newsmax.com/LarryBell/Climate-Change-Pope-Francis-United-Nations-Global-Warming/2015/09/28/id/693684.

12.   Tom Cohen, "Obama Calls for Israel's Return to pre-1967 Borders," CNN, May 19, 2011, http://www.cnn.com/2011/POLITICS/05/19/obama.israel.palestinians/; Joseph Klein, "The UN'S Propaganda War Against Israel: As Israel Defends Itself from Terror, the International Community Supports a Death Cult," *FrontPage Mag*, July 24, 2014, http://www.frontpagemag.com/fpm/237064/uns-propaganda-war-against-israel-joseph-klein.

13.   Isi Leibler, "Candidly Speaking: Global Anti-Semitism Continues to Escalate," *Jerusalem Post*, May 11, 2015, http://www.jpost.com/Opinion/Candidly-speaking-Global-anti-Semitism-continues-to-escalate-402753.

14.   Christina Park, "Yesterday's Sci-Fi is Today's Reality," *Think with Google*, November 2011, https://www.thinkwithgoogle.com/articles/yesterdays-sci-fi.html.

15.   Rob Virtue, "Putin's Boost in Battle against ISIS: China Preparing to 'Team Up with Russia in Syria,'" *Express* (UK), November 19, 2015, http://www.express.co.uk/news/world/610286/China-preparing-to-team-up-with-Russia-in-Syria-Boost-for-Putin-in-battle-against-ISIS.

16.   Ray Sanchez, "Historic Raising of the Palestinian Flag at United Nations," CNN, September 30, 2015, http://www.cnn.com/2015/09/30/world/united-nations-palestinian-flag.

17.   Tal Kopan, "Donald Trump: Syrian Refugees a 'Trojan Horse,'" CNN, November 16, 2015, http://www.cnn.com/2015/11/16/politics/donald-trump-syrian-refugees.

18. Jon Meacham, "Meacham: The End of Christian America," *Newsweek*, April 3, 2009, http://www.newsweek.com/meacham-end-christian-america-77125.

19. World Health Organization, "Sexually Transmitted Infections (STIs)," updated December 2015, http://www.who.int/mediacentre/factsheets/fs110/en.

20. Terence P. Jeffrey, "CDC: 110,197,000 Venereal Infections in U.S.; Nation Creating New STIs Faster Than New Jobs or College Grads," CNSNews.com, March 27, 2013, http://cnsnews.com/news/article/cdc-110197000-venereal-infections-us-nation-creating-new-stis-faster-new-jobs-or.

21. AIDs.gov, "The Global HIV/AIDS Epidemic," last revised November 25, 2016, https://www.aids.gov/hiv-aids-basics/hiv-aids-101/global-statistics.

22. Zoe Mintz, "Exorcisms Are on the Rise: Priests Point to Growing Fascination with the Occult," *International Business Times*, November 10, 2014, http://www.ibtimes.com/exorcisms-are-rise-priests-point-growing-fascination-occult-1721561.

23. Peter Bergen, "Why Does ISIS Keep Making Enemies?" CNN, February 16, 2015, http://www.cnn.com/2015/02/16/opinion/bergen-isis-enemies/.

24. Daniel, "Persecution of Christians Reaches Historic Levels, Conditions Suggest Worst Is Yet to Come," Open Doors, January 7, 2015, https://www.opendoorsusa.org/newsroom/tag-news-post/persecution-of-christians-reaches-historic-levels-conditions-suggest-worst-is-yet-to-come.

25. Russ Read, "Christianity in the Middle East: On the Verge of Extinction," *Daily Caller*, December 8, 2015, http://dailycaller.com/2015/12/08/christianity-in-the-middle-east-on-the-verge-of-extinction; Eliza Griswold, "Is This the End of Christianity in the Middle East? ISIS and Other Extremist Movements across the Region Are Enslaving, Killing and Uprooting Christians, with No Aid in Sight," *New York Times*, July 26, 2015, http://www.nytimes.com/2015/07/26/magazine/is-this-the-end-of-christianity-in-the-middle-east.html.

26. Alex Perala, "World Bank, Accenture Call for Universal ID," Find Biometrics, September 29, 2015, http://findbiometrics.com/world-bank-universal-id-29295.

27. "Islamic State Leader Baghdadi Goads West in Rare Audio Statement: In What Is Believed to Be His First Public Message in Seven Months, ISIL Chief Warns Israel Attacks Are Imminent," *Telegraph* (UK), http://www.telegraph.co.uk/news/worldnews/islamic-state/12069924/Islamic-State-leader-Baghdadi-goads-West-in-rare-audio-statement.html.

CHAPTER 5: READY OR NOT, HERE HE COMES!

1. johnfromberkeley, "Why Is Christianity Today Ignoring Billy Graham's End Times Prophecy?" *Daily Kos*, November 7, 2013, http://www.dailykos.com/story/2013/11/7/1253914/-Why-Is-Christianity-Today-Ignoring-Billy-Graham-s-End-Times-Prophecy.

2. Quoted in Jennifer LeClarie, "Did Pope Francis Really Just Take a Big Step Toward One World Religion?'" Charisma News, December 2, 2015, http://www.charismanews.com/opinion/watchman-on-the-wall/53547-did-pope-francis-really-just-take-a-big-step-toward-one-world-religion.

3. J. Barton Payne, *Encyclopedia of Biblical Prophecy: The Complete Guide to Scriptural Predictions and Their Fulfilment* (Grand Rapids: Baker, 1980).

4. See Douglas S. Winnail, "With So Much of the Bible Devoted to Prophecy, Why Do Most People Fail to Understand the Many End-Time Prophecies?" *Tomorrow's World*, November–December 2007, http://www.tomorrowsworld.org/magazines/2007/november-december/understanding-end-time-prophecies#sthash.pHKGWgsR.dpuf.

5. Dr. Hugh Ross, "Fulfilled Prophecy: Evidence for the Reliability of the Bible," RTB, August 2003, http://www.reasons.org/articles/articles/fulfilled-prophecy-evidence-for-the-reliability-of-the-bible.

6. "On the Road to Armageddon: How Evangelicals Became Israel's Best Friend," Beliefnet, accessed April 29, 2016, http://www.beliefnet.com/Faiths/Christianity/End-Times/On-The-Road-To-Armageddon.aspx#tCXV2zsO4gkoJa2s.99.

7. Orson Scott Card, *Ender's Shadow*, repr. ed. (New York: Tor Books, 2000), 58.

CHAPTER 6: WERE THEY MISTAKEN?

1. Joseph Tkach, "We Are Living in the Last Days," Grace Communion International, 1999, https://www.gci.org/prophecy/lastdays.

CHAPTER 7: MEET GEORGE JETSON

1. Henry Conrad, "How the Jetsons Predicted the Future," *ZME Science* (blog), August 1, 2014, http://www.zmescience.com/other/feature-post/jetsons-predicted-future/.

CHAPTER 8: MANY WILL GO TO AND FRO

1. Strong's #7751: *shuwt* (pronounced "shoot"), a primitive root; properly, to push forth; (but used only figuratively) to lash, i.e. (the sea with oars) to row; by implication, to travel. BibleTools, accessed April 30, 2016, http://www.bibletools.org/index.cfm/fuseaction/Lexicon.show/ID/H7751/shuwt.htm.

2. Strong's #7235: *rabah* (pronounced "raw-baw"), a primitive root; to increase (in whatever respect):—(bring in) abundance (X -antly), + archer (by mistake for 7232), be in authority, bring up, X continue, enlarge, excel, exceeding(-ly), be full of, (be, make) great(-er, -ly, X -ness), grow up, heap, increase, be long, (be, give, have, make, use) many (a time), (any, be, give, give the, have) more (in number), (ask, be, be so, gather, over, take, yield) much (greater, more), (make to) multiply, nourish, plenty(-eous), X process (of time), sore, store, thoroughly, very. BibleTools, accessed April 30, 2016, http://www.bibletools.org/index.cfm/fuseaction/Lexicon.show/ID/H7235/rabah.htm.

3. MG Siegler, "Eric Schmidt: Every 2 Days We Create as Much Information as We Did up to 2003," *TechCrunch* (blog), August 4, 2010, http://techcrunch.com/2010/08/04/schmidt-data/.

4. David Russell Schilling, "Knowledge Doubling Every 12 Months, Soon to be Every 12 Hours," *Industry Tap*, April 19, 2013, http://www.industrytap.com/knowledge-doubling-every-12-months-soon-to-be-every-12-hours/3950.

5. Jacob Morgan, "A Simple Explanation of 'the Internet of Things,'" *Forbes*, May 13, 2014, http://www.forbes.com/sites/jacobmorgan/2014/05/13/simple-explanation-internet-things-that-anyone-can-understand/#3a463e116828.

6. Trevor Timm, "US Intelligence Chief: We Might Use the Internet of Things to Spy on You," *Guardian*, February 9, 2016, http://www.theguardian.com/technology/2016/feb/09/internet-of-things-smart-home-devices-government-surveillance-james-clapper.

7. Parker Higgins on Twitter, "Left: Samsung SmartTV Privacy Policy, Warning Users Not to Discuss Personal Info in Front of Their TV Right: 1984," https://twitter.com/xor/status/564356757007261696.

8. CTVNews.ca Staff, "Samsung Warns Users to Watch What They Say in Front of Smart TVs," CTV News, February 9, 2015, http://www.ctvnews.ca/mobile/sci-tech/samsung-warns-users-to-watch-what-they-say-in-front-of-smart-tvs-1.2227457.

9. Jack Clark, "Scientists Ponder How to Create Artificial Intelligence That Won't Destroy Us: Researchers Take Responsibility for the Futuristic Monster They May Build," Bloomberg, December 18, 2015, http://www.bloomberg.com/news/articles/2015-12-18/scientists-ponder-how-to-create-artificial-intelligence-that-won-t-destroy-us.

10. San Shead, "A Programmer Turned Sci-Fi Author Has Predicted That Robots Could Outnumber Humans as Early as 2040," *Business Insider*, http://www.businessinsider.com.au/robots-could-outnumber-humans-by-2040-2016-1.

11. Raymond Wong, "VR Porn Is Here and It's Scary How Realistic It Is," *Mashable* (blog), January 8, 2016, http://mashable.com/2016/01/08/naughty-america-vr-porn-experience/.

12. Jill Ward, "Rise of the Robots Will Eliminate More Than 5 Million Jobs," Bloomberg Business, January 18, 2016, http://www.bloomberg.com/news/articles/2016-01-18/rise-of-the-robots-will-eliminate-more-than-5-million-jobs.

13. "Company Claims It Will Soon Resurrect the Dead—Looks to Preserve Human Brain before You Die," WND, January 3, 2016, http://www.wnd.com/2016/01/company-claims-it-will-soon-resurrect-the-dead/#l2qPS2DcdvbTeI07.99.

14. Ellie Zolfagharifard, "Could this be humanity's LAST century? Expert says 're-engineering our children' will lead to the creation of a new species," *Daily Mail* (UK), January 18, 2016, http://www.dailymail.co.uk/sciencetech/article-3405312/Could-humanity-s-century-Expert-says-engineering-children-lead-creation-new-species.html.

15. Jon Austin, "The Terminator Could Become REAL: Intelligent AI Robots Capable of DESTROYING Mankind," *Express* (UK), January 18, 2016, http://www.express.co.uk/news/science/635157/The-Terminator-could-become-REAL-Intelligent-AI-robots-capable-of-DESTROYING-mankind.

16. Sarah Buhr, "Meet Knightscope's Crime-Fighting Robots," *TechCrunch* (blog), December 31, 2015, http://techcrunch.com/2015/12/31/meet-knightscopes-crime-fighting-robots/.

17. Ellie Zolfagharifard, "Will YOU Live Forever? Presidential Candidate Claims Technology to Transform Us into Immortal Cyborgs Is Within Reach," *Daily Mail* (UK), December 30, 2015, http://www.dailymail.co.uk/sciencetech/article-3379397/Will-live-forever-Presidential-candidate-claims-technology-transform-immortal-cyborgs-reach.html.

18. Richard Gray, "Could We Soon 'Speak' Telepathically? Mind-Reading Computer Deciphers Words from Brainwaves BEFORE They Are Spoken," *Daily Mail* (UK), January 6, 2016, http://www.dailymail.co.uk/sciencetech/article-3386875/Could-soon-speak-telepathically-Mind-reading-computer-deciphers-words-brainwaves-spoken.html.

19. Rob Waugh, "10 Sex Robots You Can Actually Make Love to TODAY," *Metro* (UK), June 16, 2015, http://metro.co.uk/2015/06/16/10-sex-robots-you-can-actually-make-love-to-today-5249031/.

20. George Dvorsky, "New Technique Allows Scientists to Read Minds at Nearly the Speed of Thought," *Gizmodo* (blog), January 29, 2016, http://gizmodo.com/new-technique-allows-scientists-to-read-minds-at-nearly-1755927863.

21. Shari Miller, "Rogue 'Terminator' Robots Which Can Kill Without Human Orders Could Become Reality in Just a Few Years," *Daily Mail* (UK), February 14, 2016, http://www.dailymail.co.uk/news/article-3446483/Rogue-Terminators-kill-without-human-orders-use-years-unless-global-ban.html.

22. Ibid.

CHAPTER 9: AM I STILL HUMAN?

1. Sebastian Anthony, "What Is Transhumanism, or, What Does It Mean to Be Human?" *ExtremeTech* (blog), April 1, 2013, http://www.extremetech.com/extreme/152240-what-is-transhumanism-or-what-does-it-mean-to-be-human.

2. Zoltan Istvan, "Transhumanist Party Scientists Frown on Talk of Genetic Engineering Moratorium," *Huffpost Politics*, May 4, 2015, http://www.huffingtonpost.com/zoltan-istvan/transhumanist-party-scien_b_7167300.html.

3. Göran Hermerén, "Ethical Considerations in Chimera Research," *Development* 142 (2015): 3–5, http://dev.biologists.org/content/142/1/3.

4. James Boyle, "Endowed by Their Creator?: The Future of Constitutional Personhood," Brookings, March 9, 2011, http://www.brookings.edu/research/papers/2011/03/09-personhood-boyle.

NOTES

5. Marcy Darnovsky, "Genetically Modified Babies," *New York Times*, February 23, 2014, http://www.nytimes.com/2014/02/24/opinion/genetically-modified-babies.html?_r=0, emphasis added.

6. ResearchSEA, "World's First Genetic Modification of Human Embryos Reported: Experts Consider Ethics," ScienceDaily, April 24, 2015, http://www.sciencedaily.com/releases/2015/04/150424122312.htm.

7. Sarah Zhang, "Everything You Need to Know about CRISPR, the New Tool that Edits DNA," *Gizmodo*, May 5, 2015, http://gizmodo.com/everything-you-need-to-know-about-crispr-the-new-tool-1702114381.

8. Sarah Griffiths, "Is Technology Causing Us to 'Evolve' into a New SPECIES? Expert Believes Super Humans Called Homo optimus Will Talk to Machines and Be 'Digitally Immortal' by 2050," *Daily Mail*, February 2016, http://www.dailymail.co.uk/sciencetech/article-3423063/Is-technology-causing-evolve-new-SPECIES-Expert-believes-super-humans-called-Homo-optimus-talk-machines-digitally-immortal-2050.html#ixzz3ywOcTb7Z. Emphasis added.

9. "Tom Horn and Joe Ardis: Inhuman," Prophecy Watchers, January 5, 2016, https://prophecywatchers.com/videos/tom-horn-and-joe-ardis-inhuman/.

10. Thomas Horn, dir., *Inhuman: The Next and Final Phase of Man is Here* (n.p.: Defender Films, 2015), DVD.

11. "Editorial Reviews," Amazon.com review of *Inhuman* (documentary film), accessed May 2, 2016, http://www.amazon.com/Inhuman-Next-Final-Phase-Here/dp/0996409513.

12. Anthony Cuthbertson. "U.S. Military Plans Cyborg Soldiers WITH New DARPA Project," *Newsweek*, January 21, 2016, http://www.newsweek.com/us-military-plans-cyborg-soldiers-new-darpa-project-418128.

13. Zoltan Istvan, *The Transhumanist Wager* (n.p.: Futurity Image Media, 2013), 127.

14. Hannah Brown, "World's First Genetically Modified Human Embryo Raises Ethical Concerns," *IFL Science*, April 27, 2015, http://www.iflscience.com/health-and-medicine/world-s-first-genetically-modified-human-embryo-raises-ethical-concerns.

15. Jan Omega, "Horrifying Human Animal DNA Experiments Shows Transhumanism and Hybrids [Video]," *Inquisitr*, July 9, 2014, http://www.inquisitr.com/1343284/horrifying-human-animal-dna-experiments-shows-transhumanism-and-hybrids-video/.

16. Associated Press, "Scientists create animals that are part-human Stem cell experiments leading to genetic mixing of species," NBCNews.com, updated April 29, 2005, http://www.nbcnews.com/id/7681252/ns/health-cloning_and_stem_cells/t/scientists-create-animals-are-part-human/#.VqQXF5orJpQ.

17. "Lk Rigor," "Brain Computer Interface and Artificial Brain: Interfacing Microelectronics and the Human Visual System," SlideShare, June 1, 2014, http://www.slideshare.net/ellekaie/bio201-bciab-35363505.

18. Susan Young Rojahn, "Genome Surgery: Precise and easy ways to rewrite human genes could finally provide the tools that researchers need to understand and cure some of our most deadly genetic diseases," *MIT Technology Review*, February 11, 2014, http://www.technologyreview.com/review/524451/genome-surgery/.

19. Jennifer A. Doudna and Emmanuelle Charpentier, "The New Frontier of Genome Engineering with CRISPR-Cas9," *Science* 346, no. 6213 (November 28, 2014).

20. Leo Hohmann, "Elites Pouring Billions into Gene-Therapy Research: But Who Will Benefit from Advances in Anti-Aging Treatment?" WND, January 21, 2016, http://www.wnd.com/2016/01/elites-pouring-billions-into-gene-therapy-research/#IuVzaEb7ZA82gAqe.99.

21. Sean Martin. "Scientists Take a Step Closer to Eternal Life as They Preserve and Revive Brain," *Express* (UK), February 12. 2016, http://www.express.co.uk/news/science/643538/Scientists-take-a-step-closer-to-ETERNAL-LIFE-as-they-PRESERVE-and-REVIVE-brain.

22. Shari Miller, "Rogue 'Terminator' Robots Which Can Kill without Human Orders Could Become Reality in Just a Few Years," *Daily Mail* (UK), February 12, 2016, http://www.dailymail.co.uk/news/article-3446483/Rogue-Terminators-kill-without-human-orders-use-years-unless-global-ban.html.

CHAPTER 10: BACK TO THE FUTURE

1. Ryan Barton, "Technology's Explosion: The Exponential Growth Rate," Mainstay *Technology* (blog), January 22, 2013, http://www.mstech.com/nh-it-blog.php?show=171.

2. "World Rice Output in 2011 Estimated at 476 Mn Tonnes: FAO," *Economic Times* (New Delhi), June 24, 2011, http://articles.economictimes.indiatimes.com/2011-06-24/news/29698994_1_rice-production-paddy-production-rice-output .

3. Carl Sagan, *Billions and Billions: Thoughts on Life and Death at the Brink of the Millennium* (New York: Ballantine, 1997), 9.

4. Graham Templeton, "What Is Moore's Law?" *ExtremeTech*, July 29, 2015, http://www.extremetech.com/extreme/210872-extremetech-explains-what-is-moores-law.

5. Glyn Taylor, "The Future Is Coming Much Faster Than We Think, Here's Why," *That's Really Possible* (blog), April 7, 2014, http://www.thatsreallypossible.com/exponential-growth/.
   Quantum computing "is the area of study focused on developing computer technology based on the principles of quantum theory, which explains the nature and behavior of energy and matter on the quantum (atomic and subatomic) level. Development of a quantum computer, if practical, would mark a leap forward in computing capability far greater than that from the abacus to a modern day supercomputer, with performance gains in the billion-fold realm and beyond. The quantum computer, following the laws of quantum physics, would gain enormous processing power through the ability to be in multiple states, and to perform tasks using all possible permutations simultaneously. Current centers of research in quantum computing include MIT, IBM, Oxford University, and the Los Alamos National Laboratory," WhatIs.com, s.v. "quantum computing," accessed May 2, 2016, http://whatis.techtarget.com/definition/quantum-computing.

6. Barton, "Technology's Explosion."

7. Taylor, "The Future Is Coming Much Faster Than We Think, Here's Why," emphasis added.

8. The Emerging Future, "Estimating the Speed of Technological Advancement," accessed May 2, 2016, http://theemergingfuture.com/speed-technological-advancement.htm.

9. Vivek Wadhwa, "Why I Believe That This Will Be the Most Innovative Decade in History," *Singularity Univesity* (blog), June 25, 2012, http://www.forbes.com/sites/singularity/2012/06/25/most-innovative-decade-in-history/#f9362ff4f122.

CHAPTER 11: THE SOLUTION TO EVERYTHING

1. Mark A. Viera, *Sin in Soft Focus* (New York: Harry N. Abrams, 2003), 42-43.

2. "RFID chips: a key to more or less freedom? Euronews, June 23, 2015, http://www.euronews.com/2015/06/23/rfid-chips-a-key-to-more-or-less-freedom/.

3. The Defense Forensics & Biometrics Agency, "DFBA FAQs," accessed May 2, 2016, http://www.biometrics.dod.mil/About/faqs.aspx.

4. Electronic Frontier Foundation, "Biometrics: Who's Watching You?" September 14, 2003, https://www.eff.org/wp/biometrics-whos-watching-you.

5. Alex Perala, "World Bank, Accenture Call for Universal ID," FindBiometrics, September 29, 2015, http://findbiometrics.com/world-bank-universal-id-29295/.

6. Milland Borkar, "Biometric Technology of the Future, Today," BiometricUpdate.com, January 22, 2013, http://www.biometricupdate.com/201301/biometric-technology-of-the-future-today

7. Pooja Bhatia, "Biometric Identification That Goes Beyond Fingerprints," *USA Today*, April 19, 2014, http://www.usatoday.com/story/news/world/2014/04/19/ozy-biometric-identification/7904685/

8. Kathleen Miles, "Ray Kurzweil: In the 2030s, Nanobots in Our Brains Will Make Us 'Godlike,'" *WorldPost*, October 1, 2015, http://www.huffingtonpost.com/entry/ray-kurzweil-nanobots-brain-godlike_us_560555a0e4b0af3706dbe1e2.

9. Aaron Saenz, "India Launches Universal ID System with Biometrics," *Singularity Hub*, September 13, 2010, http://singularityhub.com/2010/09/13/india-launches-universal-id-system-with-biometrics. The posting contains a link to a second, earlier post titled "India to Biometrically Identify All of Its 1.2 Billion Citizens."

10. Michael Snyder, "The UN Plans to Implement Universal Biometric Identification for All of Humanity by 2030," *Infowars*, November 2, 2015, http://www.infowars.com/the-un-plans-to-implement-universal-biometric-identification-for-all-of-humanity-by-2030/.

11. "What Are Biometrics?" FindBiometrics, accessed May 2, 2016, http://findbiometrics.com/what-are-biometrics/; emphasis added..

12. United Nations, "Secretary-General, Addressing General Assembly, Applauds 'Agenda 2030' as Mark of Global Commitment at Dawn of New Era for Sustainable Development," press release, September 1, 2015, http://www.un.org/press/en/2015/sgsm17044.doc.htm; emphasis added.

13. Perala, "World Bank."

CHAPTER 12: MYSTERY OF THE AGES

1.   Blue Letter Bible, G1325, *didomi*, https://www.blueletterbible.org/lang/lexicon/lexicon. cfm?t=kjv&strongs=g1325.

2.   Greek Dictionary (Lexicon-Concordance), G2983, *Lambano*, http://lexiconcordance. com/greek/2983.html.

3.   Dictionary.com, s.v. "epi-" (accessed May 2, 2016), http://dictionary.reference.com/ browse/epi-.

CHAPTER 13: THE TIE THAT BINDS

1.   Stephanie Pappas, "Facts about Carbon," LiveScience, August 9, 2014, http://www. livescience.com/28698-facts-about-carbon.html.

2.   Chemistry Explained, "Carbon," accessed May 3, 2016, http://www.chemistryexplained. com/elements/A-C/Carbon.html#ixzz3yI3JMlbw.

3.   "Seen at 11: Company Developing 'Tech Tattoos' So People Can Track Their Medical, Financial Info," CBS New York, January 29, 2016, http://newyork.cbslocal. com/2016/01/29/tech-tattoos-chaotic-moon.

4.   "NBC: RFID Implants—Microchip Everything 2017—Mark of the Beast 666," YouTube video, 2:01, *NBC Nightly News* report in 2007, posted by Calgary Truth Media, April 7, 2013, https://www.youtube.com/watch?v=LZ0YPDYx6lU.

5.   Sarah Griffith, "Would YOU Be Microchipped? Kaspersky Implants Chip in Man's Hand That Could One Day Be Used to Pay for Goods and Even Unlock His Home," *Daily Mail* (UK), September 2015, http://www.dailymail.co.uk/sciencetech/ article-3221287/Would-microchipped-Kaspersky-implants-chip-man-s-hand-one-day-used-pay-goods-unlock-home.html.

CHAPTER 14: THE REVENANT NATION

1.   Josie Ensor, "Islamic State Leader Baghdadi Goads West in Rare Audio Statement," *Telegraph* (UK), January 31, 2016, http://www.telegraph.co.uk/news/worldnews/ islamic-state/12069924/Islamic-State-leader-Baghdadi-goads-West-in-rare-audio-statement.html.

2.   Mitchell Bard, Myths & Facts: A Guide to the Arab-Israeli Conflict, "Chapter 1: Israel's Roots," myth 3, Jewish Virtual Library, accessed May 3, 2016, http://www. jewishvirtuallibrary.org/jsource/myths3/MFroots.html#3.

3.   Robert Drews, "Canaanites and Philistines," *Journal for the Study of the Old Testament* 81 (1998): 61: "The name Canaan,' never very popular, went out of vogue with the collapse of the Egyptian empire."

4.   Ann E. Killebrew, *Biblical Peoples and Ethnicity: An Archaeological Study of Egyptians, Canaanites, Philistines, and Early Israel, 1300–1100 B.C.E.* (n.p.: Brill Academic, 2005), 96.

5. Jonathan N. Tubb, *Canaanites* (People of the Past) (University of Oklahoma Press, 1999)m 16.
6. Mark Smith, *The Early History of God: Yahweh and Other Deities of Ancient Israel*, 2nd ed. (Grand Rapids: Eerdmans, 2002), 6–7.
7. John William Colenso, *The Pentateuch and Book of Joshua Critically Examined, Volume 4* (London: Longman, Green, Longman, Roberts, & Green, 1864), 234.
8. "VIDEO: 'It's Not Clear If the Holocaust Is a Reality or Not,' Iran's Supreme Leader Says," *Jerusalem Post*, February 2, 2016, http://www.jpost.com/Middle-East/Iran/VIDEO-Its-not-clear-if-the-Holocaust-is-a-reality-or-not-Irans-supreme-leader-says-443006.

CHAPTER 15: FORETOLD FROM THE BEGINNING
1. Smith's Bible Dictionary, "Judah, Kingdom of," accessed May 12, 2016, http://www.bible-history.com/smiths/J/Judah,+Kingdom+of/.
2. Benjamin Blech, "The Miracle of Jewish History," History News Network, August 3, 2007, http://historynewsnetwork.org/article/38887#sthash.1djoMuZi.dpuf.
3. Mark Twain, "Concerning the Jews" (essay), Ohr Somayach, accessed May 3, 2016, http://ohr.edu/judaism/concern/concerna.htm .
4. Blech, "The Miracle of Jewish History."
5. "Arab Spring' to ISIS: The Mideast 'Misconception,'" CBN News, August 7, 2015, http://www1.cbn.com/cbnnews/insideisrael/2015/August/Arab-Spring-to-ISIS-The-Mideast-Misconception.

CHAPTER 16: THE BLESSING
1. "Jewish Biographies: Nobel Prize Laureates," Jewish Virtual Library, accessed May 3, 2016, https://www.jewishvirtuallibrary.org/jsource/Judaism/nobels.html.
2. World Heritage Encyclopedia, "LIST OF COUNTRIES BY NOBEL LAUREATES PER CAPITA," accessed May 12, 2016, http://www.gutenberg.us/articles/list_of_countries_by_nobel_laureates_per_capita.
3. Luana Goriss, "Jewish Nobel Prize Winners," About.com, accessed May 12, 2016, http://judaism.about.com/od/culture/a/nobel.htm.
4. Ilan Samish, "Nobels: Maintaining Israel's Record," Academia.edu, accessed March 2016, http://www.academia.edu/9652535/Nobels_Maintaining_Israels_record.
5. "Israel Industries : Amazing Facts about Israel," Israel Industries, July 16, 2013, http://www.israel-industries.com/israel-industries-amazing-facts-about-israel.
6. *Wikipedia*, "Portal:Israel/Did you know," accessed May 3, 2016, https://en.wikipedia.org/wiki/Portal:Israel/Did_you_know.
7. Cf. Hans M. Kristensen and Robert S. Norris, "Status of World Nuclear Forces," FAS.org, http://fas.org/issues/nuclear-weapons/status-world-nuclear-forces/; and Avner Cohen, The Worst-Kept Secret: Israel's Bargain with the Bomb (New York: Columbia University Press, 2010), xxvvi, table 1.

8. Sophie Imas, "10 Israeli Technologies That Are Changing The World," October 15, 2013, http://nocamels.com/2013/10/10-israeli-technologies-that-are-changing-the-world/.

9. Sergio DellaPergola, Arnold Dashefsky, and Ira Sheskin, eds. *World Jewish Population, 2014* (New York: Berman Jewish Databank, 2014), 5, http://www.jewishdatabank.org/studies/downloadFile.cfm?FileID=3257.

10. Bill Federer, "How Jews Helped Save THE United States," WND, January 26, 2016, http://www.wnd.com/2016/01/how-jews-helped-save-the-united-states/#xtAblvV6Lkm6GIKP.99.

11. Arnold Cusmariu, "Jewish Scientists Helped America Build the Atom Bomb," *American Thinker*, February 8, 2015, http://www.americanthinker.com/articles/2015/02/jewish_scientists_helped_america_build_the_atom_bomb.html.

12. DellaPergola, Dashefsky, and Sheskin, *World Jewish Population*, 2014, 5.

CHAPTER 17: JEWISH BELIEVERS IN THE TIME OF THE END

1. The Association of Messianic Congregations, "A Historical Survey of Prominent Jewish Believers in Messiah Yeshua," http://www.messianicassociation.org/profiles.

2. Romans 11:15, commentary from *Barnes' Notes on the Bible*, at Bible Hub, http://biblehub.com/commentaries/romans/11-15.htm. Be sure to check out all the commentaries on this passage on this web page. Every one of them says practically the same thing that *Barnes'* does.

3. "Statistics: Current Estimates of the Number of Messianics (Jews Proclaiming Belief in Jesus) in Israel," Jewish Israel, accessed May 3, 2016, http://jewishisrael.ning.com/page/statistics-1.

4. Messianic Jewish Alliance of Israel, "The Land Belongs to Israel!" July 6, 2007, http://www.mjaa.org/site/News2?page=NewsArticle&id=5142&security=1&news_iv_ctrl=1022.

5. See Carl Gallups, *The Rabbi Who Found Messiah: The Story of Yitzhak Kaduri and His Prophecies of the Endtime* (Washington, DC: WND Books, 2013); and *The Rabbi Who Found Messiah* (documentary film), directed by George Escobar (WND Films, 2013), DVD.

6. David Lazarus, "Orthodox Rabbis Bring Jesus Home for Christmas," Israel Today, December 24, 2015, http://www.israeltoday.co.il/NewsItem/tabid/178/nid/28027/Default.aspx.

7. Ibid.

8. See the websites of Messiah of Israel Ministries, http://www.messiahofisraelministries.org; and Zev Porat Ministries, zevporatministries.com.

9. See note 5.

10. The Association of Messianic Congregations, "A Historical Survey of Prominent Jewish Believers in Messiah Yeshua."

11. Ibid.

12. Ibid.

CHAPTER 18: THE WORLD WAR III ZEITGEIST

1. Stoyan Zaimov, "Franklin Graham Says Bible End Times Prophecy of 'Distress of Nations' Reflects World's Conflicts Today," *CP U.S.*, March 19, 2015, http://www.christianpost.com/news/franklin-graham-says-bible-end-times-prophecy-of-distress-of-nations-reflects-worlds-conflicts-today-135955/#grTzRHBestCsGt6z.99. Reverend Graham was quoting Luke 21:25: "And there shall be signs in the sun, and in the moon, and in the stars; and upon the earth distress of nations, with perplexity" (KJV).

2. Ploughshares Fund, World Nuclear Weapon Stockpile, updated March 2, 2016, http://www.ploughshares.org/world-nuclear-stockpile-report.

3. Grant R. Jeffrey, *Armageddon: Appointment with Destiny* (Colorado Springs: Waterbrook Press, 1997), chap. 15.

4. Leo Hohmann, "Is World War III Coming Soon?" WND, April 2015, http://www.wnd.com/2015/04/is-world-war-iii-coming-soon.

5. JTA, "French PM: Terror Attacks in France, Israel Show We Are 'in World War,'" *Times of Israel*, January 2016, http://www.timesofisrael.com/french-pm-attacks-in-france-israel-show-we-are-in-world-war.

6. Vikas Shukla, "China Warns of World War 3 Unless the US Backs Down on South China Sea," ValueWalk, May 28, 2015, http://www.valuewalk.com/2015/05/china-warns-of-world-war-3.

7. Joseph Farah, "World War III Is Shaping Up In Syria," WND, September 29, 2015, http://www.wnd.com/2015/09/wwiii-is-shaping-up-in-syria/#lSBfVqBpx0Vi565m.99.

8. "Obama Signature on Present Middle East 'Chaos' 'Hundreds of Thousands' Dead after 'Dramatic Shift in Foreign Policy toward Muslim World,'" WND, http://www.wnd.com/2015/12/obama-signature-on-present-middle-east-chaos/#0F7DltwTp1Ab4Zpf.99.

9. E, Michael Maloof, "Expert: North Korea Prepping EMP Attack on U.S.—'Test' Launch Could Turn Out to be Actual Nuclear Onslaught," WND, February 3, 2016, https://www.yahoo.com/news/global-outrage-over-north-korea-rocket-launch-074851449.html?ref=gs.

10. AFP, "Global Outrage over North Korea Rocket Launch," Yahoo! News, February 7, 2016, https://news.yahoo.com/global-outrage-over-north-korea-rocket-launch-074851449.html.

11. Jonathan Wachtel, "UN Security Council Asked to Hold Emergency Meeting Sunday on North Korean Rocket Launch," Fox News, February 6, 2016, http://www.foxnews.com/world/2016/02/06/un-security-council-asked-to-hold-emergency-meeting-sunday-on-north-korean-rocket-launch.html.

12. Richard Spencer, "Russia Warns of 'New World War' Starting in Syria," *Telegraph* (UK), February 12, 2016, http://www.telegraph.co.uk/news/worldnews/europe/russia/12153112/Russia-warns-of-new-world-war-starting-in-Syria.html.

13. Sandy Fitzgerald, "McCaul: ISIS Investigations Open in All 50 States," NewsMax, February 2016, http://www.newsmax.com/Headline/Homeland-Security-ISIS-McCaul-Terrorism/2015/11/16/id/702302/#ixzz3z3KHSC18.

14. Edward Olshaker, "Bachmann vs. the 'Fact-Checkers': Did Iran Threaten Nuclear Attack on U.S.?" *American Thinker*, December 28, 2011, http://www.americanthinker.com/2011/12/bachmann_vs_the_fact-checkers_did_iran_threaten_nuclear_attack_on_us.html#ixzz3zcPVKVK.

15. Jodi Rudoren and Diaa Hadid, "Vatican to Recognize Palestinian State In New Treaty," *New York Times*, May 13, 2015, http://www.nytimes.com/2015/05/14/world/middleeast/vatican-to-recognize-palestinian-state-in-new-treaty.html?_r=0.

CHAPTER 19: ADVANCING LIKE A STORM

1. David Samuels, "Q&A: Noam Chomsky: The World's Most Important Leftist Intellectual Talks about His Zionist Childhood and His Time with Hezbollah" *Tablet*, November 12, 2010, http://www.tabletmag.com/jewish-news-and-politics/50260/qa-noam-chomsky.

2. This brief paraphrase of Ezekiel 37–39 is my attempt to concisely capture the spirit, message, and contextual truth of these chapters.

3. Chris Schang, "The Gog and Magog War of Ezekiel 38–39," Rapture Forums, accessed May 4, 2016, http://www.raptureforums.com/EndTimesEvents/thegogandmagogwarofezekiel3839.cfm. Dr. Arnold Genekowitsch Fruchtenbaum (born September 26, 1943) is the founder and director of Ariel Ministries, an organization that prioritizes evangelization of Jews.

4. *NAS Exhaustive Concordance of the Bible with Hebrew-Aramaic and Greek Dictionaries*, s.v. 983. "*betach*," http://biblehub.com/hebrew/983.htm.

5. Schang, "The Gog and Magog War of Ezekiel 38–39."

6. Joel C. Rosenberg, "PROPHECY Q&A," http://www.joelrosenberg.com/ezekiel-38-39-faq/.

7. American Public Opinion Polls: Gallup Polls on American Sympathy Toward Israel and the Arabs/Palestinians, "In the Middle East situation, are your sympathies more with Israel or with the Arab Nations/Palestinians*?" Jewish Virtual Library, updated March 2015, https://www.jewishvirtuallibrary.org/jsource/US-Israel/gallup.html.

8. Gallup, "Latest Gallup Poll Shows Young Americans Overwhelmingly Support Palestine," Mint Press News, August 4, 2014, http://www.mintpressnews.com/latest-gallup-poll-shows-young-americans-overwhelmingly-support-palestine/194856.

9. European Council on Foreign Relations, "What Palestinians Can Expect from Europe," October 2014, http://www.ecfr.eu/article/commentary_what_palestinians_can_expect_from_europe331.

10. Imogen Bell, ed. *Eastern Europe, Russia and Central Asia*, 3rd ed. (London and New York: Europa, 2002).

11. Alan Moore, "The Killing Joke," Genius, http://genius.com/Alan-moore-the-killing-joke-annotated.

12. Edward R. Kantowicz, *The Rage of Nations* (Grand Rapids: Eerdmans, 1999), 149.

13. Golo Mann, *Die Zeit* (Hamburg), August 30, 1985, quoted in *Watchtower,* February 15, 1986.

14. KONDA Research and Consultancy, *Religion, Secularism and the Veil in Daily Life* (2007), http://www.konda.com.tr/en/raporlar/2007_09_KONDA_Religion_ Secularism_and_the_Veil_in_Daily_Life_Survey.pdf.

CHAPTER 20: PASS THE TURKEY, PLEASE

1. "Erdogan: 'Democracy in the Middle East, Pluralism in Europe: Turkish View,'" *Journal of Turkish Weekly,* October 12, 2004, http://www.turkishweekly.net/2004/10/12/article/ erdogan-democracy-in-the-middle-east-pluraliism-in-europe-turkish-view/.

2. Asli Kandemir, Nick Tattersall, and Dominic Evans, "Turkish presidency says Erdogan's Hitler comments misconstrued," Reuters, January 1, 2016, http://uk.reuters.com/ article/uk-turkey-erdogan-hitler-idUKKBN0UF1T320160101.

3. Unless otherwise noted, this chapter's history of the Turkish people was collected from the following sources: Turkish Cultural Foundation, "A Brief Outline of Turkish History," TCF, http://www.turkishculture.org/general-1067.htm; *Wikipedia,* s.v. "Turkic peoples," accessed May 4, 2016, https://en.wikipedia.org/wiki/Turkic_peoples; *Encyclopædia Britannica Online,* s.v. "Turkic peoples," accessed May 4, 2016, http:// www.britannica.com/EBchecked/topic/609972/Turkic-peoples.

4. Peter B. Golden, *Introduction to the History of the Turkic People: Ethnogenesis and State-Formation in Medieval and Early Modern Eurasia and the Middle East* (Wiesbaden, DEU: O. Harrassowitz, 1992), 12: ". . . source (Herod.IV.22) and other authors of antiquity, Togarma of the Old Testament, Turukha /Turuska of Indic sources, Turukku of Assyrian . . ."

5. Norman Golb and Omeljan Pritsak, *Khazarian Hebrew Documents of the Tenth Century* (Ithaca: Cornell Univ. Press, 1982).

6. "Bangsa Turki Kuno: Asal-Usul dan Persebarannya," (The Turkish Nation Ancient: Origins and Spreading), Salaamatan (Useful Science) (blog), December 2015, http:// salaamatan.blogspot.com/2015/12/bangsa-turki-kuno-asal-usul-dan.html.

7. James Arlandson, "The Truth about Islamic Crusades and Imperialism," *American Thinker,* November 2005, http://www.americanthinker.com/articles/2005/11/the_ truth_about_islamic_crusad.html.

8. Raymond Ibrahim, "The Islamic Genocide of Christians: Past and Present," *FrontPage Mag,* April 27, 2015, http://www.frontpagemag.com/fpm/255940/islamic-genocide-christians-past-and-present-raymond-ibrahim.

9. Robert Davis, *Christian Slaves, Muslim Masters: White Slavery in the Mediterranean, the Barbary Coast and Italy, 1500–1800* (Early Modern History), 2003 edition (Hampshire, UK, and New York: Palgrave Macmillan, 2003).

10. "American Peace Commissioners to John Jay," March 28, 1786, Library of Congress, accessed May 4, 2016, http://hdl.loc.gov/loc.mss/mtj.mtjbib001849; Making of America Project, *The Atlantic Monthly, Volume 30* (Atlantic Monthly Co., 1872), 413, https:// books.google.com/books?id=nWQCAAAAIAAJ&pg=PA413#v=onepage&q&f=false.

11. Dennis Prager, "You Don't Know What Obama Said at the Mosque," February 8, 2016, WND, http://www.wnd.com/2016/02/you-dont-know-what-obama-said-at-the-mosque/. The president made these comments in a February 2016 speech before a Muslim audience at an American mosque. From the WND article: "Why did Obama say this? Even Muslim websites acknowledge that 'Islam' means 'submission' [to Allah], that it comes from the Arabic root 'aslama' meaning submission, and that 'Islam' is in the command form of that verb. That's why 'Muslim' means 'One who submits,' not 'One who is peaceful.'"

12. Liz Sly, "Turkey's Increasingly Desperate Predicament Poses Real Dangers," *Washington Post*, February 20, 2016, https://www.washingtonpost.com/world/middle_east/turkeys-increasingly-desperate-predicament-poses-real-dangers/2016/02/20/a3374030-d593-11e5-a65b-587e721fb231_story.html.

CHAPTER 21: CALIPHATE RISING

1. Barry Strauss, "4 Jarring Signs of Turkey's Growing Islamization: Erdogan Is Set on Making the Formerly Secular Nation an Islamic Country, and It's Working," *Atlantic*, May 31, 2013, http://www.theatlantic.com/international/archive/2013/05/4-jarring-signs-of-turkeys-growing-islamization/276425.

2. Muhammad Wajid Akhter "The End: The Anniversary of the Abolition of the Caliphate,"MuslimMatters.org, June 24, 2010, http://muslimmatters.org/2010/06/24/the-end-the-anniversary-of-the-abolition-of-the-caliphate.

3. Reuters, "Turkey's Secularists Alarmed over Rise of Islamic 'Moralism,'" *Jerusalem Post*, November 18, 2013, http://www.jpost.com/Middle-East/Turkeys-secularists-alarmed-over-rise-of-Islamic-moralism-332081.

4. Pew Research Center, "Mapping the Global Muslim Population," October 7, 2009, http://www.pewforum.org/2009/10/07/mapping-the-global-muslim-population.

5. Joel Richardson "Ezekiel's Magog: Russia or Turkey?" WND, June 2012, http://www.wnd.com/2012/06/ezekiels-magog-russia-or-turkey/.

6. Bill Federer, "Islam Is the Cause of Turkey's Violent History," WND, http://www.wnd.com/2015/10/islam-is-the-cause-of-turkeys-violent-history/?cat_orig=faith.

7. "Erdogan: 'Democracy in the Middle East, Pluralism in Europe: Turkish View,'" *Journal of Turkish Weekly*, October 12, 2004, http://www.turkishweekly.net/2004/10/12/article/erdogan-democracy-in-the-middle-east-pluraliism-in-europe-turkish-view/.

CHAPTER 22: THE DAMASCUS DILEMMA

1. Krista Klaus, "Israel, Syria Conflict: 9 Quotes That Illustrate Recent Struggles," NewsMax, August 29, 2014, http://www.newsmax.com/FastFeatures/israel-syria-conflict-quotes/2014/08/29/id/591736/#ixzz3zPo9jDMm.

2. Anthony Sharwood, "Syria Explained in 10 Simple Points. A Western Perspective on the Crisis," news.com.au, September 9, 2015, http://www.news.com.au/world/middle-east/syria-explained-in-10-simple-points-a-western-perspective-on-the-crisis/news-story/4463e6f61181946100517266bd648009.

3. "Syria: The Story of the Conflict," BBC News, February 3, 2016, http://www.bbc.com/news/world-middle-east-26116868.

4. Unless otherwise noted, the information in this section was adapted from: Sharwood, "Syria Explained in 10 Simple Points"; and "Understand the Syrian Conflict in Five Minutes," YouTube video, 5:41, a MintPress News summary of the Syrian conflict, posted by SyrianPerspective, June 8, 2014 https://www.youtube.com/watch?v=2XbfH4rCMJA; and BBC, "Syria: The Story of the Conflict."

5. Ruth Pollard, "Syrian War: Russia's Support for Bashar al-Assad Explained," *Sydney Morning Herald*, September 29, 2015, http://www.smh.com.au/world/syrian-war-russias-support-for-bashar-alassad-explained-20150928-gjwuyp.html#ixzz3ztxFeBah.

6. Mary Chastain, "ISIS Fighter Claims Turkey Funds the Jihadist Group," Breitbart, July 30, 2014, http://www.breitbart.com/national-security/2014/07/30/isis-fighter-claims-turkey-funds-the-jihadist-group.

7. Ibid.; Sharwood, "Syria Explained in 10 Simple Points."

8. Pollard, "Syrian War."

9. Jerome Corsi, "Putin Aim in Syria 'to Destroy Europe,'" WND, February 11, 2016, http://www.wnd.com/2016/02/putins-aim-in-syria-to-destroy-eu/#OQqYZs4LiyRBkd8i.99.

10. Sean Adl-Tabatabai, "Pentagon Stunned as Thousands of Chinese Troops Enter ISIS War," YourNewsWire.com, December 28, 2015, http://yournewswire.com/pentagon-stunned-as-thousands-of-chinese-troops-enter-isis-war/.

11. Kurt. Nimmo, "Russia Warns of World War If Syria Conflict Not Resolved: Medvedev Says Saudis Must Call Off Planned Invasion," *InfoWars*, February 11, 2016, http://www.infowars.com/russia-warns-of-world-war-if-syria-conflict-not-resolved.

12. Billy Hallowell, "Why Some Believe These 'End Times' Bible Verses Could Hold the Key to the Syrian Crisis," TheBlaze, September 8, 2013, http://www.theblaze.com/stories/2013/09/08/why-some-believe-these-end-times-bible-verses-could-hold-the-key-to-the-syrian-crisis.

13. Drew Zahn, "Biblical Doom of Damascus 'Right Before Our Eyes': Students Of Prophecy Warn Nations Aligning to Fulfill Isaiah 17," WND, August 31, 2013, http://www.wnd.com/2013/08/biblical-doom-of-damascus-right-before-our-eyes.

14. Billy Hallowell, "Bible Expert Joel Rosenberg Delivers 3 Reasons Why Those Dismissing Syria-Related Prophecies May Be Dead Wrong," TheBlaze, September 12, 2013, http://www.theblaze.com/stories/2013/09/12/end-times-bible-expert-delivers-3-reasons-why-those-dismissing-syria-related-prophecies-may-be-dead-wrong.

15. Zahn, "Biblical Doom of Damascus 'Right Before Our Eyes.'"

16. Saudi Press Agency, "'Raad North' the Biggest Military Exercise in the History of the Region . . . Led by Saudi Arabia, February 14, 2016, http://www.spa.gov.sa/viewstory.php?lang=ar&newsid=1466877 (translated to English).

17. Juliet Eilperin, "Making Terrorism Link, Obama Says Climate Instability Can Lead to 'Dangerous' Ideology," *Washington Post*, December 4, 2015, https://www.washingtonpost.com/news/energy-environment/wp/2015/12/04/making-terrorism-link-obama-says-climate-instability-can-lead-to-dangerous-ideology.

18. Al-Alam, "350,000 Saudi Arabia Soldiers Maneuver, Preparing for Syria War?" February 9, 2016, http://en.alalam.ir/news/1787755#sthash.uKmC3Hfj.dpuf.

CHAPTER 23: DEADLY CONNECTIONS

1. Alan Greenblatt, "Twenty Years Later, First Iraq War Still Resonates," NPR, February 24, 2011, http://www.npr.org/2011/02/24/133991181/twenty-years-later-first-iraq-war-still-resonates.

2. Kanan Makiya, "The Arab Spring Started in Iraq," *New York Times*, April 6, 2013, http://www.nytimes.com/2013/04/07/opinion/sunday/the-arab-spring-started-in-iraq.html?pagewanted=all&_r=0.

3. Remarks by the President on the Middle East and North Africa, the White House, Office of the Press Secretary, May 19, 2011, https://www.whitehouse.gov/the-press-office/2011/05/19/remarks-president-middle-east-and-north-africa, emphasis added .

4. Con Coughlin, "The Arab Spring Turns Sour for America," *Telegraph* (UK), September 12, 2012,, http://www.telegraph.co.uk/news/worldnews/middleeast/syria/9538493/The-Arab-Spring-turns-sour-for-America.html.

5. Lucy Rodger et al., "Syria: The Story of the Conflict," BBC, March 11, 2016, http://www.bbc.com/news/world-middle-east-26116868.

6. Coughlin, "The Arab Spring Turns Sour for America."

7. Sharyl Attkisson. "How Arab Spring Opened the Door to Terrorism's Ugly March," *Daily Signal*, March 12, 2015, http://dailysignal.com/2015/03/12/arab-spring-opened-door-terrorisms-ugly-march.

8. Caroline Glick, "'Arab Spring' to ISIS: The Mideast 'Misconception,'" CBN, August 2015, http://www.cbn.com/cbnnews/insideisrael/2015/August/Arab-Spring-to-ISIS-The-Mideast-Misconception/?Print=true.

9. Eliza Griswold, "Is This the End of Christianity in the Middle East?" *New York Times Magazine*, July 26, 2015, http://www.nytimes.com/2015/07/26/magazine/is-this-the-end-of-christianity-in-the-middle-east.html.

10. Douglas Ernst, "DHS Warns: Isis Trojan Horse Coming to America: Homeland Can't Locate 122,000 with U.S. Visas Revoked over Terror Ties," WND, December 17, 2015, http://www.wnd.com/2015/12/feds-warn-isis-trojan-horse-coming-to-u-s.

11. Remarks by President Obama to the Turkish Parliament, press release, White House, Office of the Press Secretary, April 6, 2009, https://www.whitehouse.gov/the-press-office/remarks-president-obama-turkish-parliament.

12. Bruce Gottlieb, "What's the Name of Saddam Hussein?" Explainer, *Slate*, November 16, 1998, http://www.slate.com/articles/news_and_politics/explainer/1998/11/whats_the_name_of_saddam_hussein.html.
13. Peter Beaumont, "Saddam Paradox Divides Iraqis," *Guardian* (UK), July 3, 2014, http://www.theguardian.com/world/2004/jul/04/iraq.
14. Kate Green, "Al-Sadr Tones Down Fiery Commentary," *Michigan Daily*, November 10, 2003, https://www.michigandaily.com/content/al-sadr-tones-down-fiery-commentary.
15. Beaumont, "Saddam Paradox Divides Iraqis."

CHAPTER 24: HATED BY ALL NATIONS

1. Sharyl Attkisson, "How Arab Spring Opened the Door to Terrorism's Ugly March," *Daily Signal*, March 12, 2015, http://dailysignal.com/2015/03/12/arab-spring-opened-door-terrorisms-ugly-march. Sharyl Attkisson, an Emmy award-winning investigative journalist, is a senior independent contributor to the *Daily Signal*. She hosts the Sunday morning news program *Full Measure* and wrote the *New York Times* best seller *Stonewalled*.
2. Simon Tomlinson, "Christians Face Being Wiped Out from the Middle East within TEN YEARS as They Are Killed by ISIS or Forced to Flee Persecution, Warn Catholic Aid Groups," *Daily Mail*, October 10, 2015, http://www.dailymail.co.uk/news/article-3311716/Christians-face-wiped-Middle-East-TEN-YEARS-killed-ISIS-forced-flee-persecution-warn-Catholic-aid-groups.html#ixzz3zczDT18L. See also Perry Chiaramonte, "On the Brink: Christianity Facing Middle East Purge within Decade, Says Group," Fox News, November 9, 2015, http://www.foxnews.com/world/2015/11/05/christianity-could-be-completely-erased-from-middle-east-in-less-than-decade.html.
3. Ibid. Tomlinson, Simon. "Christians face being wiped out..."
4. Eliza Griswold, "Is This the End of Christianity in the Middle East?" *New York Times Magazine*, July 26, 2015, http://www.nytimes.com/2015/07/26/magazine/is-this-the-end-of-christianity-in-the-middle-east.html.
5. Ibid.
6. Open Doors USA, "Christian Persecution," accessed May 5, 2016, https://www.opendoorsusa.org/christian-persecution.
7. Cristina Corbin, "Some 100,000 Christians Killed Per Year over Faith, Vatican Says," Fox News, June 2, 2013, http://www.foxnews.com/world/2013/06/02/vatican-spokesman-claims-100000-christians-killed-annually-because-faith/.

CHAPTER 25: THEY'RE COMING TO AMERICA

1. Remarks by the President to the UN General Assembly, United Nations Headquarters, press release, White House, Office of the Press Secrety, September 25, 2012, https://www.whitehouse.gov/the-press-office/2012/09/25/remarks-president-un-general-assembly.

2. Ed Pilkington, Ryan Felton, and Nicky Woolf, "'Beyond Terrifying': Muslim Americans Shocked by Trump and Carson Quotes," *Guardian*, November 20, 2015, http://www.theguardian.com/us-news/2015/nov/20/muslim-americans-outrage-donald-trump-ben-carson; see the embedded article, "Donald Trump: we need to track all Muslims in America."

3. Pilkington, Felton, and Woolf, "'Beyond Terrifying.'"

4. Fox News, "Krauthammer Slams Obama's 'Mechanical' Tone on Terror; Coach Suing School for Religious Discrimination Speaks Out," *Kelly File*, December 7, 2015, http://www.foxnews.com/transcript/2015/12/17/krauthammer-slams-obama-mechanical-tone-on-terror-coach-suing-school-for/.

5. Douglas Ernst, "DHS Warns: Isis Trojan Horse Coming to America: Homeland Can't Locate 122,000 with U.S. Visas Revoked over Terror Ties," WND, December 17, 2015, http://www.wnd.com/2015/12/feds-warn-isis-trojan-horse-coming-to-u-s.

6. Fox News, "Krauthammer Slams Obama's 'Mechanical' Tone on Terror."

7. Susan Jones, "Homeland Security Chair: 'We Don't Have the Ability to Monitor' the 2000 Syrian Refugees Already Here," CNSNews.com, December 9, 2015, http://www.cnsnews.com/news/article/susan-jones/homeland-security-chair-we-dont-have-ability-monitor-2000-syrian-refugees.

8. Ibid.

9. Jesse Byrnes,. "FBI Investigating ISIS Suspects in All 50 States," *The Hill* (blog), February 25, 2015, http://thehill.com/blogs/blog-briefing-room/233832-fbi-investigating-isis-suspects-in-all-50-states.

10. *Los Angeles Times*, "Everything We Know about the San Bernardino Terror Attack Investigation So Far," December 14, 2015, http://www.latimes.com/local/california/la-me-san-bernardino-shooting-terror-investigation-htmlstory.html.

11. Ernst, "DHS Warns."

12. Richard Lardner, "The Top NATO Commander in Europe Says Terrorists, Criminals and Foreign Fighters Are Part of the Daily Refugee Flow into Europe," *U.S. News & World Report*, March 1, 2016, http://www.usnews.com/news/world/articles/2016-03-01/general-says-terrorists-in-daily-refugee-flow-to-europe.

13. Remarks by the President at Cairo University, press release, White House, Office of the Press Secretary, June 4, 2009, https://www.whitehouse.gov/the-press-office/remarks-president-cairo-university-6-04-09.

14. John Flavel's "Warning to an Ungodly Nation," *Zwinglius Redivivus* (blog), April 7, 2015, https://zwingliusredivivus.wordpress.com/2015/07/04/john-flevels-warning-to-an-ungodly-nation/.

15. Loren Gutentag, "CIA Director Brennan: ISIS' Attempts to Attack US 'Inevitable,'" NewsMax, February 15, 2016, http://www.newsmax.com/Newsfront/John-Brennan-CIA-Director-ISIS-attacks/2016/02/15/id/714373/#ixzz40Febp6vK.

CHAPTER 26: THE DEMONIC DELUGE

1.   C. S. Lewis, *The Screwtape Letters*, repr. ed. (New York: Harper, 2015), ix.

CHAPTER 27: EMISSARIES OF DECEIT

1.   Joseph P. Laycock, "Why Are Exorcisms as Popular as Ever?" *New Republic*, December 28, 2015, https://newrepublic.com/article/126607/exorcisms-popular-ever.

2.   Sputnik, "Mass Exorcism Needed: Mexico Swept by Wave of Satanic Killings," March 12, 2016, http://sputniknews.com/latam/20160312/1036173443/mexico-exorcism-crime.html#ixzz42hTCxPMp.

3.   Andrew Chesnut, "The Extraordinary Exorcism of Mexico," *Huffington Post*, June 16, 2015, http://www.huffingtonpost.com/r-andrew-chesnut/the-extraordinary-exorcis_b_7585508.html.

4.   James Kaplan, "Robin Williams," January 1999, *US Weekly*, http://www.maryellenmark.com/text/magazines/us%20weekly_new/925B-000-028.html.

5.   "Crazy in Love—Beyonce Admits Spirit Coming into Her," YouTube video, 2:22, television interview, posted by "cmberriTV," April 25, 2010, https://www.youtube.com/watch?v=HNXNxscgMgU.

6.   "Oprah & Denzel Summon Spirits," YouTube video, 2:03, excerpt from Good Fight Ministries DVD release *Hollywood Unmasked*, posted by Good Fight Ministries, June 4, 2008, https://www.youtube.com/watch?v=D5oOY2C9wdI.

7.   Ibid.

8.   Shirley MacLaine, *Going Within: A Guide for Inner Transformation*, repr. ed. (New York: Bantam, 1990), 25.

9.   Peter Nowak, "U.S. Leads the Way In Porn Production," *Canadian Business*, June 5, 2012, http://www.canadianbusiness.com/blogs-and-comment/u-s-leads-the-way-in-porn-production-but-falls-behind-in-profits.

10. Damon Brown, "PCs in Ecstasy: The Evolution of Sex in PC Games," *Computer Games* magazine, May 2006.

11. U.S. Department of Justice, quoted by Covenant Eyes, "Porn and Your Teens," accessed May 4, 2016, http://www.covenanteyes.com/pornstats/.

12. Jill Manning, "Pornography's Impact on Marriage & the Family" (Testimony of Jill C. Manning before the Subcommittee on the Constitution, Civil Rights and Property Rights, Committee on Judiciary), November 9 2005, http://www.heritage.org/research/testimony/pornographys-impact-on-marriage-amp-the-family.

13. Ibid.

14. Unless otherwise noted, the following statistics were taken from: Tech Mission, "Statistics on Pornography, Sexual Addiction and Online Perpetrators," Safe Families, accessed May 5, 2016, http://www.safefamilies.org/sfStats.php.

15. Covenant Eyes, "Porn in the Church Teens," accessed May 4, 2016, http://www.covenanteyes.com/pornstats/

16. Dr. David Kyle Foster, "Pornography: Power over Pornography Addiction," *Mastering Life*, emphasis added, http://www.masteringlife.org/index.php/mastering-life/articles/pornography.

17. Sarah L Shannon, "The Global Sex Trade: Humans as the Ultimate Commodity," *Crime & Justice International* 15, no. 28 (May 1999), http://www.cjimagazine.com/archives/cji67d3.html?id=288.

CHAPTER 28: DID GOD REALLY SAY . . . ?

1. Heather Clark, "'Pope Francis' Calls for Collaboration with World's Religions, Those Who 'Meet God in Different Ways,'" Christian News, January 9, 2016, http://christiannews.net/2016/01/09/pope-calls-for-collaboration-with-worlds-religions-those-who-meet-god-in-different-ways/, emphasis added.

2. On the Road to Armageddon: How evangelicals became Israel's best friend, http://www.beliefnet.com/Faiths/Christianity/End-Times/On-The-Road-To-Armageddon.aspx#tCXV2zsO4gkoJa2s.99.

3. *Strong's Concordance*, "5172. Nachash" Bible Hub, http://biblehub.com/hebrew/5172.htm.

4. *Strong's Concordance*, "3789. Ophis" Bible Hub, http://biblehub.com/greek/3789.htm.

5. See George Brown Tindall and David E. Shi, *America: A Narrative History*, 7th ed. (n.p.: W. W. Norton, 2006), chap. 35, "Rebellion and Reaction in the 1960s and 1970s," http://www.wwnorton.com/college/history/america7/content/multimedia/ch35/documents_01.htm.

6. Joseph P. Laycock, "Why Are Exorcisms as Popular as Ever?" *New Republic*, December 28, 2015, https://newrepublic.com/article/126607/exorcisms-popular-ever.

7. See U.S. Fish and Wildlife Service, International Affairs, "CITES," http://www.fws.gov/international/cites/; "Endangered Species Act," https://www.fws.gov/international/laws-treaties-agreements/us-conservation-laws/endangered-species-act.html.

8. Adapted from Ray Pritchard, "Faded Glory: Why Christ Had to Come," Keep Believing Ministries, November 30, 2003,, http://www.keepbelieving.com/sermon/faded-glory-why-christ-had-to-come/.

9. Chris Woodward, "Barna: Many Pastors Wary of Raising 'Controversy,'" OneNewsNow, August 1, 2014, http://www.onenewsnow.com/church/2014/08/01/barna-many-pastors-wary-of-raising-controversy#.U-ED1KO0uSr.

10. Barna Group, "What Do Americans Believe About Jesus? 5 Popular Beliefs," Barna, April 1, 2015, https://www.barna.org/barna-update/culture/714-what-do-americans-believe-about-jesus-5-popular-beliefs#.VsIs1LQrJpQ.

11. Lee Strobel, *The Case for the Real Jesus: A Journalist Investigates Current Attacks on the Identity of Christ* (Grand Rapids: Zondervan, 2007), 108–9.

CHAPTER 29: DENIZENS OF DARKNESS

1. Pew Forum on Religion and Public Life, *U.S. Religious Landscape Survey: Religious Affiliation: Diverse and Dynamic,*. February 2008, http://www.pewforum.org/files/2013/05/report-religious-landscape-study-full.pdf, 5, 12.

2. "On the Road to Armageddon: How Evangelicals Became Israel's Best Friend," Beliefnet, August 23, 2004, http://www.beliefnet.com/Faiths/Christianity/End-Times/On-The-Road-To-Armageddon.aspx#tCXV2zsO4gkoJa2s.99.

3. Pew Research Center, "America's Changing Religious Landscape," May 12, 2015, http://www.pewforum.org/2015/05/12/americas-changing-religious-landscape/.

4. American Culture & Faith Institute, "God's People Want to Know," September 24, 2015, http://www.culturefaith.com/gods-people-want-to-know-2/.

5. I first heard this illustration from Dr. William Lile, OB/GYN, also known as Pro Life Doc. Dr. Lile is a nationally renowned pro-life activist and appears in numerous radio and television markets, speaks at universities, schools, churches, and pregnancy resource center conventions around the nation. His website is www.prolifedoc.org.

6. International Suicide Statistics, Suicide.org, accessed May 6, 2016, http://www.suicide.org/international-suicide-statistics.html.

7. Tara Parker-Pope, "Suicide Rates Rise Sharply in U.S." *New York Times*, May 2, 2013, http://mobile.nytimes.com/2013/05/03/health/suicide-rate-rises-sharply-in-us.html?referer=

8. Casey Leins, "U.S. Suicides Hit Highest Rate in 25 Years," *U.S. News & World Report*, October 8, 2014, http://www.usnews.com/news/newsgram/articles/2014/10/08/us-suicides-hit-highest-rate-in-25-years.

9. Ibid.

10. Maggie Fox, "Anxiety Drug Overdoses in U.S. Hit Record Levels," *Time*, February 19, 2016, http://time.com/4230374/anxiety-drugs-overdose-study/.

11. Karl Payne, "Removing Demonic Oppression," *Leadership Journal*, Spring 2012, http://www.christianitytoday.com/le/2012/spring/removingdemonic.html; Ron Phillips, "Symptoms of Demonic Operation." *Charisma*, April 16, 2013, http://www.charismamag.com/spirit/spiritual-warfare/17397-symptoms-of-demonic-operation.

12. Lloyd Sederer, "A Blind Eye to Addiction," *U.S. News & World Report*, June 1, 2015, http://www.usnews.com/opinion/blogs/policy-dose/2015/06/01/america-is-neglecting-its-addiction-problem.

13. Venetia Robertson, "The Beast Within: Anthrozoomorphic Identity and Alternative Spirituality in the Online Therianthropy Movement," *Nova Religio* 16, no. 3 (2013): 7–30, http://www.academia.edu/1851789/The_Beast_Within_Anthrozoomorphic_ Identity_and_Alternative_Spirituality_in_the_Online_Therianthropy_Movement_ Nova_Religio_16_3_2013_. Venetia Robertson is a PhD candidate and postgraduate teaching fellow in the Studies in Religion Department at the University of Sydney, Australia. She received a double major in studies in religion and history, completed an honors year in 2010, and received the University of Sydney Medal for her academic results. Her PhD thesis analyzes other-than-human identity subcultures as a nexus between spirituality, popular culture, and the Internet. http://sydney.edu.au/arts/ religion/postgraduate_research/student_research.shtml#Robertson.

CHAPTER 30: THE SHEMITAH SHAKING

1. Jonathan Cahn, "Shemitah Impact? See Evidence For Yourself," WND, January 20, 2016, http://www.wnd.com/2016/01/the-sword-of-the-shemitah-and-how-it-just-changed-your-world/#scPKhygdHkrLQefV.99.
2. Evelyn Cheng, "Dow Closes Down Triple Digits, Posts Worst Opening Day in 8 Years," CNBC, January 4, 2016, http://www.cnbc.com/2016/01/04/us-markets.html.
3. The information in this section is taken from "What Is Shemittah?" Chabad.org, accessed May 6, 2016, http://www.chabad.org/library/article_cdo/aid/562077/jewish/ What-Is-Shemittah.htm.
4. Jonathan Cahn, *The Mystery of the Shemitah: The 3,000-Year-Old Mystery That Holds the Secret of America's Future, the World's Future . . . and Your Future!* (Lake Mary, FL: FrontLine, 2014).
5. "Holy Shemitah! Bible Cycle Unlocks U.S. Future," 9-1-14, http://www.wnd. com/2014/09/holy-shemitah-u-s-history-repeating-itself/#eoKT44H3GGolgbdT.99.
6. Ibid.
7. Cahn, *The Mystery of the Shemitah*, 260.
8. Ibid., 240
9. Cahn, "Shemitah Impact?"
10. Joel McDurmon, "Just When You Thought the Shemitah Hype Was Over," American Vision, September 15, 2015, https://americanvision.org/12471/just-when-you-thought-the-shemitah-hype-was-over.
11. Jonathan Cahn, "The Sword of the Shemitah—and How It Just Changed Your World," *Charisma*, January 2016, http://www.charismanews.com/opinion/54575-the-sword-of-the-shemitah-and-how-it-just-changed-your-world.
12. Ibid.
13. Ibid.
14. Marcus Leroux, "Markets Suffer Their Worst Start to the Year Since Great Depression," *New York Times*, February 19, 2016, http://www.thetimes.co.uk/tto/public/assetfinance/ article4667135.ece.

15. Cheng, "Dow Closes Down Triple Digits."

16. Lucinda Shen, "Investors Have Lost $1.78 Trillion So Far This Year," *Fortune*, February 11, 2016, http://fortune.com/2016/02/11/investors-have-lost-1-78-trillion-so-far-this-year/.

17. Don Lee, "Some Countries Are Using Negative Interest Rates to Fight Slowdowns: Is the U.S. Next?" *Los Angeles Times,* February 19, 2016, http://www.latimes.com/business/la-fi-negative-interest-rates-20160219-story.html.

18. Washington Post Staff, "The Complete Transcript of Netanyahu's Address to Congress," *Washington Post*, March 2015, https://www.washingtonpost.com/news/post-politics/wp/2015/03/03/full-text-netanyahus-address-to-congress.

19. Jack Minor, "Obama's Iran Deal Falls on Ominous Bible Date," WND, April 2015, http://www.wnd.com/2015/04/obamas-iran-deal-announced-on-ominous-bible-date.

20. Kia Makarechi, "Pope Francis Continues to Do Whatever He Wants, Because He's the Pope," *Vanity Fair*, May 14, 2015, http://www.vanityfair.com/news/2015/05/pope-francis-palestine-climate-change.

21. Adam Liptak, "Supreme Court Ruling Makes Same-Sex Marriage a Right Nationwide," *New York Times,* June 26, 2015, http://www.nytimes.com/2015/06/27/us/supreme-court-same-sex-marriage.html. See also "UNITED STATES v. WINDSOR," Cornell University Law School, Legal Information Institute, accessed March 2016, https://www.law.cornell.edu/supremecourt/text/12-307.

22. Penny Star, "Obama Administration Advances Gay Agenda at African Leaders Summit," CNS News, August 6, 2014, http://cnsnews.com/news/article/penny-starr/obama-administration-advances-gay-agenda-african-leaders-summit.

23. Simon Tomlinson, "The Pope's New World Order: Francis Calls for the 'Goods of the Earth' to Be Shared by Everyone—Not Exploited by the Rich at the Expense of the Poor," *Daily Mail,* February 20, 2016, http://www.dailymail.co.uk/news/article-3153552/The-Pope-s-new-world-order-Francis-calls-goods-Earth-shared-not-exploited-rich-expense-poor.html.

24. Steve Almasy and Eliott C. McLaughlin, "Planned Parenthood Exec, Fetal Body Parts Subject of Controversial Video," *CNN*, July 15, 2015, http://www.cnn.com/2015/07/15/health/planned-parenthood-undercover-video/.

25. Alan Blinder and Tamar Lewin, "Clerk in Kentucky Chooses Jail over Deal on Same-Sex Marriage," *New York Times*, September 3, 2015, http://www.nytimes.com/2015/09/04/us/kim-davis-same-sex-marriage.html.

26. Pete Souza, "In Photos: Pope Francis Visits the White House," White House blog, September 15, 2015, https://www.whitehouse.gov/blog/2015/09/25/photos-pope-francis-visits-white-house.

27. "Pope Francis' Address to Congress (as Prepared for Delivery)," *CNN*, September 24, 2015, http://www.cnn.com/2015/09/24/politics/pope-francis-congress-speech/; Carl Gallups, "The Words the Pope Did Not Say to Congress," WND, September 25, 2015, http://www.wnd.com/2015/09/the-words-the-pope-did-not-say-to-congress/.

28. Patrick Goodenough, "Israeli Ambassador: UN 'Would Vote to Declare That the Earth Is Flat, If the Palestinians Proposed It,'" *CNS News,* September 11, 2015, http://cnsnews.com/news/article/patrick-goodenough/israeli-ambassador-un-would-vote-declare-earth-flat-if-palestinians.

29. Ali Younes and Patrick Strickland, "Palestinian Flag Raised at UN for First Time," Aljazeera, September 30, 2015, http://www.aljazeera.com/news/2015/09/palestinian-flag-raising-symbolic-step-150930124248791.html; Goodenough, "Israeli Ambassador."

30. Somini Sengupta, "Pope Francis to Address U.N.'s Largest Gathering of World Leaders," *New York Times,* September 25, 2015, http://www.nytimes.com/2015/09/25/world/americas/pope-francis-un-general-assembly.html.

31. Michael R. Gordon, "Russia Surprises U.S. with Accord on Battling ISIS," *New York Times,* September 27, 2015, http://www.nytimes.com/2015/09/28/world/middleeast/iraq-agrees-to-share-intelligence-on-isis-with-russia-syria-and-iran.html.

32. Oren Dorell, "Netanyahu: Nuclear Deal with Iran Unleashes a 'Tiger,'" *USA Today,* October 1, 2015, http://www.usatoday.com/story/news/world/2015/10/01/israel-prime-minister-netanyahu-united-nations-iran/73141398.

33. "Russia Joins War in Syria: Five Key Points," BBC News, October 1, 2015, http://www.bbc.com/news/world-middle-east-34416519.

34. Anna Nemtsova, "Russia Ramps Up WWIII Talking Points," *Daily Beast,* October 7, 2015. http://www.thedailybeast.com/articles/2015/10/07/russia-ramps-up-wwiii-talking-points.html.

35. "Obama Puts Nuclear Deal into Effect, but Iran Still Likely Months Away from Sanction Relief," Fox News, October 18, 2015, http://www.foxnews.com/politics/2015/10/18/obama-puts-nuclear-deal-into-effect-but-iran-still-likely-months-away-from.html.

36. Rob Virtue, "Putin's Boost in Battle against ISIS: China Preparing to 'Team Up with Russia in Syria.'" *Express,* November 19, 2015, http://www.express.co.uk/news/world/610286/China-preparing-to-team-up-with-Russia-in-Syria-Boost-for-Putin-in-battle-against-ISIS.

37. Geoffrey Aronson, "China to Open Its First Naval Base in Africa," Al Jazeera, December 22, 2015, http://www.aljazeera.com/indepth/opinion/2015/12/china-opens-naval-base-africa-151222141545988.html.

38. Jennifer LeClaire, "Did Pope Francis Really Just Take a Big Step Toward One World Religion?" *Charisma News,* December 2, 2015, http://www.charismanews.com/opinion/watchman-on-the-wall/53547-did-pope-francis-really-just-take-a-big-step-toward-one-world-religion.

39. "Saudi Arabia Forms Muslim 'Anti-Terrorism' Coalition," Al Jazeera, December 2015, http://www.aljazeera.com/news/2015/12/saudi-arabia-forms-muslim-anti-terrorism-coalition-151215035914865.html.

40. Elise Harris, "In First Prayer Video, Pope Stresses Interfaith Unity: 'We Are All Children of God,'" Catholic News Agency, January 7, 2016, http://www.catholicnewsagency.com/news/in-first-video-message-pope-francis-stresses-unity-we-are-all-children-of-god-39381/.

41. Precious Silva, "Russia Pushes for World War 3, Putin Affirms Possibility," *Morning News USA*, February 17, 2016, http://www.morningnewsusa.com/russia-pushes-world-war-3-putin-affirms-possibility-2358284.html.
42. Jamie Gangel et al., "Antonin Scalia, Supreme Court Justice, Dies at 79," *CNN*, February 15, 2016, http://www.cnn.com/2016/02/13/politics/supreme-court-justice-antonin-scalia-dies-at-79/.
43. John Coumarianos, "Opinion: Chilling Ways the Global Economy Echoes 1930s Great Depression Era," Market Watch, February 19, 2016, http://www.marketwatch.com/story/chilling-ways-the-global-economy-echoes-1930s-great-depression-era-2016-02-19.
44. Patrick Hosking and Philip Aldrick, "Global Fears as Markets Lose Faith In Central Banks," *Times* (UK), March 7, 2016, http://www.thetimes.co.uk/tto/business/economics/article4707169.ece.

CHAPTER 32: PERSPECTIVE

1. Carl Gallups, *Be Thou Prepared: Equipping the Church for Persecution and Times of Trouble* (Washington, D.C.: WND Books, 2015), xvii.
2. Bob Unruh, "Attacks on Christians in U.S. Double in 3 Years," WND, February 22, 2016, http://www.wnd.com/2016/02/attacks-on-christians-in-america-double-in-3-years/#Mkv9Qi6x3VSQqvBP.99.
3. Kelly Shackelford, gen. ed., *Undeniable: The Survey of Hostility to Religion in America*, 2016 ed, (Plano, TX: First Liberty Institute, 2016), 9. https://firstliberty.org/wp-content/uploads/2016/02/2016_Undeniable.pdf.
4. Ibid., 5.

CHAPTER 33: THE INGATHERING

1. "World Wide Web Inventor Uses Anniversary to Campaign for Internet Rules," *Herald Scotland,* December 25, 2015, http://www.heraldscotland.com/news/14167629.World_Wide_Web_inventor_uses_anniversary_to_campaign_for_internet_rules/?ref=mr&lp=19.
2. Lucinda Borkett-Jones, "We Are Living in the Midst of the Greatest Turning of Muslims to Christ in History," *Christianity Today,* June 17, 2015, http://www.christiantoday.com/article/we.are.living.in.the.midst.of.the.greatest.turning.of.muslims.to.christ.in.history/56393.htm.
3. David Garrison, *A Wind in the House of Islam* (Monument, CO: WigTake, 2014).
4. Borkett-Jones, "We Are Living in the Midst of the Greatest Turning of Muslims to Christ in History."
5. Admin, "Al-Jazeerah: 6 Million Muslims convert to Christianity in Africa alone each year," *Muslim Statistics,* December 14, 2012, https://muslimstatistics.wordpress.com/2012/12/14/al-jazeerah-6-million-muslims-convert-to-christianity-in-africa-each-year/.

6. *International Standard Bible Encyclopedia Online*, s.v. "Sinim, Land of," accessed May 9, 2016, http://www.internationalstandardbible.com/S/sinim-land-of.html; emphasis added.
7. "Sinim," Bible Hub, accessed March 2016, http://biblehub.com/topical/s/sinim.htm.
8. Eleanor Albert, "Christianity in China," Council on Foreign Relations, May 7, 2015, http://www.cfr.org/china/christianity-china/p36503.
9. Dr. Michael Brown, "Does the Bible Really Say That Things Will Only Get Worse?" Charisma News, July 15, 2013, http://www.charismanews.com/opinion/in-the-line-of-fire/40236-does-the-bible-really-say-that-things-will-only-get-worse.

CHAPTER 34: ENGAGE AND ADVANCE

1. Robert I. Fitzhenry, ed. *The Harper Book of Quotations*, 3rd ed. (New York: Harper Collins, 1993), 356.
2. Veronica Neffinger, "Franklin Graham Says World Turmoil Is Sign of Jesus' Coming," *Christian Headlines,* February 18, 2016, http://www.christianheadlines.com/blog/franklin-graham-says-world-turmoil-is-sign-of-jesus-coming.html.
3. Cheryl Chumley, *The Devil In DC: Winning Back the Country from the Beast in Washington*, (Washington, D.C.: WND Books, 2016), 283.

INDEX

A

Abdrahaman, Sidi Haji, 162
Abdullah II of Jordan (king), 143
Abi-Talib, Ali Ibn, 19
"abomination of desolation," 90, 209–10
abortion, 225, 231, 244
Abraham (patriarch), 115
Adams, John, 161–62
Adams, John Quincy, 122
Afghanistan, 153, 159, 168, 182, 186, 261
Africa, 268, 271. *See also* North Africa
Agence France-Presse (AFP), 145
Ahasuerus (Persian king), 25
Ahmadinejad, Mahmoud, 119
Akash, Mariam, 170
Albania, 160
Al Jazeera, 33, 268
al-Qaida, 182
al-Sadr, Muqtada, 188
America, how Jews saved, 130–31
American Academy of Matrimonial Lawyers, 217
American Family Radio, 226
American Revolution, 130, 131
American Tract Bible Society, 270
America's Top 10 Most Admired Men (Gallup list), 13
Anatolia, 158–59
Anglo-American Committee, 115
answer, our biblical responsibility to give people the (to the world's problems), 255–56

Antichrist, 52–54, 84, 86, 92, 107, 108, 110, 111, 147, 148. *See also* beast (of Revelation)
anti-Semitism, 14, 24, 34
"anti-terrorism" coalition, 246
anxiety, 17, 18, 23, 118, 147, 263
anxiety drug overdoses, 233
apostasy, 34, 52, 220, 222, 224–25, 232, 246
Arabs, 114, 119, 152, 271
Arab Spring, 164, 170, 171, 182–86, 190, 197, 261
Arab states of the Persian Gulf. *See* Gulf States
Armageddon: An Appointment with Destiny (Jeffrey), 152–53
Armenians, 160
Artificial Intelligence, 68, 86
Asia, 158, 159, 168, 271
Asia Minor, 159
Assad, Bashar al-, 2, 29, 171, 172–73, 174, 245
Associated Press (AP), 29, 233
Association of Messianic Congregations, 139
Assyrians, 160, 269
Aswan, 270
Ataturk rebellion, 163–64. *See also* Kemal, Mustafa (Ataturk)
Atlantic, 165
Attkisson, Sharyl, 185, 190, 301n1 (chap. 24)
Austria-Hungary, 163

311

churches and Christian properties, number destroyed daily, 194

Churchill, Winston, 132

CIA, 67

Clapper, James, 66

Clausewitz, Karl von, 272

Clemens, Samuel. *See* Twain, Mark

climate change, 61, 177, 242, 244, 245

Clinton, Hillary, 183

CNBC, 17, 235, 241

CNN, 10, 46

Colmes, Alan, 14

Comey, James, 199

"coming of the Lord"; "coming of the Son of Man," meaning of the terms, 45

Company of Biologists, 73

Computer Games magazine, 216

Congress of the United States, 23, 25–27, 161, 173, 228, 241–42, 244, 278

Constantinople, 159

Coolidge, Calvin, 130–31

Cooper, Henry, 144–45

Coptic Christians, beheading of, 141

Council on Foreign Relations, 271

Crimea, 160

CRISPR/Cas9, 75, 79

Croatia, 2

CSI 300, 17

Cunningham, Solveig, 233

Cush, 153

cybernetics, 76. *See also* genome engineering; transhumanism

cyborgs, 68, 77–78

D

Daily Mail (UK), 69, 75–76, 190–91

Daily Signal, 185, 190

Damascus, 171, 172, 174, 175–77

Danes, Claire, 211

Daniel (prophet), 37, 41, 63–65, 80, 81, 84, 90, 106

DARPA, 77

David (king), 26, 124, 138, 277

Davis, Kim, 243

"day of the Lord"; "that day," meaning of the terms, 45

death, elusiveness of, 89

Defense Advanced Research Projects Agency. *See* DARPA

demonic outpouring, scriptures regarding the last-days, 206–8

demon possession, 206, 209, 211, 214, 215

demons, 34, 205, 207, 208–9, 210, 212, 213, 223

Destroyer, 187–89

Development (journal), 73

Devil in DC, The (Chumley), 276

DFBA (U.S. Department of Defense Forensics and Biometrics Agency), 93

"digital immortality," 75–76

divorce, role of Internet, pornography in, 217

Djibouti, 174

DNA, 72, 75, 79, 87–88, 105–8

doctrinal illiteracy among Christians, 226

DOMA, 242

Dow (index), 17, 235, 240, 241

drug overdoses, 233

E

earthquakes, 9

Eastern Europe, 153

economic crashes occurring in Shemitah years, 237, 238

Ediboglu, Mehmet Ali, 166

Einstein, 62, 141, 274

electromagnetic pulse (EMP), 145

Encyclopedia of Biblical Prophecy (Payne), 45

"end-time," meaning of the term, 45

Egypt, 27, 113, 115, 166, 178, 183, 184, 236, 268

Erdogan, Recep Tayyip, 157, 165–67, 169

Esther (queen), 24, 278

ethical considerations of chimera research and development, 73–74

Ethiopia, 153, 171

Euphrates River, 32, 144, 168, 181, 195

Europe, 12, 14, 34, 128, 137, 142, 153, 155, 158, 271, 186, 198, 200, 271

European Council on Foreign Relations, 152

Europeans, 161

European Science Foundation, 8

European Union, 173

Express (UK), 7, 9–10, 18

exorcisms, international fascination with, 35

Exorcist, The (Blatty), 225

Ezekiel Option (Rosenberg), 150, 151

Ezekiel 38, 55, 120, 126, 150–51, 152–54, 158, 168, 169, 174, 177, 187

Robertson, Venetia, 306n13 (chap. 29)
robots, 68–69, 71, 86, 206
Roe v. Wade (1973), 225, 231, 238
Roman Catholic Church, 211
Roman Catholicism, 230
Romania, 160
Romans (imperial), 43, 55
Rosenberg, Joel C., 150–51, 176
Ross, Scott, 125
Russell 2000 Index, 240
Russia, 1, 2, 11, 12, 14, 18, 28, 29, 30, 34,
    129, 142, 143, 144, 145–46, 147, 153,
    154, 158, 163, 166, 168, 169, 172–73,
    174, 178, 187, 245, 261, 276

S

Saddam Hussein, 180–81, 182–83, 186,
    187–89, 261
safety, meaning of the Hebrew word in
    Ezekiel 38, 150
Sagan, Carl, 83, 259
same-sex marriage (aka gay marriage), 226,
    231, 243
Samson Option, 181
Samsung, 66
San Andreas fault, 10
San Bernardino, California (terrorist attack),
    199, 200
S&P 500, 240
Santorum, Rick, 19–20
Sarah (wife of Abraham), 115
Satan, 45, 89, 92, 167, 168, 208, 212, 213,
    219, 222, 223–24, 226, 258, 271
Saudi Arabia, 1–2, 146, 177, 182, 191, 246,
    268
Saudi Press Agency, 177–78
Satanism, international fascination with, 35
Scalia, Antonin, 246
Schmidt, Eric (Google CEO), 64–65
Schneier, Bruce, 66–67
science, 10, 60, 69, 71, 72–76, 92, 95,
    127–28
science fiction, 60, 69, 71, 79, 84
ScienceDaily, 74–75
Screwtape Letters, The (Lewis), 205
scriptures
    predicting the return of Israel, 126
    regarding the last-days demonic
    outpouring and proliferation of evil,
    206–8

Scythians, 168
Second Coming, 50, 51, 53–54, 276
secularization of American culture, 225
Sekulow, Jay, 140
Seljuk Empire, 158–59
September 11, 2001, terrorist attacks (aka
    9/11), 39, 46, 163, 182, 186, 197, 261
seven churches of Asia Minor, 167
700 Club, 141
sex robots, 68, 69, 206
sexual exploitation, solicitations (online), 218
sexually transmitted infections (STIs),
    34–35
sexual revolution, 225
Shackelford, Kelly, 264
Shanghai Composite Index, 240
Shcherbak, Yuri, 143
Shemitah year, 235–40, 247
Shia Muslims, 159
Shiite, percent of Islamic populate that is, 19
Singapore, 268
"Singularity," the, 87
Sinim, 270–71
Six-Day War, 152
"666," 90, 93, 100, 103–6, 107
Slate.com, 187–88
Smith, Mark (scholar), 115
Smith, Shepard, 8
Snyder, Michael (founder of the *Economic
    Collapse* blog), 44
social media, 199, 267
Sodom, 232, 243, 274, 275, 277, 284n10
Solomon, Haym, 130–31
Somalia, 268
sorcery, 206
southeastern Europe, 153
"spirit of *nachash*," 224. *See* apostasy; *nachash*
Stalin, Joseph, 119
"State of Palestine," 34, 147, 244
St. Clair, Arthur (revolutionary general), 131
stem cell(s), 73, 78
stock market, 17, 235, 240
substance addiction, 232
Sudan, 153, 160, 178
suicide, 232–33
Sunni Muslims, 20, 159, 172
Supreme Court of the United States, 140,
    228, 242–43, 246
surveillance, 66, 93
synthetic biology, 76, 87–88

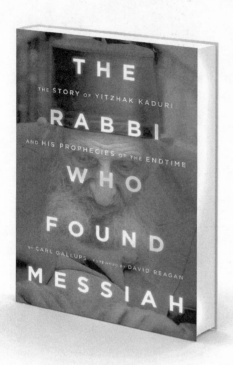
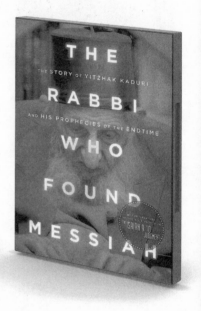

"This book is EPIC!"

—JIM BAKKER, HOST OF *THE JIM BAKKER SHOW*

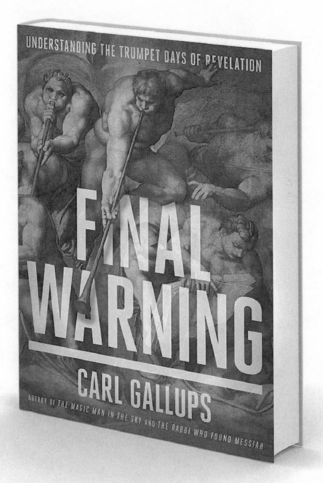

Whether one is a believer or not, the Bible provides many clues about the future of us all. In FINAL WARNING beloved pastor and best-selling author Carl Gallups explores the stunning visions of the Apostle John as found in the seven trumpets of Revelation and overlays them on major events in the 20th and 21st centuries. Gallups has scoured historical, military, and journalistic sources to address these questions and more. An incredible journey of contextual biblical understanding and astounding prophetic possibilities await as you discover why today's signs could be the final warning.

WND BOOKS • WASHINGTON DC • WNDBOOKS.COM

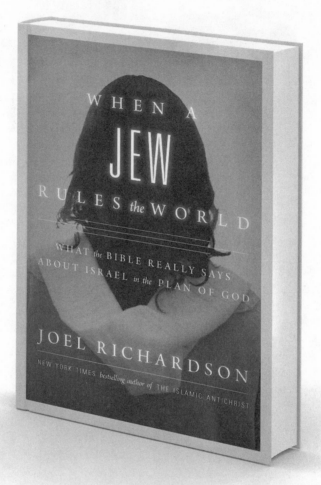